William J. Potter

Twenty-Five Sermons of Twenty-Five Years

William J. Potter

Twenty-Five Sermons of Twenty-Five Years

ISBN/EAN: 9783337087685

Printed in Europe, USA, Canada, Australia, Japan

Cover: Foto ©Lupo / pixelio.de

More available books at **www.hansebooks.com**

TWENTY-FIVE SERMONS

OF

TWENTY-FIVE YEARS

BY

WILLIAM J. POTTER.

BOSTON:
GEO. H. ELLIS, 141 FRANKLIN STREET.
1885.

*Copyright,
1885,
By William J. Potter.*

CONTENTS.

		PAGE
PREFATORY LETTER		v

I.	APOSTOLIC SUCCESSION	1
II.	THE SOUL'S REST	20
III.	GOD IN NATURE	32
IV.	MERCY AND JUDGMENT	48
V.	SELF-SACRIFICE	56
VI.	THE RELIGION OF THE AFFECTIONS	71
VII.	ENDURANCE	88
VIII.	CHILDHOOD'S INSTINCT AND MANHOOD'S FAITH	103
IX.	PURE RELIGION	116
X.	CHRISTMAS LEGEND AND FACT	130
XI.	THE EDEN OF THE SENSES AND THE EDEN OF THE SOUL	143
XII.	THOUGHTS AND CONDUCT	158
XIII.	EASTER TRUTHS AND TRADITIONS	171
XIV.	OPTIMISM	189
XV.	MUTUAL SOCIAL RESPONSIBILITY	204
XVI.	HEART IN NATURE	224

XVII.	WAITING FOR ONE'S SELF	240
XVIII.	THE SILENT REVELATION	256
XIX.	THE RELIGION OF HUMANITY	271
XX.	WHAT DO WE WORSHIP?	288
XXI.	GOD IN HUMANITY	304
XXII.	THE PERMANENCE OF MORALITY	323
XXIII.	THE PRACTICALITY OF THOUGHT	340
XXIV.	THE GLORIOUS GOD	355
XXV.	A TWENTY-FIVE YEARS' MINISTRY	376
APPENDIX		401

PREFATORY LETTER.

Dear Friends and Parishioners:

FOR more than two years, I had cherished the thought that, if I should remain your minister twenty-five years, I would print a volume of discourses selected from those years, and have it ready as a surprise gift to you on the twenty-fifth anniversary. But the pressure of ordinary work delayed my entering on the execution of this purpose until last summer's vacation; and then I found that the task of preparing and getting through the press such a book was too great for the limited time at command. The anniversary came, and only a beginning had been made. In an unguarded moment, I expressed to one of you my disappointment at not having completed this intention; and thus I let out my secret. From that time, the purpose became yours; and you now make the gift to yourselves. You asked and urged me to put the thought into action, and made it easier to do so; and you, especially, are responsible for the frontispiece and Appendix to the volume, which formed no part of my plan. I have only selected and arranged for you the discourses and seen the book through the press.

This book, therefore, has been made chiefly for your eyes. It may be regarded as, in a sense, a memorial record of our twenty-five years of parish life together. With this end in view, it contains the first and the last discourse of the quarter-century, and, with one exception, one from each of the successive years between, in chronological order. For one twelvemonth, though still your minister, my ministry was in soldiers' hospitals and near battle-fields. As that twelvemonth did not entirely synchronize with the calendar year, I might have found some sermon with the date 1864 attached to it; but I came across nothing which it seemed worth while to print. I had left some of my physical vigor in Virginia, and it took several months to recover mental elasticity. This plan of selecting the sermons from the whole period of the twenty-five years is one, I am well aware, which involves a risk. Possibly, it involves some *moral* risk to assume that anything I wrote in the earliest part of my ministry can be worthy of preservation. But there is also a risk that the plan may cause some misunderstanding in regard to my present intellectual beliefs. As explained in the anniversary discourse,— the last in the book,— my views have undergone considerable

change in this period. Hence there are among my
earlier discourses many which I could not write in
just the same way to-day; and some of those chosen
for this volume come, in a measure, under this class.
I have chosen none, however, the main lesson of
which I should not still stand by and hold important; and, if certain incongruities in respect to subordinate ideas and phraseology may appear between
the earlier and later discourses, they are a part of the
record of my ministry which I have no wish to conceal, and which may have, indeed, a certain interest
and value.

With one exception, I have allowed myself to
change only verbal infelicities; and that exception
seems to me of sufficient importance specially to
note. The discourse on "The Religion of the Affections," numbered VI., was quite recently repeated,
and was included in the volume by the request of a
number of persons who then heard it. At the repetition, I inserted a modifying, cautionary clause on
introducing the argument from the doctrine of immortality; and this I have permitted to stand in the
sermon, which is otherwise printed substantially as
first delivered in 1865. The discourses are, for the
most part, dated at the time of their first or only
delivery in our own church. In two or three cases,
where they had been to a considerable extent rewrit-
ten, the date when they were given in their new

form is attached; as, for instance, number XXI. was delivered in several places and several years before the date here assigned it, when it appeared in revised form. In the anniversary sermon, one quite important paragraph, accidentally omitted in the delivery, has been inserted. As you know, I have not in late years held to the custom of taking texts, either from the Hebrew and Christian Scriptures or elsewhere. My habit is to use a text, from whatever source, only when the text actually suggests the sermon. But sometimes I have written a quotation as a motto at the head of a sermon, without referring to it in the delivery; and in a few instances, for the sake of uniformity, I have prefixed such mottoes to sermons chosen for the volume, where they were wanting.

Had I been called to select a volume of discourses for the general public, I should have chosen such as would have a more logical connection on some one line of thought. But for you, as a memorial volume of these years during which we have lived and worked together, I have judged that a more miscellaneous selection, as regards topics, would be more acceptable and useful. Selecting thus from the wide variety of subjects which have engaged our thoughts in the Sunday service, I have had, however, two leading aims: first, to choose those discourses that seemed to touch most closely the permanent problems of moral and religious life; and, second, to choose those that attempted to throw some light on the specially perplexing problems of modern religious thought. With the hope that these sermons, thus chosen, which, as a congregation, you have listened to from the pulpit, may now be a help to some of you in the nearer companionship of your homes, I respond to your kindly expressed wish, and put them into your hands.

Sincerely your friend,

WM. J. POTTER.

NEW BEDFORD, May 1, 1885.

SURE the dumb earth hath memory, nor for naught
    Was Fancy given, on whose enchanted loom
Present and Past commingle, fruit and bloom
Of one fair bough, inseparably wrought
Into the seamless tapestry of thought.
So charmed, with undeluded eye we see
In history's fragmentary tale
Bright clews of continuity,
Learn that high natures over Time prevail,
And feel ourselves a link in that entail
That binds all ages past with all that are to be.

JAMES RUSSELL LOWELL.

I.

APOSTOLIC SUCCESSION.

"Other men labored, and ye are entered into their labors."—JOHN iv., 38.

"Therefore, seeing we have this ministry, as we have received mercy, we faint not."—II. COR. iv., 1.

As I recall the succession of able men who with eloquent lips and earnest hearts have ministered to the spiritual wants of this Society, in the privacy of your homes and from this desk, and into whose labors among you, responsive to your call, I this day enter, my heart trembles with conflicting emotions of fear and hope: of fear, lest I shall wear but unworthily the pastoral mantle now fallen upon me from these past prophets and only demean offices hallowed to your hearts by so many memories; of hope, when I think of the warm hands with which you have welcomed me here to begin my life's work, so near the scenes among which began my life. Ay, I am tremulous with joyous pride, when I remember the nature of the work into whose long succession of laborers you have now admitted me, and see that this day the dream of my life is fulfilled. Confirmed by this realization of my childhood's hopes, inspired by a conviction of the worthiness of the office before me, and reading in the unanimity of your invitation and in the ready consent you have given to my requests for certain changes in some of your forms of service that you will freely and candidly listen to my thought, though it may not always agree with your own, and not be swift to censure deficiencies which must become apparent to you from a closer intercourse, I am emboldened to say with Paul, "Having therefore this ministry, as I have received mercy, I faint not."

Into the lengthening succession of the ministry, then, I now enter, and to its holy offices, under the blessing of God, here consecrate my powers. And the thoughts which the occasion presses upon me group themselves naturally around this topic,— *the true doctrine of Apostolic Succession.*

You know the old doctrine that goes by this name, which asserts that no ministry is valid unless it can be traced back, by the successive laying on of priestly hands, to the grace which Jesus himself communicated when he commissioned the first apostles. According to this view, the Holy Spirit can flow only through certain ecclesiastical channels, and spiritual validity is made dependent on physical manipulations. The minister does not go immediately and for himself to the fountain of grace which gives worth and spiritual life to his ministrations; but — standing at the end of this long conduit, reaching back through all the ramifications and disturbances of ecclesiastical history for eighteen hundred years — he is dependent for such supplies as tradition may have saved for him from a past age through the hands of pope and prelate. The Scriptures, interpreted by the traditions and official voice of the Church,— this is the channel, and this only, through which his spirit may receive divine truth. And when we remember the worthless character of not a few of those who have stood in this priestly line of succession, and see through what gross and sordid hands this legacy of truth has sometimes had to pass; and when we think with what rubbish and corruption the channel of ecclesiastical history has been clogged and befouled,— is it strange that those who trust to this resource for their supplies of grace should often find them both scanty and stale? What wonder if they should sometimes discover that what they had taken for aqueducts of pure water should turn out to be offensive sewers, bringing down the filth and poison of effete centuries!

But this view, though its shadow linger yet in several of the Protestant sects, is distinctly declared and maintained as a dogma only by the Roman Catholics and the High Church party of the Episcopal denomination, and need not detain us longer. The fact of the Reformation and the consequent springing up of new sects, and often under the leadership of teachers on whom no priestly hands had been laid in consecration, necessitated the abandonment of the doctrine that ministerial grace is transmitted from the first apostles through an unbroken chain of physical communication, and gave rise to the *second* form of the doctrine of Apostolic Succession, which, for sake of distinction, though not held very strictly by all the Protestant sects, yet found to some extent in all or nearly all, I shall call the *Protestant* view of the doctrine.

According to this view, it is not necessary, in order to validate the ministerial office, that the laying on of priestly hands should have been maintained in unbroken succession from the first apostles. The impossibility of tracing such a genealogy through the confused history of the Middle Ages and the meagre annals of the first centuries of the Church, if there were no other objections, is deemed a sufficient argument against the claim. But the real succession and validity, it is maintained, are spiritual; and the laying on of hands is only emblematic of grace already possessed, or, at best, is only a form of giving ecclesiastical validity, not substantial and spiritual qualifications. And this were all clear and rational, if it were only the real doctrine held; that is, if the doctrine, as it is really held, were what the plain sense of these words indicates. But, in point of fact, there is hardly a Protestant sect that does not practically reproduce, with more or less strictness, in its own limits the Roman Catholic idea of validity. It is not necessary, indeed, for the Protestant preacher's validity that he should have received grace through the unbroken priestly order of the Church from the original apostles; but it is deemed necessary that he should have received it from hands of his own faith. The Calvinist minister needs not, in order to prove his legitimacy, to show that the hands which were laid upon him received grace from some prelate's hands, which were made gracious by some previous prelate's hands, and so on back to the original grace in Galilee; but he must show that the hands of Calvinists have been laid upon him. Should it be said that this form is only emblematic of approbation and fellowship on points of doctrine, I reply that the fancied explanation points to the very root of the error and, instead of refuting my statement, proves it; for it shows that the substantial and spiritual qualifications — of the possession of which, it is said, the form of ordination is only symbolic — must have come through certain channels and have a certain church stamp upon them. Whatever may be said of individual societies, there is no sect — no, not even the most liberal — that dares to trust a minister freely with the Divine Spirit. He must have that Spirit, indeed; but he cannot breathe it in like the free air of heaven by contact with his own lungs. He must have it measured out for him by prescription of some theological authority, and inhale it artificially through the sponge of a creed. It is not the Divine Spirit coming to *him* and showing him truth, but that Spirit as it once came to Luther or Calvin or Swedenborg or Wesley or Fox; and if, perchance, it should come to him with some word not told to them, and he should use his freedom to utter it, most likely he will be disfellowshipped and excommunicated therefor. And so essentially there is no difference between the Catholic and the common Protestant doctrine of ministerial succession. The papal priest succeeds to apostolic grace and truth by hereditary descent from the first apostles. The Protestant minister succeeds to the apostolic inheritance by tradition from the founder, or founders, of his special sect. The only difference is that the Protestant thinks that the line of hereditary descent from the first apostles has been broken, so that corruptions entered the Church, and that this failure has been mended by the truth having been reshown to the founders of his own sect. But both the Catholic and Protestant parties agree that of religious truth, at least for this world, there has been a final revelation; and each of these two great bodies, as well as each of the numerous smaller Protestant sects,— with hardly a complete exception,— claims that its own interpretation of that revelation is a finality, so that a new minister only succeeds to the old office of expounding Scriptural truth according to the creed and commentaries of his own faith, travelling over the same road trodden by his predecessors for, it may be, hundreds of years; while those who put themselves above the Scriptures, and claim the continuance and efficacy of the same revealing Spirit which manifested itself in them, are denounced as heretics and infidels. The sect that still claims the present guidance of the Holy Spirit as above Scripture — that of the Society of Friends, or Quakers — makes, at least in its largest section, no proper exception to this judgment; for it practically neutralizes the doctrine by making the authenticity of the living spoken Word of to-day depend upon agreement with the literal written words of eighteen centuries ago. And so there is succession, but no advancement. Churches are built, decay, and are succeeded by others, generation after generation of priests passes away, and yet there is no progress, no going beyond the creed of the fathers, no getting out of the catechism.

Notice that I am here stating the principle on which the sects stand rather than actual facts with regard to them. As a matter of fact, not even the strictest sect, I believe, is able to resist the general current of progress, which is shown, however, rather by a prudent silence on some of their most discreditable articles of faith than by boldly expunging them from the creed. In principle, however, no progress can be admitted. The Orthodox must hold to Calvin or Edwards, the Methodist must not depart from Wesley, the Quaker cannot go beyond Fox and Barclay; and even in our own free denomination there are many who would draw lines each side of Channing, to pass over which in either direction should be deemed sufficient cause for non-fellowship. So that, with the partial exception of Liberal Christians, whatever advancement the sects make in religious truth is made not in consequence but in spite of their principles. And this advancement of particular sects, in spite of their creeds and their own efforts, is the result of a general movement in the knowledge of truth by which the whole civilized world is going forward: which brings us to the *third* view under our topic,— the true and philosophic order of Apostolic Succession and ministerial validity. Let us distinguish the points carefully.

1. That is a narrow conception of revelation, and, as I believe, unsupported both by enlightened views of the nature of God and by the history of the religious development of man, which maintains that in religious truth there is no progress,— that the Christian of to-day has no better ideas of God and man

and the relation between them than the Christian of eighteen centuries ago. It would indeed be strange if, while science and art and philosophy are progressive, religion — which embraces them all, the science, art, and philosophy of life — should stand still, and have no new word for eighteen hundred years. Nor does the history of Christianity bring us to any such singular result. So far as Christianity is a revelation of God, it is so, not because it laid down a platform of doctrines and put a finality to all religious thought and inquiry, but because it entered the world as a vitalizing, organizing power, bringing truth gradually to light and building up society according to its dictates. Truth, indeed, is one, absolute, eternal, infinite. But, for this very reason, the revelation of religious truth, as of all other truth, to a finite, progressive being must be always gradual, partial, and progressive. The case would not be altered by the supposition that the revelation of religious truth is through supernatural means and at special seasons. For even though the Creator, by methods above the ordinary laws of spiritual influence, should have so acted upon a few minds, the writers of the Bible, that they saw and uttered truths which otherwise they would not have seen, yet the minds of other persons — that is, of the world at large — could not see and comprehend these truths until elevated to the same condition of seeing, which must occur either suddenly by supernatural agency or gradually by natural growth and development; and, as the former process is not claimed by the hypothesis except in the case of those to whom the truth was first shown, it follows that to the world at large the revelation must be gradual and progressive. And, moreover, this must be so from the very nature of the mind itself. Our powers are not given us in full maturity, but as germs to be developed, we know not to what destined end. To this law of growth, the religious faculty, including religious perception as well as sentiment, is certainly no exception : else, why all this organizing of means, of preaching and prayer and missions, to make men more rationally religious? The elevation of the soul, the enlargement and quickening of the truth-seeing faculty within us, is, in fact, the test of the growth of character. And as not even Omnipotence can make the blind see without first opening their eyes, so he cannot reveal truth to the soul unless the soul be first opened to receive it ; and as the soul, in the natural order, opens by gradual development, so the revelation must be gradual and progressive. What is true of the individual is also true of the race, since the race advances only through the progress of individuals. Religious truth, then, in process of revelation to the world, must be progressive.

2. What are the agencies through which this revelation is effected? First and foremost is the Divine Spirit, the source or vital atmosphere of the truth itself which is to be revealed. This is the primary and permanent agency acting through and above all others. It is Infinite Being revealing itself, Absolute and Infinite Truth making its way into finite, individual consciousness. The Divine

Spirit is only a form of conception for God. It is God going forth, as it were, from himself,—the Eternal Word issuing from Absolute, Unchangeable Being, and seeking incarnation and articulation in finite, personal form. This Eternal Word carries truth with it, by virtue of its very nature; for truth is its life and substance. This is that "Wisdom" which "in all ages, entering into holy souls, maketh them friends of God and prophets." In every finite soul, then, in which this Word comes to consciousness, and just in proportion to the extent of that consciousness, is truth revealed.

And so the finite soul becomes a second and subagency in the revelation of truth. For though in every human being there is planted, as its vital organic principle, a germ of this eternal substance of the Divine Spirit, which will develop, as the faculties open, into religious principles and character, yet, as in science and art and every department of knowledge there have always been individuals who have seen farther than the mass of men, and have therefore been special instructors in their respective branches of knowledge, so in all ages have men appeared in whom the religious consciousness has been so elevated that they have seen farther than mankind in general into the secrets of religious truth, and become its special revealers to the world. These are the Spirit's witnesses, through whom the higher truths of religion are confirmed, if not announced, to humanity at large. They stand along the course of history as the guides of the race, as the prophets of human destiny. Their souls are the reflectors of divine truth, so placed that they throw the rays upon the common human heart, and start into life and organic form the germs of truth before lying latent there. Through these prophetic souls, the common religious consciousness of the race is quickened to greater activity and elevated to a higher point of vision and a more extended spiritual horizon. And, then, as out of this elevated religious consciousness a new generation is born, so the prophets of this newer generation — even if, their feet standing on this higher plane, they do not see farther into the mysteries of truth than their predecessors — will at least have a better vantage-ground from which, with the truth they do see, they can act practically upon the world. And thus the common religious consciousness of the race is elevated to still higher reach; and this elevation, in its turn, becomes a new stage by which succeeding prophets shall rise to yet larger vision, and make to the underlying world still broader revelations of Infinite Wisdom. As scientific men take up their respective sciences where they were left by the preceding generation, and so go on from these results to fresh discoveries and new generalizations, so each generation of religious teachers, standing on the ground won by the preceding age, should attain to broader views and help build to more perfect completion the temple of religious truth. And this is the true divine order of Apostolic Succession.

3. If we would follow the line of this succession, we must get above denominational distinctions and take a broad philosophic view of religious develop-

ment, not merely within the *limits* of sects, but in the *production* of sects. We shall then see that the true Apostolic Succession does not lie within denominational boundaries, but overleaps them, and that, in the race of true prophets, validity is proved rather by departure from than conformity to the established order of creeds and churches. Who does not see that Paul, though he had never seen Jesus in the flesh and was regarded with jealousy by the original apostles as an interloper and innovator of dangerous doctrines, was yet a truer apostle of Jesus than were they? Paul, with his idea of the universality of the gospel, embracing the Gentile world, was the really Christian apostle; while the twelve were little more than partially reformed Jews. Again, Wiclif and Huss and Luther, Calvin and Zwingle, though trampling on the authority of the Church and introducing new doctrines and ecclesiastical usages, were yet, by spiritual descent, more legitimately priests of Christianity than were the popes and bishops who excommunicated them. So, in England to-day, it is not the High Church party, trying to stand so straight by ecclesiastical tradition and the Thirty-nine Articles that it leans backward toward Rome,— it is not this party that is carrying out, by true succession, the principles of the Reformation, but rather the heresy-suspected leaders of the Broad Church party,— Jowett, Whately, Stanley, and the lamented Arnold and Robertson, or even the open dissenters. Fox and Wesley and Bunyan denounced Church and priest; yet, by the laying on of spiritual hands, they were more legitimately successors in God's line of priesthood than the Archbishops of York or Canterbury. So, if we were to look for the true successors of Fox and Penn, we might not find them in the sect that, from the effort to stand upon *their* protest against forms and ceremonies in religion, has become the most severely formal of all religious denominations. The cause of the persecuted Independents, who fled from the tyranny of the English Church to find an asylum in New England, is better upheld now by the liberal sects than by those who still subscribe to the Puritan creed. And to come still nearer home, when I read the sublime pleas of Channing for the fullest liberty of religious inquiry and the formation of religious opinions untrammelled by the authority of great names or ecclesiastical organizations, and when I remember his earnest protestations against imposing upon the convictions of a single soul the bondage of a creed or making articles of faith the test of religion, I can but ask whether those who call themselves "Channing Unitarians," because, forsooth, they adopt his beliefs, are, in reality, so truly his followers as those who, entering into his labors and adopting his methods of fearless inquiry and criticism, have taken up the results of his thought and advanced to still greater victories over the degrading errors of the popular theology and to still clearer visions of religious truth. It behooves us, at least, to inquire whether to *stand* where Channing stood is to be his *follower*. None, I am sure, quicker than he would rebuke the attempt to build a sect upon his creed by cutting off all inquiry beyond. To stop at his results, as though all truth were found, is not to honor, but to defame his memory. The only church that can be an honest monument to his name and truly claim him as its great apostle is that which, with the largest freedom of religious inquiry and indefinite progress in religious truth, combines the utmost charity to opponents in opinion and love to all men. Away, then, with that childishness that talks of there being "no more road in the direction we have been going"! It is as ludicrously short-sighted as the opinion of the commissioners appointed, two hundred years ago, by the Colony of Massachusetts Bay, to lay out a public road into the wilderness ten miles west from Boston, who, in their final report, congratulated the General Court on the completion of the work, even at the great and unexpected cost, as there would never be need of a road any farther in that direction! Nay, it is worse than short-sightedness, this talk of turning our forces, fatigued with the long march, to seek repose in the dreamy sanctity of venerable ecclesiastic rites and a "mystic church organization." It is infidelity to our Protestant inheritance, infidelity to the spirit of the age, infidelity to the great trusts we have assumed for humanity by virtue of our position, infidelity to the guiding Providence of God, and a cowardly distrust of the powers he has committed to man.*

We may see, then, from the foregoing illustra-

---

*The references in the above sentences are to the then much discussed sermon of Dr. Bellows, on "The Suspense of Faith," given at Cambridge in the preceding summer, 1859.

tions, how the lineage of the true apostolic succession runs; that it is not identical nor parallel with ecclesiastical lineage, but crosses and denies its legitimacy; that it is not to be found intact in any one church or sect, but breaks through churches and sects, and follows always the line of development in religious ideas; that, finally, God's priesthood are not ordained by the laying on of ecclesiastic hands, but by the revelation of truth to the soul. And in this priestly succession stands many a one without mitre or surplice, unfrocked, and unconsecrated by ecclesiastic hand,— many a one who never stands in pulpit or speaks in the priestly name. So, too, there is many a surpliced or cassocked preacher, many a one whose ecclesiastic validity is amply authenticated by all the forms of the Church, and who may speak from the pulpit every Sunday with priestly authority to the people, who yet has no part in this apostolic succession of God's priesthood and (to adopt with a little variation.Dr. Channing's phraseology) no validity of the Spirit's grace, though all the unctuous hands of Rome, Geneva, Princeton, or Cambridge, have been laid upon him. But to whomsoever and wheresoever the truth is shown, if it be but uttered again, in public or in private speech, by pen or spoken word, there is a prophet of God; one who stands by true commission in the eternal order of the Spirit's priesthood. And all they to whom the truth is shown, by whomsoever or wheresoever shown, and *who strive faithfully to live thereby*, whether in the limits or out of the limits of ecclesiastic lines, constitute the true Broad Church, the real Catholic Church, which breaks over all the partition walls of sect, and joins in one spiritual fellowship the true and holy souls of all nations, ages, and religions.

My friends, I pray that it be into no merely ecclesiastical order of ministerial succession that I now enter among you. If I felt that I had no validity save what came to me through the churchly ceremonies of last week, severely simple though they were, I should not stand here to-day. I do not come among you to help build up a sect, or to fill your pews, or to perform merely the priestly office in your homes. I come to speak to you whatever of truth may by God's grace be shown to me. I ask only that you may listen by the same grace. I believe that the mission of Unitarian Christianity is higher and larger than simply to make a new religious sect or to open new places for Sunday worship or to fill old ones,— namely: to liberalize and spiritualize all sects, to make all society religious and all life worship; and all ecclesiastical organizations, forms, rituals, ministers, missions, houses of worship, the very Church itself, are nothing, and worse than nothing, if they do not effect this.

This morning's sun brought the birth of the eighteen hundred and sixtieth year of the Christian era. Eighteen hundred and sixty years since that Life appeared in Galilee, which seemed so divine a thing that it became the measure of time and named the civilized world! In these years, what successions of priests have come forth in the name of Christ, and passed away; how numberless the churches dedicated to his memory; what countless crowds of worshippers have knelt at his altars; how various the sects claiming his authority for their doctrines and practices; what conflicting systems of theology have been built upon his words; what imposing pageantries of ritual and ceremony, what costly and complicated organizations, what a vast array of ecclesiastical machinery, what wealth and enginery of material and political forces, have gathered around that humbly born life in Nazareth! But what more? Has that life been lived? Do we *dare* to live it yet? Does it appear in society, in government? Do we yet trust the principles of peace that this Prince of Peace proclaimed? Count our armies. See our bristling forts. Look at Christian Europe in arms to-day. No: 'we have no faith in Christ. We dare not trust the principles he uttered, till the whole world shall adopt them. Do we yet enact his precepts in our laws? A slave woman comes to you, flying for freedom, for purity, for life. You must violate your laws, if you will give her humane shelter. You must hang the men who go down to the tyrant's house, with chivalrous hearts, to set her free. Look into the world of business. Does Christ's life appear there? Does the merchant always dare to follow the laws of justice and strict honesty, when they interfere with what he calls the laws of trade? *No:* the Christian sects do not dare to live Christ's life yet. For centuries, now, the civilized world has borne his name. It has prayed to him and through him; it has called him Son of God, nay, God himself; it has invented ingenious devices of theology by which he may save mankind; men have preached him, read him, admired him, worshipped him; but who yet dares to live as he lived, with no authority but Truth, no law but Right, no master but God? With all its massive and wide-spread organizations, with all this ecclesiastical machinery and power,— nay, with all its victories, for it has them,— how little, when we consider its resources, has Christianity done toward *Christianizing* society!

And, if we were to look for the cause of these small results, we should find it, I believe, to be chiefly that there has been too much organization, too much mechanism, too much Church. The power has been nearly spent in moving the machinery. It is an historical fact that, so far as Christian truth or the moral essence of Christianity has made progress in society and appeared in the reform of laws and social institutions, it has done so, not through the organic action of the Church, but against it. And, at this very day, it is the most powerful and strongly organized Christian sects that most stand in the way of the progress of religious truth and social reforms. It is not the "organic, instituted, ritualized," imperial Church, with its mystic sanctity and symbols, with its sacred days and usages made venerable by centuries of repetition, that is to bring the kingdom of God; nor yet is that kingdom to come through the priests of this Church, made such only by ecclesiastic grace. But wherever a single soul bows with more passionate devotion to truth, and resolves to follow the truth wheresoever it may lead, through whatsoever road, and though losing all things else, even life itself, there is a member of God's Church and a true minister in the line of his priesthood.

It is into the order of the holy priesthood of this inorganic, spiritual Church that I pray this day to enter. It is into the membership — yea, ministry — of this Church that I invite you. If I can lift any souls among you to more ennobling truth, to purer love, to stronger virtue, if I can quicken your spiritual vision and lead any of you to see more clearly the infinite beauty of a life proportioned to the laws of Eternal Rectitude, then will these New Year's vows of consecration be crowned indeed with blessing, being followed in due season by seed-time showers and hopes, maturing summer suns, and autumn harvests of ripened souls.

January 1, 1860.

II.

THE SOUL'S REST.

"Return unto thy rest, O my soul."—PSALM cxvi., 7.

"THERE would seem," says a living writer and one of the greatest of living preachers,* "to be an incurable variance between the life which men covet for themselves and that which they admire in others; nay, between the lot which they would choose beforehand and that in which they glory afterwards. In prospect, nothing appears so attractive as ease and licensed comfort; in retrospect, nothing so delightful as toil and strenuous service."

The truth of this remark is being repeatedly impressed upon us both by public and private circumstance. It does seem as if Providence had conditioned us to a lot of labor and struggle,—nay, forced it upon us,—while our first aim is to smooth our path and prepare the way for an after happiness which consists in rest and passive pleasure. The Creator leaves no soul at ease. If inherited circumstances give you the perilous opportunity, you may try the problem of an inactive life, resistless to any inclination or whim that the hour may give birth to; but be assured that, for as many hours

* James Martineau.

thus spent, nature, which is the working of divine laws, will demand in payment an equal number of hours of weariness and disgust, of aching nerves and empty heart,— a gnawing consciousness of a destiny unfulfilled and of faculties craving a rest they have not yet attained. If inheritance, fortunately, has not put your life to such a hazard, then you are forced to an existence of toil, of body or mind, in order to keep that very existence. The earth will not yield you bread till you have ploughed and tilled; and, in the furrow where you plant your seed, God grows weeds as well as corn, in order to task your energies still the more. You must fell the forests before they shelter you; spin the cotton, weave the wool, before they clothe you; build the ship and invent compass and chart before you can bring the ends of the earth to serve your needs. We are thrown upon a world of wild, half-savage material forces, which we must either tame and subdue to service or be destroyed by them. Yet all the time, throughout the struggle, we cry for respite and rest; and the most prevailing motive that spurs on these toiling millions of men and women all around the globe is the hope that by and by toil will cease in competency, and struggle be rewarded with independent ease.

Just so it is with our moral and spiritual condition. We cannot get food for our intellects, we cannot clothe our souls in the virtues, we cannot ornament them with the graces of character, we cannot build up good society and good institutions around us, we cannot have good governments, good laws, and good charitable organizations, we cannot be safe in our houses or in the street, we cannot do away with evil institutions, with crime and corruption and vices,— our own or those of the community,— we cannot, I say, have or do any of these things without labor and study and struggle and assiduous culture. We are thrown upon a world of wild, unregulated *moral* forces, which we must also tame and bring to service, or they, too, will work our destruction.

Yet all the time, as in the physical, so in this moral struggle, we sigh for rest; and the strongest incentive that urges us along the path of conflict is the hoped-for ease to come at the end. We are driven to the battle, not so much that the truth and the right may be victorious as for the sake of the peace that will follow. Wearied with the assaults of passion, we long for an untempted virtue. Our comfort invaded by the dust and din of contending forces, we yearn for the quiet of neutrality, and for the sake of ease are not infrequently tempted into dishonorable treaties with vices that ought to be recognized only to be exterminated.

And so, generally, the moral condition which we covet is just the reverse of that to which we have been born. Born for contest, we ask for repose. We would skip, if possible, the drill and the discipline, and clutch at once the prizes of victory. How many of us go through life like complaining school-children,— doing our tasks, it may be, but longing for the time when books shall be put aside and all lessons come to an end! Questions, it may be, besiege the intellect, demanding of it activity and decision; doubts, perhaps, of the old settlement of religious things in which we have been educated, — doubts and questionings and conflicts and searching inquiry, which are the providential order of removing error and bringing in the light of truth. Yet, tired of the intellectual struggle, appalled by the view that seems to keep man's reason in constant tension and humanity in continual march, we are often tempted to escape the responsibilities that our faculties impose upon us, and, suspending reason, to sink back on the soft cushions of ecclesiastical authority. Thus it is that some struggling souls, shrinking from the conflict and from the inevitable conclusions that the Protestant principle of individual inquiry forces upon them, seek for rest and try to lull all religious questionings to sleep on the ready-made bed of the Church of Rome.

Or it may be that it is a moral contest we have entered upon,— a contest with social evils around us or with the nearer evils in our own breasts. But we find that the battle goes hard against us. Society is slow to acknowledge its sins, and still slower to remove them. Public opinion frowns upon our efforts. Friends, even, regard our schemes as Utopian, and evidence only of amiable weakness. And the very classes of society we would help, not infrequently suspect and resist the aid that we offer. With so much against us, it is not strange if we should often be sorely tempted to give over the battle, and let ourselves float smoothly along with the stronger current of popular opinion, leaving it to God (as we say, in phrase that sounds more pious than it is), who has permitted evil, to take care of it. And this fallacious rest we often try, too, when the moral struggle is with ourselves. Our evil habits too strong for one encounter, our vices too deeply rooted to be washed out by mere *tears* of repentance, the passions — avarice, selfish ambition, carnal appetite — from continued indulgence grown inordinate in their demands, and all the forces of our being having fallen under the control of our lower nature, conscience, maimed and bleeding, is often tempted to retire from the hard contest on the high ground of moral law, to try the flattering repose offered by the code of social respectability. And hence it is that very many come to accept as the standard of their lives, not what the highest moral truth *demands*, but what the common decencies of society will *allow;* while only a prayer is left that He who has made us with passions, and thrown this conflict with them upon us, will somehow grant us rest from their tyranny on a higher level hereafter. Religion, too, or much that passes in its name, not infrequently fosters this easy faith, and, instead of nerving us to strong encounter with evil, degenerates into plaintive whining over the ills of earth and sighing for the rest of heaven.

But, notwithstanding the prevailing extent of this desire for repose and the fallacious arguments with which we attempt to cover our own delinquencies in the matter, human nature, in its inmost heart, is sound, and honors no repose which is not honorably achieved by contest and victory. Human nature is to be judged, not by the standard which individual

men live by, or even set for themselves, but by that
which they most admire in others; and that must
be regarded as the aim of humanity at large, which,
though exhibited in the attainment of but a single
individual, gathers about it the greatest number who
applaud and revere it. What craven spirit was ever
admired in history or in fiction? Who but the
brave, who but those who against all obstacles
have contended manfully and unflinchingly and kept
their integrity to the bitter end, have ever been
adopted as the models or worshipped as the heroes of
mankind? How immeasurably more has the world
admired the character of Socrates for refusing to
avail himself of the plan of his jailer, who had been
bribed to aid his escape! And yet few are the persons in all history whose moral sense would not
have been confused by such an offer. And, if the
Athenian sage had faltered and used the proffered
means of saving his life, we should have found, I
will not say merely apologies for, but defences of
the act even as a duty,— as, indeed, in thousands of
similar cases has been done, and as most of us perhaps would be likely to do, if the case were to come
home to ourselves to-day. But, such an example of
unmoved integrity once set, humanity is true enough
to recognize it as a higher order of virtue than flight,
however guiltless, would have been, and to bow
before it in admiring reverence, though few may
have the courage to be its imitators. And when we
come to that most admired character of all, the
name highest and most beloved of history, what is
it that has made Jesus to be regarded as the proto-

type of all human perfections, worshipped indeed as God himself, and the word "Christian" to be a synonyme of all that is most elevated in virtue and most amiable in character? What is it but that Jesus stood, like Divine Majesty itself, firm for the truth, unyielding before corruption and hypocrisy, gentle and forgiving, yet bearing faithfully the burdens of his mission, not flinching before violence nor swerving for adulation, and meeting the cross with such a spirit of love and of triumph that he consecrated it as "a thing of beauty" forever?

And, moreover, we admire such character as this for its own sake, for a majesty and divineness in itself, and not for any after good it may issue in. Nay, our admiration would be sensibly diminished, if we could for a moment suppose such a character sustained only by the hope of some after blessing as a reward; nor can we conceive that all these excellences were practically annihilated at the grave by the soul's then passing into a condition of absolute repose.

These two points, then, seem to be clearly established: first, in the midst of the toil, trials, and struggles of our lot there is an instinctive craving within us for rest; and yet, secondly, the standard of life which we also instinctively place the highest, and which, at the bottom of our hearts, we do most really admire, is that in which there is the least of rest. Solve this seeming paradox, and we shall answer the question of *what the soul's rest is.*

We crave for rest, it is true; and the desire is so universal that it must be regarded as instinctive.

But, like all our instincts, the desire is blind. Instinct does not see and *consciously* choose its end, but gives only direction toward a certain satisfaction which human nature requires in order to fulfil its destiny. What is the extent and character of that satisfaction, not any one instinct or desire, but the whole nature, must determine. What, then, is the kind of rest which the human soul demands, and which alone can satisfy its desires?

Rest and motion, used in their primitive meaning, referring to material things, have both a relative and an absolute sense. A body is at absolute rest when it keeps the same position with regard to a fixed point in space; in motion, when it departs from such a point. But two bodies, though both in motion, are relatively at rest when they keep the same position with regard to each other. Now, how can these terms, or more particularly the term "rest," be used of spirit, or of mental and moral life? Not, I answer, in an absolute sense at all. The very word *spirit* implies life, movement, energy,— the very opposite of inertia and passivity, which are the characteristics of matter. To spirit, then, there can be no such thing as absolute rest. It can have, evidently, only relative rest,— the rest that depends on unison of movement. And the rest, therefore, which our human spirits crave, and which can alone satisfy their needs, is not the rest of inactivity and inertia, but the rest of harmony.

But harmony with what? Harmony with the Divine Spirit,— harmony with the Universal Spirit, — whose aim and movements we may know by its *pulse-beats* in our consciousness ; by our best affections and aspirations and the voice of conscience, which, as they assert their supreme authority within us, lay down also the laws of our being's guidance. There can be no rest for us but in obedience to these laws of our being, which are the laws of God ; no rest for our bodies but in obeying the laws of health,— not overtasking, not undertasking our physical powers, but giving to each just the action that it needs to keep it in vigorous, healthy life. And very much, I am satisfied, of this plaintive, unmanly sighing for rest, which often passes for religious aspiration, is nothing but the jar and creaking of shattered nerves. Yet physical laws are subordinate, and must sometimes be broken, in order that higher laws may be obeyed. For, again, there can be no rest for our moral and spiritual natures,— no rest for our hearts, no rest for our minds, no rest for our aspirations and consciences, — unless we faithfully follow their highest bent and laws of action. Have we evil habits and vices? There can be no rest but in meeting them, struggling with them, conquering them. Are there social evils around us for which by omission or commission we are in any way responsible? There can be no rest but in entering the field of conflict against them. Are there miseries to be alleviated, broken spirits to be healed, wrongs and oppressions to be righted, poverty to be enriched with sympathy, ignorance with instruction? Then there can be no rest but in taking upon ourselves, in some form, the office of the comforter and savior. Is there any wisdom and light in the heavens above us, not yet penetrated by our mental vision? Then there is no rest for our intellects but in constant ascent, according to the laws of mental progress, through the successively ascending fields of infinite science. Finally, is there any ideal of life still above us, sometimes, perhaps, for a moment seized and then again floating away beyond our present reach, but radiant there in the clear sunshine, with heavenly beauty? Then there can be no rest for our souls but in daily striving, aspiring, ascending, till we attain and realize it.

The rest, then, that our natures crave is not the repose of passivity, of listlessness, of sleep, but the rest of healthy spiritual life,— of life in accordance with the laws of our being, which are laws of progressive activity, and, if obeyed, put us into harmony with the spirit and peace of God. The rest that we want is like the rest you may have in a railroad car, where, though you may be moving with immense rapidity, yet with respect to the whole train you are relatively in repose, because you are in harmony with it and the mighty force that takes it forward. Or, better, it is the rest of the heavenly bodies, which, though all may be in rapid and varied movement, are yet at peace with regard to each other, because moving according to the harmony of a divine law. And such rest as this we can have, though in the midst of labor and trial and conflict. It is the rest to which Jesus invited the "weary and heavy-laden"; the rest, not of those who have thrown their burdens off or would impose them upon others, but of those who have taken upon them the yoke of God's law, and find the "yoke easy" and the "burden light," because, through obedience to this law, a mighty strength and a mighty peace have come into their being. Such rest have martyrs had, while flames and tortures unspeakable destroyed with slow cruelty the body to let the spirit free. And such rest can every one of us possess, whatever our lot or toil or duty or trouble, who will bow unreservedly to the mission and the laws of the divine Spirit within us, and follow it by whatsoever path, through whatsoever conflicts, to whatsoever end it may lead.

O ye "weary, heavy-laden" souls, return unto your rest! "*Return*,"—the word is well chosen. This rest is yours by the demand of your natures. It is yours by the original endowment and laws of your being. It is yours by your place in creation's plan. It is yours by the dreams of your youth, by the prayers that went up from the homes of your childhood. *Return* to it,— to this rest prefigured in your natures, promised, by the Highest Giver, in your earliest hopes of what your life might be, and still longed for, with secret longings unutterable, in your inmost hearts. You have tried, it may be, the rest of ease and the rest of travel; tried the comforts and the luxuries of wealth; tried the tempting path of fame; tried the ways of selfish pleasure; ay, tried, perhaps, the lusts of appetite: but the vulgar enjoyment of the hour once past, the selfish excitement over, your real self with you alone again, and there comes back, week in, week out, this same old weariness of heart, emptiness of aim, and crying for a rest that none of these things can give. Let go these husks, then, and return to the old home love, to the dreams of your childhood, to the noble, heroic, faithful manly or womanly life that floated in ideal before the vision and won the admiration of your youth. Return to the highest demands of your natures, which are a revelation of God's demands upon you; and, behold, the infinite peace of God shall flow without measure into your being, and give you the rest that is everlasting.

January 20, 1861.

NOTE.— This discourse was also preached in the Unitarian church in Washington, July 21, 1861, the day of the first battle of Bull Run. As the congregation came out of the church, the booming of cannon could be distinctly heard across the Potomac.

III.

GOD IN NATURE.

"And the earth was without form, and void; and darkness was upon the face of the deep. And the Spirit of God moved upon the face of the waters."—GEN. i., 2.

"Consider the lilies of the field, how they grow."—MATT. vi., 28.

I HAVE coupled these texts together as a convenient indication of the course of thought I wish to present this morning on the manifestation of God in Nature, or the *Divinity of the Material Universe.* Whether we look into these old Jewish records or into the still older Hindu, into the fables of Grecian Hesiod or the Eddas of Scandinavia, we find everywhere that the earliest problem of human thought which language has preserved is the problem of creation,—the *Whence* and *How* of the universe. We open the latest issues of the modern printing-press, and behold, in book and review, the great question of the scientific world to-day is this same old problem of the origin of things. The problem is not, perhaps, strictly a religious one either in its old or its new shape; that is, all the immediate obligations of morality and practical religion are clear enough, and would remain the same whether the world was made in six days or in six thousand years, or is still in process of making. And the better it will be for us, the sooner we arrive at that mental state wherein, careful only for the truth, we shall become indifferent as to the effect upon religion whether this or that particular theory of the universe shall finally be established. Still, this problem of creation, though not directly connected with religious practice, has always been, and is necessarily, associated with religious thought; and there is such an interdependence among our faculties that it may well be doubted whether truth in thought does not finally connect itself with truth in character, and whether any religious sect can long continue to hold, *for the sake of its theological creed*, a scientific falsehood without corresponding narrowness appearing somewhere in its moral and spiritual life. That, indeed, is a very limited view of the practical in religion which looks only to the giving of homilies that can be converted at once into daily habits. The well-balanced religious life, though it must always include outward work, yet is vastly more than that. It is a life of intellectual as well as of moral and spiritual fidelity. The springs of religion lie deep and are wide-spread; and that is but a superficial religious culture which does not plough into the subsoil and develop the riches of every field of our complex natures.

We may find, then, ample grounds on which to discuss, even from a practical stand-point of religious truth, the theme to which I ask your attention in this discourse.

And, first, see what a change has been wrought,

by the progress of knowledge, in the popular view of this subject. Egypt, Greece, and Rome, which successively led the human race in civilization and enlightenment, all divided the administration of the material universe among many deified rulers. The earth, the air, the sea, and woods they peopled with unseen beings, by the immediate fiat of whose wills the various changes and operations of nature took place. Whether the sea raged or stood still, whether the wind blew from the north or from the south, whether the earth clothed itself in its spring garments of green or the autumn leaf fell sere to the ground, a god, a spirit, was believed to be there, immediately and consciously acting. But science has changed all this. Mother Ceres has been banished from the earth, and her tender housewifely care of the spring buds, summer flowers, and autumn harvests is now only a beautiful myth. We have not yet traced the laws of the wind; but we do not believe longer that any capricious Æolus locks them up in his cave, and lets them out at his pleasure. No Neptune lives for us in the sea, to command its waves. No Aurora breaks for us each morning the gates of darkness, bringing light and life upon the earth. In place of these beautiful, poetic imaginings, we now have positive science; for this simple faith, we now have demonstrated facts; instead of these living, personal deities, we now have physical laws; and, (may it not be added?) instead of religion, we have — too often — only philosophy.

Now, the advance of science is neither to be stayed nor deprecated. We must submit our theologies to its discoveries and analysis as well as all other departments of our knowledge and experience. We must modify and advance our theological views to conform to the assured conclusions of science, or else our religious faith must suffer detriment; and, because this has not generally been done, we may well doubt whether Deity is to Christendom so real and vital a presence as to the devotees of these old religions whom we have been so forward to commiserate and enlighten. The unity of God is a great truth; but, if we cannot hold it without sacrificing the universality of God, then it may well be questioned whether, in our entire view of the divine nature, we have made much advance upon the religious beliefs of Greece and Rome. If we cannot maintain ourselves at the elevation of Jesus, where with clear vision we can gaze at the spiritual oneness of Deity and at the same time feel that he who inhabiteth eternity and sitteth upon the arch of the heavens dwells also in the lowliest human soul and clothes the humblest lily of the field, then we may well go back to learn the preparatory lessons that heathenism has for us. If we cannot believe in the unity of God without falling into those dreary theological systems which banish him from the earth and from the daily changes of nature to a distant throne in the remotest heavens, from which we must imagine him to rule and judge the universe with the cold, calculating reserve of a human sovereign; if we cannot hold the unity of God without giving him form, and circumscribing him in space, and picturing him with all the attributes of a finite ruler,— then I am not sure that it would not be better for us to leave our Bibles for a while and take some lessons in the warmer faith of the old Pagan mythology. Better than this one cold, distant, deified despotism the myriad human deities of Greece and Rome. Better let go the unity of God than his universality.

But we need not take this backward step. Christianity appears originally to have held the recognition of both ideas. A fine statement of their unity was made in the apocryphal book called "The Wisdom of Solomon," before the advent of Jesus. But the Christian Church and Christian theology have too often failed to comprehend this finely harmonized doctrine, which Jesus by virtue of his spiritual genius seems to have assumed, of universal and infinite unity,— of one spirit pervading the whole universe, of mind and matter, of nature and man. In order to prove one creator and governor of the world, Deity has been banished outside of the world.

Incalculable harm, in one way, has been done to religion by such works as Paley's. You know the old argument, the analogy drawn from a watch: if a person should stumble suddenly upon a watch, and examine its mechanism, and see how exquisitely all its parts were adapted to each other and each to its office, he must necessarily conclude that it was the work of an intelligent contriver and maker. In like manner, as the argument runs, from studying the universe,— its adaptation of part to part and each part to its object,— we must conclude that it, too, is the work of an intelligent author. Now, the universe unquestionably discloses marks of nicest adaptation and the most consummate wisdom. But there is always danger, in using the argument from analogy, that we push it too far ; and this is peculiarly the danger when we reason from finite things to infinite. And so the majority of persons, I suppose, who adopt Paley's argument, follow it up till they have pictured to themselves the whole act and plan of creation, and creation and creator have become as definite conceptions to them as the making and maker of a watch. And, going so far, it is almost impossible that they shall not push the analogy still farther; and, since a watch, having once been made and its machinery set in motion, passes out of the maker's hands, to go henceforth by the forces brought together and shut up within it, so they conceive that the world, having been made and put into operation by its maker, was left henceforth to go of itself, in accordance with certain forces and laws impressed upon it in the beginning. Moreover, this analogical result seems to harmonize with the Mosaic account of creation ; and hence the Christian Church has very generally accepted it, and branded as heretics all who could not square their opinions on this intricate subject of cosmogony by the childish belief that the world was made like a watch.

But, in the presence of modern science, how puerile all this is ! Let us suppose an omniscient, all-powerful Creator ; a Being infinite in wisdom, whose every impulse and every thought at every moment must be equally and absolutely perfect, and no act of whom, on account of this infinite perfection, could ever fall a hair-breadth short of its intent. Shall we think of such a Being as compelled, like imperfect, plodding man, to weigh means against results, to study effects, to sit down, as it were, to deliberate, to form a plan of the universe, and then mechanically to construct the universe thereby? And when to the conception of such a Being the attribute of omnipresence is added, how can we think of him, the all-comprehending, the all-pervading spirit and energy, as shut out, by any mechanism external to himself, from any part of creation, from any atom of matter, from any point of space, from any manifestation of life? Throw away, I beseech you, this god, that only comes in to round a syllogism or to flank an analogy. It is an idol, as much as the wooden or brazen images of heathendom. Confessedly, this whole analogical argument only proves *an* author of the universe: it does not reach the Infinite. Moreover, as an argument, it is irremediably vitiated by the fact that the watch itself, which is assumed as the known side of the analogy, involves all the mysteries which the analogy is to explain. An intelligent mind must have put together all these wheels and cogs and balances: that is true. But what is the secret power that holds those shining metallic atoms so solidly together? What is that force we call the elasticity of the spring? What gives hardness to the wheels, that they act and react upon each other with unvarying order? We must fathom all these secrets before we have found out the infinite God. And the question is not whether these various forces are not ultimately to be referred to an infinite Being as cause, but how they are related to such a Being now.

Again, the popular conception of the relation between the universe and Deity meets another objection. No sooner have people satisfied themselves of the harmony of what they call their natural and revealed ideas of God — that is, the harmony between the conception of a Creator making the world by a specific act, as a man makes a watch, and the account in the first chapter of Genesis — than Science steps in and says, "With my divining-rod, I have read the secrets of the earth,— yea, the deep things of God that were written on the stones and in the great mountains ages before the Twelve Tables of Moses' Law were made or Adam became a living soul; and I declare unto you that neither in six days nor in six thousand thousand was the earth created, and that by no specific, clearly defined acts, but through an almost infinite series of progressive stages of action, did it come to its present form." Nay, there is a theory of the universe, sometimes stigmatized as an attempt to account for creation without the hypothesis of a creator, which asserts that the whole universe is developed, under the operation of physical laws, from a condition of simple primordial atoms as germs, like a tree from a seed or a bird from an egg; and millions upon millions of years would not take us back to the beginning of the process. This theory may not yet be scientifically established, but how soon it may be no one can tell. And no religious opinions and prejudices ought to stand, or can stand permanently, in the way of its establishment, if science can show it to be true. Clearly, then, we must be prepared to change our conception of the relation between the universe and Deity. Already, by the advanced positions which science has taken, we are driven to this dilemma: we must either abandon our old analogical idea of God as a creator and ruler of the universe, in the common acceptation of those words, — an idea of him formed from the nature of a finite being,— or else we shall be compelled to place him farther and farther from the universe, until he is banished to the remotest corner of conceivable space, and the period of his active power is pushed to the utmost limit of conceivable time, and he shall have become an infinitesimal rather than an infinite Being; and then will be fulfilled the prediction of a certain school of philosophy, that religion, as a childish superstition of our race, will, as the race matures, yield up her sovereignty, and finally disappear before the full light of science.

That this fate will ever befall humanity at large I have no fears. For, although no fair deductions of science, however much they may conflict with our religious notions, can be denied, I should still maintain that religion, properly conceived, represents the normal attitude of the human soul, and is not to be lost out of the world so long as human nature endures. Between science and true religion there can be no conflict: it is only our false religious ideas that science winnows away. The right adjustment will come at last. For the future of the race, then, I have no fears. But for ourselves in the midst of the present conflict between the old and the new,— how are we, as individuals, to keep our own faith in the ever-living presence of Deity fresh and active, notwithstanding the invincible batteries of modern science? how save ourselves from the calamity of accepting an atheistic world? How shall we receive the latest conclusions of scientific research,— ay, be ready to receive all possible future conclusions, — and still with the old Hebrew proclaim that "the earth was without form, and void," till "the Spirit of God moved upon the face of the waters," or, with Jesus' religious sensitiveness to natural beauty, see the hand of God in the gorgeous array of the lilies?

My answer to this question is that, contrary to what has been the prevailing teaching of Christian theology, *we must bring God back into the universe.* We must conceive of Deity as in nature,— not simply as at the beginning of it or as over it, but as *in* it; as a power pervading its laws, energies, unfoldment, life. Science is no atheist. It has no conflict with the existence of Deity,— only with our analogical conception of him as creator of the world, according to a pre-arranged plan, in a definite period of time, and by a definite series of acts, as a great Machinist. Science finds everywhere gradation, development, progress from cause to effect,— a law of evolution instead of a miracle; but it, none the less, everywhere finds that incomprehensible power which religion has named Deity. Wherever we find law, wherever we find order and system and beauty, there we find elements in their very nature eternal, divine. In the orbits of the stars, in the budding and flowering of trees, in the upspringing grass and ripening fruit, in the strata of the mountain ranges, in the speechless sublimity of the Alps and the spoken sublimity of the ocean,— in short, wherever in nature the imaginative or the scientific eye be cast, we are reading no past thought of a distant, historic Deity, but standing face to face with the vital potency of a present Omnipotence. Science opens a way into the universe,— not that God may go out, but that we may see him all the more clearly there.

And, first, we are to bring God back into the universe by asserting his immanence in matter. And by this I mean something more than that he is immanent in the material universe. I do not mean that the universe is made, as it were, something apart from him, and that then he as Spirit flows in to dwell in it; nor, again, that chaotic matter first exists as something apart from him, into which a vitalizing divine Spirit is afterwards infused. But I mean that matter is by its very nature penetrated and possessed by a divine energy; that it is not an absolute creation, not a beginning *de novo*, but a manifestation of, or issue from, the one eternal substance of Deity; and that, could we get back behind all specific forms of matter to its primordial essence, we should find it an inherent, eternal part of the divine nature. It is impossible for our minds to conceive of the absolute creation or annihilation of matter. Every existing, every possible *form* of matter is subject to change,— to beginning and end. Decay, departure, death, as also new forms of life, are all around us. The rock crumbles to pieces and is converted to soil, and by and by, in another form, its particles are drawn up to color the rose or to flavor our fruit; mountains are reared and worn again to plains; even the stars, our emblem of eternity, are sometimes lost from their courses. But, in all this round of endless change, not one atom of matter is ever lost; nor can we conceive how even Omnipotence can destroy it or create. There seems, in fact, to be no reason, either analogical or ontological, or from the human consciousness, for supposing that matter in its essence is not equally eternal with spirit, or mind. Consciousness gives us no idea of the absolute causation of matter, but only of mind acting upon matter already existing. The greatest *a priori* reasoners have affirmed the eternity of matter. Even though we were to accept the first chapter of Genesis as a literal account of the process of creation, we do not get beyond the creation of the existing world,— that is, the beginning of a certain order, or of determinate forms, of matter, and not the absolute origin of matter itself; while experience and analogy both go to show that matter — if, indeed, it be not necessary to the existence of spirit — is, at least to our human comprehension, necessary to its manifestation and expression.

I would say, therefore, that spirit and matter are, in their essence, equally eternal, and equally elements in the primal origin of things. We might call the one the active, the other the passive side of the divine nature. In absolute Being, or God, we may conceive that the two coexist in perfect unity, making indeed one substance; and, in any form of manifested being, the two must be wedded before spirit can come to personal consciousness or give any other utterance of itself. Without matter, spirit could never be organized into soul: without spirit, matter would remain forever "without form, and void." *

Here, then, we have the key to the true process of creation,— still, for convenience, using the word "creation," though the idea be essentially changed; and the first chapter of Genesis, childish considered as science, becomes sublime, considered as a poetic representation of creative activity. "The Spirit of God moved upon the face of the waters." Spirit is pictured as brooding over the chaotic mass of matter. It moves upon chaos; and, behold, the chaotic mass takes shape, and separates into a myriad forms of life and beauty. The upper and the nether firmaments, stars and planets, land and seas, herb, grass, and tree, fish, bird, and beast, all come, through the slow gradation of ages, in their order; and all in some sort prefigure, and prepare the way for, something higher, higher yet, till we come to man. Creation, beginning with the primal germ of being, is the action of spirit, or mental energy, upon matter, by which matter becomes organized into various forms of being, activity, and life. It is only, indeed, with regard to our human comprehension,

---

* Infinite Being, as Spinoza maintained, may have many other attributes; but these two, mind and matter, are the only ones that come within human cognizance.

that we speak of its having a beginning. With reference to absolute Being and the whole infinity of things, creation can have no beginning and no end. It is only a term to mark a certain change of form, — a kind of change which is going on from everlasting to everlasting. Spirit, by its very nature, is an organizing, vitalizing force. By its own inherent impulse, it must ever seek to express itself in law, symmetry, order, and life. And the whole history of the material universe may be summed up as the effort of spirit to possess and vitalize matter, and so to organize itself in material forms.

Hence, as a second means through which we are to keep our faith fresh in the presence of God in nature, we are to consider him as manifested in the *laws of nature*. Christian theology has laid so much stress upon the *supernatural* as the peculiar method of divine manifestation that it has tended to establish, has in fact directly inculcated, the doctrine that the regular and ordinary operations of nature are less immediate revelations of the divine character; that what we call natural physical laws were ordained, indeed, of God in the beginning, yet now only in a distant and secondary way execute his intent. But, in reality, when science has revealed to us a law or taught us to observe a method of nature, we have reached no past thought or plan of Deity, but his present action. What we name the plan of the universe is no *fore-thought* of God, but our *afterthought*. The laws of nature are no mould into which the past thought of the Almighty has been run, but the immediate outgoing of his present energy, the divine purpose and thought in process of action at this very moment. Every new physical law discovered, instead of being another secondary cause and so removing the great First Cause still farther off, ushers us, in fact, into the more immediate presence of divine power. Science may speak of secondary causes, but to Religion there is no such thing. Where Science shrinks from naming it, Religion recognizes the omnipresent, all-pervading One, bows its head, and adores.

And so, while we have escaped their errors, we may still have all the advantages of the old religions. We may hold to the divine unity, and yet not lose the more practical doctrine of the divine universality. Nature, though no longer peopled with divinities, is filled, inspired with Divinity. One omnipresent Power pervades and energizes all things. We do not call him Neptune, but the same Deity still controls the tidal waves and rules the sea. The offices of Ceres and Aurora, of all benign, all fatherly and motherly providences, are henceforth combined in one great Love that streams forever through the universe. One power clothes the fields with summer green and mantles them with winter snow; brings the seasons in their order, and provides tender care for every great and every little thing; moulds the great orbs of the stars; paints no less the lily's leaf and the passing cloud.

Do we ask at once for absolute perfection,— that all disorders, both from man and nature, be at once discarded? We ask for an impossibility, for a finite and temporal infinity. Perfection is our aspiration:

toward that, the whole universe is advancing; and infinite wisdom and infinite benevolence are justified so long as the aim and movement of things are upward.

September 8, 1861.

IV.

MERCY AND JUDGMENT.

"Their thoughts the meanwhile accusing or else excusing one another."— ROM. ii., 15.

THE moral integrity of human society is kept, in great measure, by the reciprocal action of the two sentiments, justice and mercy. No individual, perhaps, can ever really forgive himself for any lapse in his own conduct from the strict line of rectitude; but, with regard to one another's conduct, we are not only made judges, but have the power also of pardon. More than this: we are forbidden to judge, unless our judgment be tempered with mercy. This, I take it, is the meaning of what both Jesus and Paul say with reference to judging the character of others; for, so long as we are endowed with a moral sense,— that is, so long as we are human,— it is impossible that we should make absolutely no judgment of one another's conduct. We are so constituted by nature that we are necessarily judges of each other. It is, indeed, by this interaction of conscience upon conscience that the moral education of society proceeds: only, it is provided that, as we are to judge one another, so we are to forgive one another; as every man's conscience is to exact entire justice from every other man, so every man's heart is to be ready with pity and pardon for another's frailty. Judgment is necessary, but mercy is to "rejoice against judgment"; "for he shall have judgment without mercy that hath showed no mercy."

In the common order of things in human society, we see continually how these two forces are made to balance and regulate each other. Justice and mercy, exaction and forgiveness, penalty and pardon, accusation and excusation, the father's law, the mother's love,— between these two poles flow the moral life-currents of humanity. That action would be absolutely right which should be vitalized alike from both of these sources,— which should combine justice and mercy in such perfect proportions that they should flow into one sentiment and be undistinguishable from each other; which should be kind because it is just, and just because it is kind. In the last analysis of moral issues, the action which is conformed to the strictest equity is the highest benignity. With absolute Being, we can conceive no conflict between justice and tenderness. In a perfect Being, justice would be but the impartial distribution of love.

But, in man, these two sentiments are not yet brought to this perfect oneness. Both are present, and both are necessary to the well-being of society; but the moral balance between them is preserved by their action and reaction upon each other. The exactions of justice become sometimes severe. Then mercy pleads, often with a mistaken tenderness,— with blind excess of good will doing a wrong, which only a severer equity can set right again.

And so there is conflict, struggling of force with force: we accuse and yet excuse one another; but, by and by, justice gets done, and mercy also triumphs.

Society is most healthy when these two forces are most nearly balanced,— when mercy follows most swiftly upon severity, or, better, when the spirit of love goes along with the spirit of accusation. The scribes and Pharisees would have left the woman whom they accused of sin fallen and hopeless. Jesus lifted her up, and said unto her, "Go, and sin no more." Without looking with weak indulgence on the past, he yet opened to her the hopes of the future. In this act, he shows us the exquisite mean between the moral judgment that condemns the sin and the moral compassion that reclaims the sinner. But society has not yet learned to keep this golden mean. We are continually running between the two extremes of unjust severity and mistaken indulgence; in one case exercising judgment without mercy, in the other showing mercy without judgment.

First, we exercise judgment without mercy. Great, almost irreparable, is the wrong that is done by condemnation of the vicious without appeal. With the doors of our houses, we shut against them also, in many cases, the doors of repentance and reformation. Keeping them from the paths of honest industry till they have established an honest character, we force them into courses of dishonor, and give them no chance to win a good name. In the severity of our judgment upon their past lives, we condemn them to sin as a punishment, and to a dark future of misery and moral despair; and with moral despair comes moral ruin. What worse fate can we conceive for a man who has run the ways of wickedness and learned their barrenness, and now desires sincerely to regain his virtue and his reputation, than to find all the avenues to virtuous associations barred against him? Suppose that the prodigal son in the parable — when, weary of sin, the memory of the old home love and innocence had been revived within him, and he had resolved to return to his father's house — had found, instead of the welcome which he did receive, the father's heart hardened against him and the door closed, and no opportunity given him for expressing his contrition and making amends for the wrong he had done: *would he have been saved?* What burden could have been imposed upon him more fitted than such a repulse to crush out every reviving memory and desire of better things,— every aspiration for the old home virtue and pure domestic joys? Yet this is what society — society, too, that is called Christian — is doing every day. Thousands of human beings are this moment kept in the degradation of vice, because no human ear will listen to their penitence and no hand is reached out to welcome and aid their returning footsteps. Nay, their own fathers and mothers often suffer their hearts to close against these their erring children. I doubt not there are those among the vicious and abandoned of this city who would this hour gladly go back to the pure homes of their childhood, if they could be sure that they would still find there a father's and a mother's heart. But they feel that the house would be shut against them, that every honest mode of livelihood shrinks from them, that even this so-called house of God is not open for such as they! God pity them, for they find few friends and little pity on earth!

On the other hand, though judgment without mercy is so ruinous, not less ruinous is mercy, or compassion, without moral judgment. The safeguards of society are at once torn down and the whole fabric exposed to destruction, so soon as the vicious are allowed without question to stand on the same footing and receive the same honors with the virtuous. We can do no greater wrong to society than when, through a fiction of words, we call men moral by relaxing the severity of the moral law. Without elevating them in the least, we debase the moral standard of the whole community, and excuse them from all effort to elevate themselves. If men are thieves, let us call them so, no matter how high they stand in social position : only be sure they are thieves before we call them so. If men are drunkards and libertines, let us give them those names, though they be members of cabinets or churches : only be sure that the accusation is true before we repeat it. Nothing is so strong an indication of, as well as help to, the corruption of public morals as the prevalent disposition to cover up flagrant vices and crimes under an evasive phraseology. Let it be understood that a lie is a *lie*, and not merely "misrepresentation" or "evasion,"—words that have a much less culpable sound. The hard word *theft*, which is as destructive of a man's pretences to morality, if it hit him fairly, as a well-aimed cannon ball is fatal to his body, is too often softened into "embezzlement," "defalcation," "financial irregularity,"—weak paper bullets which do little execution. If a boy takes a loaf of bread from a baker's window, he is sent to jail as a thief. If a man steals a railroad, he goes at large; and a considerable portion of society look upon him with admiration for his financial ability. If a young man is given to inebriety and lust, we call him "a little wild"; and younger men and boys are rather left with the impression that to be "a little wild" is the proper thing for a young man. Now, all such concealment of vice under fine names is weakly to excuse it; and weakly to excuse vice is to put a premium upon it. Let us not deaden the sting of a just accusation of guilt by words of velvet. Let us use the plain Anglo-Saxon terms: they are the words that, true and sharp as steel, carry home to a man the real meaning of his deeds. The courtly Latin has been used to tell lies and cover up crime from the beginning of the English language.

We must make it understood that sin is sin, and not merely an inherited taint of the blood; that evil is evil, and not merely a misfortune of circumstances; that guilt is guilt,—to be got rid of, not by finely worded confessions of piety and theories of substituted punishment, but by real pain and struggle and hearty honest work. Let us not by any feeble sentimentality weaken the force of the old law, that "the way of the transgressor is hard." There are times when the greatest unkindness you could do a man would be to show him that you lightly excuse his vices. Many a mother smooths the road to ruin for her sons, because she overlooks too readily their childish faults. It isn't that she has too much love, too much heart, but that her love does not look through the far-seeing eye of moral judgment; her heart is not what Solomon calls "a wise and an understanding heart." No : let no mistaken tenderness, public or private, blind us to the enormity of immoral deeds. For very self-preservation, society must wear the ermine and sit in the seat of judgment. Let no man feel that the eye of the community is not upon him. Let no man feel that he can sin, and escape the court of public opinion. There may be forgiveness for him, but let him not feel that he is forgiven before he has been brought to trial. The accusation and the sentence must come before the pardon. If any will waste their substance in riotous living, let them know distinctly that husks must be their food and the swine their company ; that only for such as return are the feasts and the joys of the Father's house.

We see, then, that the moral judgment that condemns and punishes guilt, and the moral tenderness that overlooks and pardons guilt, are equally injurious when they appear apart from each other. Many are the victims whom society has crushed apparently to moral death by the severity of a moral judgment,—just, perhaps, at first, but upon which no pardoning mercy followed. Equally many are the victims who have been surfeited to moral death by kindness,— who have been lured to their graves by friendly (so they were meant) excuses for their sins. The problem is to combine these two ; to be both just and kind at the same time ; to let the conscience pronounce with unflinching manly voice the word *guilty*, and execute with firm hand the punishment, while the heart trembles with its full motherly burden of healing and redeeming love. "Behold," exclaimed St. Paul, "the goodness and the severity of God!" In that phrase, we have the wondrous unity we seek. In the divine laws, justice and mercy are brought into concord, are atoned. "*On them which fell* [*i.e.*, who sinned], *severity; but toward thee, goodness, if thou continue in his goodness: otherwise, thou also shalt be cut off,*"— so severely kind are the great laws of God. Very pitilessly do they accuse us, if we violate them ; for a yielding pity would be our ruin. Very pitilessly do they condemn and punish us, if we continue in disobedience ; for the severity of our punishment is our salvation. And yet the same laws, if we will but turn to obedience, if we will continue in goodness, are our consolers and our healers. While we are scourged, we are blessed ; while we are accused, we are redeemed. Into the divine laws are infused equally the father's firmness and the mother's compassion ; and, though they pronounce us sinful and condemn our sins, they yet fold strong arms of love around us to lift us up and save.

March 16, 1862.

V.

SELF-SACRIFICE.

"Whosoever shall seek to save his life shall lose it; and whosoever shall lose his life shall preserve it." — LUKE xvii., 23.

NO ONE saying of Jesus seems to have been impressed so deeply on the memory of his disciples as this. Six times does it appear in the Gospels in nearly the same words, and as having been uttered on several different occasions; while the same sentiment appears in many other forms, and is the keynote of many discourses. Paradoxical as is the sentence in expression, its meaning is clear. The word *life*, as every one must immediately see, is used in two senses: first, for the material, temporal life; and, secondly, for the spiritual and eternal life. Hence, dropping the form of paradox, we should read the text thus: Whosoever shall seek to save his material and temporal life shall lose the higher and eternal life of the spirit; and whosoever subordinates and stands ready even to let go his material and temporal life shall find the higher and eternal spiritual life. In other words, one may seek only the pleasures and pursuits of this life of earth, be absorbed wholly in them; but, if so, then this life of earth is his all. To say nothing of what is possible hereafter, here, at least, he loses the life of heaven,—

loses the life of those nobler principles, pursuits, and joys that properly belong to spiritual and moral beings. On the other hand, if one's life is entirely subordinated to, swallowed up, and lost in these high motives of the spirit, then, though he may lose what the world regards as the necessities and triumphs of earthly success, he finds the fairer fortune, even here upon the earth, of that life which has no end.

In my last discourse, I spoke of the sacrifice of Christ,— of the real efficacy of his blood toward the redemption of the world. Contrary to the customary theological teaching, I endeavored to show how his death, with its results, falls into natural harmony with the great providential laws of human progress; and, explaining the doctrine of his sacrifice thus, we saw how it culminated in this saying which I have taken for my text to-day,— "Whosoever is ready to lose his life shall find it." That is, the doctrine taught by the sacrifice of Christ is the doctrine of self-sacrifice,— *rest not for salvation in the sacrifices made for you, but in the sacrifices you make;* and it is to this subject, the true doctrine of self-sacrifice, that I wish to call your attention in the present discourse.

Our thoughts at a time like this turn naturally, turn by necessity, to the topic of sacrifice. When every week is bringing us intelligence of battle-fields, with their marvellous tales of endurance and heroism, their horrors of carnage and blood, with a strange blending of a beautiful and divine tenderness therewith, we are led inevitably to the question, What is the meaning of all this destruction and agony and blood? Is there not some universal law by which the world is spiritually redeemed through suffering and self-sacrifice? We can hardly, I think, however closely we may be cased in the old dogmas of atonement and redemption by blood, go through with the scenes of this national conflict without putting a more universal and rational idea into these doctrines; while some of us, perhaps, will be brought to see a greater moral efficacy in the sacrifice of physical life than we have been wont heretofore to believe in. My own thoughts on this subject I find strikingly expressed by one * who went over the battle-field of Fort Donelson soon after that terrible contest; and, though the printed sermon in which they are contained has doubtless been read by many of you, I will yet quote the exact words, because they have more vivacity coming from one who spoke of what he himself saw. " As I went over this battle-field," he says, " and thought on the dead heroes and of all they died for, I kept repeating over each one, 'He gave his life a ransom for many'; and I wondered, when I thought of how we had all gone astray as a people, and how inevitable this war had become, in consequence, as the final test of the two great antagonisms, whether it may not be true in our national affairs as in a more universal sense,— 'without the shedding of blood there is no remission of sins.' And so, by consequence, every true hero fallen in this struggle for the right is also a saviour to the nation and the race." And do we not all feel that there is a deep truth in this statement, and that

* Robert Collyer, Unitarian *Monthly Journal*, April, 1862.

the language is as reverent as it is true and tender? Not indeed that every soldier who falls for a righteous cause is put on the same level with Jesus, but that both fall by the same law of redemption through sacrifice. The rudest stone thrown into the air falls to the earth by the same law that draws Jupiter through the infinite spaces of the heavens, but that is not to put the stone on the same grade of existence with the planet. What is meant is that whoever gives his life for the right enters by that act, according to the elevation of his motive, into the spirit of the sacrifice of Christ, and helps, in proportion to the worth of his life, to redeem the world from error and from sin. The more precious the life, the more valuable becomes the testimony, the greater the price; and the greater also — for divine providence balances every account with perfect exactness — the moral value which the world receives in return: the costlier the blood, the greater the redemption. Yet we may be allowed to feel that not even the humblest and obscurest man who gives his life for the right falls in vain. And I speak not now of what will be attained by a victory of arms, but of the moral worth of the mere act of sacrifice. No sacrifice, not even the smallest, falls fruitless. The poorest woman, who with her tears sends forth her sons to battle, does something for the remission of our country's sins; and the blood of the unnamed private soldiers, trickling unnoticed and neglected into the soil where they bravely fell, shall yet spring up a fountain of pure water, clear as crystal, to cleanse us from the foulest iniquities.

Paul somewhere teaches the doctrine that, by the death of Jesus, God's righteousness was made manifest; that, by permitting so holy and perfect a being to suffer a cruel and ignominious death at the hands of evil men, God showed his love of goodness and his hatred of sin. In ordinary times, it seems a strange, dark doctrine; and I remember when, on one occasion, our theological professor, by a *lapsus linguae*, reversed the phrases, and said, " Paul taught that God, by permitting the violent death of so holy a being as Christ, showed his love of sin and hatred of goodness," a member of the class exclaimed that that was a more logical statement than the one he meant to make. And so at first sight it seems. We are at least moved to exclaim: " If God had wished to manifest his righteousness, would he not have saved the righteous being, and brought the guilty to destruction? How, pray, did he show his love of goodness by permitting goodness to be sacrificed, or his hatred of sin when he allowed sin to triumph?" But the criticism, though natural, is superficial. Paul spoke out of a deep and extraordinary experience, and it is only when events call forth a deeper life than we commonly know in our own souls that we understand the transcendent truth of his thought. That truth, I think, is made clear to us now. God's righteousness is manifested by the greatness of the sacrifices which he demands shall be made for it. He shows his love of goodness by infusing into human hearts a spirit which is willing and firm to endure the most cruel agony and death rather than to forswear the good and the true. He shows his abhorrence of evil by nerving human souls with a strength almost omnipotent, and capable of bearing tortures unspeakable rather than to yield to the seductions of evil. It is in morals as in material things : value is measured by the price paid.

So, when God calls upon men to give for the truth, to give for righteousness, those things which are counted the dearest among earthly possessions, he shows that he counts truth and righteousness as dearer than all things else. Wealth is dear: men will toil early and late for it; and, to a certain extent, we are bid by the divine laws to seek it for the better comfort of our bodies and the higher refinement of our minds. But the same divine laws tell us clearly that virtue is dearer, for you must pay the whole price of your wealth rather than lose your virtue. Home and family are dear: what, indeed, is more precious than these little household structures which your hearts have builded? They are dearer than your wealth, for you seek wealth that you may adorn and elevate these; and you instinctively call the man worse than mean who lets his dollars stand between him and his home. And yet you let go home and family, when you recognize a higher voice calling you to service in the broader household of your country or humanity. You tear yourself from the cradle of your own child that you may save the liberties of strangers' children. Wife, sister, father, mother,— you give them all up ; for it is better that you see them in want, or see them no more, than that all the households in the land should be imperilled by the outbreak of national wickedness, or continue to stand under the traitorous protection of a flag stained with crime against domestic sanctity. Life is dear,— this life of the body on the earth. Instinctively, we cling to it. We let go everything that we have gained and toiled for a whole life long rather than let go the life itself. Of all temporal things, it is counted dearest; and, as men advance in civilization, they grow into the opinion that life, of all things, is sacred and inviolable. We may, under certain conditions, take men's property, we may take them from their homes, we may take their liberties, but life is the last thing we can take; and many there are who deny that the right ever comes to man to take it at all. Life, then, is held to be the most precious and inviolable of human possessions. But see what vast numbers there have been and are — the brave army of soldiers and the still braver army of martyrs — who hesitate not to pay this highest price of all for the sake of truth. So is it shown that truth, that principles of right, are valued above all things,— above wealth, above home and family, above life.

And thus it is that by the sacrifice of these things — by the sacrifices and sufferings and death of the righteous — the righteousness of God is made manifest. By the value of the things we are called upon, by our higher natures, to give rather than to yield the truth, or in order to ransom us from evil, does God show the price he sets upon goodness and his abhorrence of iniquity. "What shall a man give," exclaimed Jesus, "in exchange for his soul?"

No answer was needed, for every true man's heart answers that there is nothing costly enough to purchase that. The kingliest blood, the manliest form of flesh, cannot be weighed for a moment against the imperishable virtues and principles of the immortal spirit. Was the worth of Jesus' life inestimable? How much more inestimable, then, the worth of that truth, of those principles, for the sake of which all the wealth and beauty of that life were given! So we are learning now, through the severe lesson of tears and blood, how the everlasting righteousness of God may be manifested, not only by life, but by the sacrifice of life. We are learning, what perhaps in our ease and prosperity we were in danger of forgetting, that there are many things higher and holier than this life of flesh, and many things which we had better die rather than do or allow to be done. And we are learning also, through the costliness of the sacrifice, the infinite worth of those things for which the sacrifice is made,— national justice and righteousness and purity. What, indeed, could better teach us the value that God sets upon these things than the greatness of the price we are now called to pay for them? That the most precious blood of the race is being poured out in ransom; that the bone and sinew of the nation are being laid upon its altar; that lives of the richest promise,— the pride of our homes, the pride of our colleges,— lives rich in culture, in virtue, of the noblest manhood and the saintliest purity,— are being freely offered up in sacrifice,— herein, my friends, does God reveal to us the inestimable worth of that national purification and of those eternal principles of righteousness for which this most precious of all offerings is being made. By the value of the life given may we measure the value of that higher life which is to be obtained.

If we were to state the reason, then, of the rational Christian doctrine of self-sacrifice, it would be this: that no private life can be of so much importance as the life of humanity; no personal ends can stand in the way of universal; no temporal, physical good is of any worth, which cannot be held consistently with eternal principles of right. The doctrine does not militate against the just claims of individuality. It enjoins no sacrifice of our personal being, no surrender of that sacred entity within us which we call our selfhood. Rather does it draw the line in our being between things temporal and things eternal, between material things and spiritual things, and bid us seek our life and ground our being in those things that are eternal and spiritual. Instead of demanding the sacrifice of our individuality, it bids us find it in a higher sphere. Letting go all merely private and selfish ends and aims, our being re-comes to us enlarged by universal relations and elevated into divine and everlasting proportions. Whether we continue to wear this body of flesh or whether it fall away,— in the body or out of the body,— it is of little moment. The personal existence does not necessarily cease: the *life* goes on, only a certain manifestation of it vanishes.

It is to be remembered, too, that goodness, manhood, culture, are not sacrificed, only certain personal and temporal manifestations thereof; but the sublime qualities themselves are saved. Good men die, but goodness survives: good men die, that goodness may survive. Did holiness expire on the cross of Christ? Did wickedness triumph in his death? Nay, rather did holiness appear more holy. Jesus, lifted upon the cross, drew all men unto him; while wickedness was stripped of its disguises and revealed in its real form, so odious that men shrank from it and could not help then but choose the truth. Are the virtues of your friends buried in their graves? Nay, rather does death transfigure to your vision their characters, so that the grave generously veils their faults, while it allows their virtues to spring up with a diviner grace and beauty. Of our soldiers, too, who fall in battle for the redemption of the nation, we forget the evil, and remember only that they were patriots and heroes. Blest mode of death, by which a man's sins are washed from memory by his own blood, and only his virtues — his single virtue, perhaps — survive in remembrance to describe his character and give example to the world! And, as it seems to our vision, so doubtless it is in reality. No man, however worthless and ignoble he may have been, can give his life for a great cause without feeling that with his body something of his low selfishness drops off from him; while a higher life, from the cause he suffers for, is infused into his spirit. This, too, must be the experience, not only of those who fall in the terrible contest, but of those who, though ready to fall, are yet spared.

It is impossible but that something of the deeper and mysterious verities of life should have been revealed to them. The same observer whom I have already quoted says again: "I noticed one feature in this camp that I never saw before: the men do not swear and use profane words as they used to do. There is a little touch of seriousness about them. They have taken the Eternal Name for common purposes a thousand times; and we feel as if we could say with Paul, 'The times of this ignorance God passed by.' But on that fearful day, when judgment-fires were all aflame, a voice said, 'Be still, and know that I am God'; and they are still under the shadow of that awful name." Thus it is that by sacrifice of this life of earth, even by the agony and sweat and blood of the battle-field, the higher verities of God and eternity are revealed.

This doctrine of self-sacrifice is not only the doctrine of Christianity, but the doctrine of human nature. There is within us all, if we will but heed it, the germ of a natural instinct — let us call it divine — which prompts us to give ourselves for others; and, however far short most of us may fall of its requirements, there is yet, I think, no man sunk so low in selfishness who will not appreciate and applaud a pure act of self-sacrifice performed by another. Let a stranger — one entirely unknown to the whole community — rush into the street, exposing his own life in order to snatch a child from being trampled to death by a frenzied horse, and instantly you know that stranger has a noble manhood, and you wish to take him by the hand

and call him brother; and in all the crowd of bystanders is there one so mean, so insensible to every manly sentiment, as not instinctively to pray that he might have the same brave and self-forgetful spirit? Human nature at its inmost heart is true, and teaches the same gospel as did Jesus,—" not to be ministered unto, but to minister"; not to save, but to give ourselves. See how friend will give himself for friend. See how, in every true marriage relation, the husband sacrifices himself for his wife and wife for husband. See how father and mother give themselves unweariedly for their children. What, indeed, will not a mother do to save her child? Her own life, mature and rich in womanly usefulness, is not so precious to her as that yet unfolded bud of life in her arms. The world outside might say, Better that the child be sacrificed than the mother. But she judges and acts by a diviner instinct, and knows that, though she loses her life, she finds a higher life in the action of that love that prompts the sacrifice; and, the sacrifice once made, the world outside acknowledges also the higher divinity of the deed.

The subject is far from being exhausted; yet time remains only for one thought in conclusion, and that an important one. *There must be some object for which sacrifice is made, some worthy object;* else the doctrine finds no valid justification. Sacrifice for the mere sake of sacrifice is neither morality nor religion. It is only a poor asceticism which narrows, worries, and wearies the soul more than it elevates. But sacrifice of self for the sake of some object held dearer than self; sacrifice of self out of love for another, or love for the truth, or love for humanity, or love of country,— this it is that saves us ; for only this lifts us out of the circle of self, and gives our life a higher and more universal sweep. He who gives himself, not merely for the sake of self-discipline, but for the sake of love, finds a higher spirit of love pervading his whole being. He enters into a sphere of loftier affection, of holier action. He becomes one with those higher objects for which he gives himself, and so finds his life brought more into harmony with absolute and eternal aims. Whoever dies for the truth dies that he may live more truthful ; whoever dies for humanity becomes more humane; whoever dies for God becomes more Godlike.

And, at this day, what our nation in its time of trial has needed, and still needs most of all, is the more openly avowed and inspiring purpose of a holy cause. Let our struggle be expressly for justice and humanity. As the armies of treason are gathered avowedly for the defence of a government founded on slavery, let the loyal men of the nation take up the challenge, and rally under the holier and more chivalrous title, "Defenders of liberty." Let the principles of our heroic fathers,— dead, but in their graves still speaking,— universally applied, even as they hoped and prophesied, inspire us. Not the Union alone, but "*Liberty and Union*, now and forever, one and inseparable,"— let that be our aim ; and so let us rally to make this land actually in the future what it has been only ideally in the past, the home where the oppressed of every nation and race and people may lift themselves up to manhood, and be counted members of one family on earth as they are children of one Father in heaven. Not, I believe, until we are ready to give ourselves for an object like this, shall we be strong enough for victory or worthy to achieve it.

Go forth in this faith, ye brave and freedom-loving hearts! Your country calls you; humanity needs you. And, though the human voices that summon you do not as yet all thrill with the stirring tones of freedom, yet go in faith. The notes of liberty, still somewhat muffled, shall yet ring clear throughout the land, and the world shall own you as the brave army of freedom's defenders. Meanwhile, rally to the summons that comes up from the deep instincts of your hearts; rally to the cry of humanity crushed to the earth; rally to the voice that comes down from the Lord God of justice in the heavens! And for us who must remain at home,— let us not grow weary in upholding the great cause for which our country struggles; let us stand firmly for the right; and, though the result we pray for comes not yet, though wickedness seems still to triumph and the counsels of weak men to prevail, yet let us still labor on, giving ourselves — our word, our deed, our treasure — to our country's life, confident that the right must win at last, and our sacrifices be blessed with a victory for humanity and a peace that shall be enduring. And, oh, may the Spirit of Infinite Compassion instil into all our hearts the gentler mercies and humanities that the hour demands. Let the sick, the wounded, the suffering, the bereaved, have our constant sympathy, our constant care. Tender in heart, just and firm in aim, helpful in hand, so may we strive to do the duties of the time; and so, over the ruin and waste, the shattered hearts and broken households of this conflict, may new life spring up, with fairer moralities and nobler societies and juster legislation! Though we go forth in weeping, yet, bearing precious seed, we shall doubtless come again with rejoicing, bringing with us costly sheaves of God's harvested truths. Our brothers, lifted upon the cross of battle, shall draw all our hearts to greater reverence for the sacred principles which they have died to save. From these red fields of carnage, planted with the blood of our bravest and best, shall spring up richer crops of virtue, even trees of righteousness whose leaves shall be for the healing of all nations; and, over the desolation caused by the demon of war, we will rear new and fairer temples to the Prince of Peace.

May 10, 1863.

NOTE.— This sermon was first preached in April, 1862, with the exception of the last two paragraphs. Besides its repetition at New Bedford, with these paragraphs added, it was given in fifteen other places in 1862 and 1863, where it was believed it might be of service in helping on the enlistment of soldiers for the national army.

VI.

THE RELIGION OF THE AFFECTIONS.

"Then said Jesus, Let her alone: against the day of my burying hath she kept this. For the poor always ye have with you; but me ye have not always."—JOHN xii., 7, 8.

HUMAN nature is many-sided; and religion, which in its full sense is the perfect satisfaction of all human needs, must offer some truth and present some obligations for every side. The natural affections of our hearts have therefore an appropriate place in the complete religious life. I wish ‹to speak to-day of the religion of the affections; and the theme was well illustrated in the domestic scene in the house of Lazarus and his sisters as described in the Fourth Gospel, where Jesus, on being rebuked for allowing Mary to waste the precious ointment upon his person when it might have been sold and the proceeds given to the poor, rebuked in turn his critic, on the ground that, while the poor were always at hand and always to be cared for, there was also a legitimate place for the expression of personal affection, and that the legitimate time and manner of such expression, if allowed to pass, might never return. The poor are always with us: the demands for charity and general philanthropy are ever at hand. But our heart-friends do not remain always where they can receive the demonstrations of our love.

It has been very commonly represented that religion denies, as some religions have denied, these natural affections of the human heart which bind persons together in families, in friendships, in social and kindred circles. It is said that religion includes love to God and love to man,— that is, a universal love for the whole race of mankind,— but that it does not embrace the special affections, such as the conjugal, filial, parental, friendly, fraternal, social, and the like. Therefore, the Roman Catholic Church considers it the highest grade of the religious life to forsake all ties made by such affections, and, in retirement from the affairs of the world and from all the joys and loves of a home, to devote one's self to works of so-called piety toward God and of general charity toward man. Its constant question of the world is, Why this waste of wealth on the selfish demands of the heart, when it might have been given to relieve the sufferings of the poor or to save souls from eternal torments? Francis of Assisi, founder of the powerful order of Franciscan monks, renounced his father's rich inheritance, cut himself off from all ties of home and friendship, put on à robe of the coarsest cloth, and went through the country begging alms to build churches. He visited hospitals, and washed the feet and kissed the loathsome sores of lepers, left his bed empty and slept upon the ground, mixed his food with ashes to make it less palatable; and for twenty years he travelled thus as a friendless beggar through many lands, doing, indeed, a vast missionary work and performing acts of the most self-denying and self-mortifying charity, but all the time repelling and crucifying every natural affection and love of his heart. And this, says the Catholic Church, is the highest type of religion; and Francis of Assisi is made a saint. Elizabeth of Hungary abandoned her own children, dismissed her maids when she found herself loving them too well, and devoted herself to caring for the sick and giving alms to the children of the poor; and the Roman Catholic Church canonizes her therefor. There have been women who have wrought with equal patience, devotion, and self-sacrifice in their own homes, loving their own children and caring for their own households; but the Church of Rome has never made them saints, nor does it even regard their faithfully and heroically performed duties as religious. There have been men who, without renouncing the world or the natural life of the heart, have performed as great deeds of philanthropy as Francis d' Assisi; yet, in the eye of the Church of Rome, they have not made the first step toward saintship.

Protestantism has denied, indeed, this extreme view of self-denial and self-mortification. Protestantism does not assert that the highest religious duty is to crucify the natural affections of the heart, nor that to indulge them is sinful or irreligious. It does not demand that a man or woman, in order to be holy and saintly, must withdraw from the world and from all social and domestic life. And yet Protestantism, as a general thing, has not ventured to assert that religion embraces the natural affections of the heart. Though it does not, like Catholicism, call them irreligious and make war upon them, neither does it call them religious. It has regarded them, generally, as a neutral field between religion and irreligion; as a fruitful source of temptations, idolatries, snares, delusions, and spiritual conflicts,—as belonging to "the things of the world," good in their places, but transient and perishable, and to be watched lest they usurp too great a place, and interfere with the claims of religious duty and the eternal interests of the soul. But Protestantism hardly more than Catholicism has dared to affirm that there can be any religion in the life of the natural affections themselves; and Jesus, it is said, has shown us by his life how the natural affections of the heart for home and kindred and friends are to be denied, that one may live the more wholly to God and the truth. Even the liberal, learned, and brilliant French biographer of Jesus, Renan, thinks that Jesus was in many things an ascetic,—that he "preached war against nature," voluntary "poverty" and "celibacy," and "total rupture with kin."

Now, Jesus' own example cannot, I believe, be rightly drawn to the support of any ascetic view of religion. That certain sayings reported of him, torn from their connection and from the general spirit of his teaching and practice, are capable of such an interpretation, I admit; and it would be strange if he should not have had some tinge of the asceticism that belonged to the purest religious sects of his time; but the general moral and religious influence of his life and the aggregate weight of his teaching are decidedly the other way. On account of his freedom from ascetic practices, he was even stigmatized as "a man gluttonous and a wine-bibber," an associate with "publicans and sinners." He does not appear to have practised self-denial for the mere sake of self-denial. He did not preach the abandonment of home and friends, of earthly goods and social ties, as a virtue in itself; yet he was as ready as Francis d' Assisi to make these sacrifices whenever the cause of truth and virtue demanded it. The distinction is here: ascetic religion seeks ways of self-denial and self-sacrifice for their own sake; true religion accepts self-denial and self-sacrifice when self stands in the way of something greater than self. Francis of Assisi slept on ,the bare ground, though there were beds all around him, for the mere sake of mortifying and deadening the body: Jesus "had not where to lay his head," because often, under the necessities of his mission, persecuted from town to town, the earth and sky were the only hospitality offered him.

Nor is it true that Jesus abandoned all social and domestic ties, and denied himself the support of the love and sympathy of congenial hearts. It is probable that his mission drew him away somewhat from his own family and kindred; for they could not understand, more than his old neighbors, the source of this strange power that he possessed as a teacher, and the misunderstanding became a cause of partial alienation. But, though under the exigencies of his work, the *home* was in great measure lost, home joys and ties and affections were not lost. His little band of disciples was his family. With them, he worked and travelled and lived. And, when his human love craved a warmer and more interior home, there were three disciples, Peter, James, and John, who seemed to form an inner circle within this little flock of followers, and to whom his heart went out in its deepest intimacies and most earnest cravings for sympathy. Nor was he without domestic shelter and hospitality and love. The house of Simon Peter, in the village of Capernaum, became his home while in Galilee, where he was cared for like an own son. He was a frequent guest at the house of Zebedee; and, occasionally, some of the wealthier citizens invited him under their roofs and to their tables. There were devoted women, like Salome, Joanna, and the faithful Mary Magdalen, who followed him, bound by no merely technical religious tie, but held by the tie of gratitude and love and personal devotion. But the most beautiful of all these ties of private affection was that which bound him to the family at Bethany,— to Lazarus and his sisters. Here seems to have been his home during his work in Judea; and his visits to this house, when the burdens of his toilsome service appear for a time to have been laid aside, while his nature refreshed itself with home affections and delights, are like bright oases in the midst of the stormy desert of his public life. Here, aside from faithful discipleship, was pure and exalted friendship. Here was not only religious fellowship, but love, sympathy, communion of hearts. Here not only stern duty, but the voice of affection was heard; and Jesus was for the hour transformed from the public teacher and religious reformer into the cordial companion and, possibly, tender lover.

In view of intimacies and friendships like these, it is a great error to suppose that Jesus lived and died in ascetic denial of the claims of the heart. If his own example is to be considered as settling the question, it is certain that, while he did not allow the natural affections of the heart to thwart or interfere with the ruling purpose of his career, he yet did not sacrifice them, but gave them a large and sacred place in the completed temple of his religious life.

Again, Jesus draws some of his sublimest religious lessons from these natural human affections. How does he illustrate the bond of religious discipleship but by the terms "brother," "sister," "mother"? How does he teach the perfect providence of the Infinite Power but by the argument, "If ye then know how to give good gifts unto your children, shall not your Father in heaven give good things to them that ask him?" How does he declare the quick, pardoning mercy of Heaven toward sinning men and women but by that exquisite portrayal of a human father's forgiving love for a wandering child in the parable of the Prodigal Son? Where, in fact, did Jesus find the word that best and oftenest expressed his conception of the character and government of Deity, and is the key to the whole edifice of his religious ideas, but in the parental relation of the human family? In short, it is in these intimate human relations, in these home affections, sympathies, and services that are often considered without the pale of religious duties, or even as standing in the way of religious duties, that Jesus found the most apt illustrations of the special religious truths he had to teach. He took these common, inborn affections of the heart that bind the human family together, lifted them up, as it were, into a higher and purer atmosphere, and showed how, both in their origin and in their issue, they are a type of our relations to infinite Being and infinite providence. Shall we, then, in the face of these teachings and habits of Jesus, dare to assert on the ground of his example that there is anything irreligious, or contrary to the spirit of religion, in the natural affections of the heart? " Let them alone," says this great teacher of duty: "restrict not the heart, mutilate not its loves, forbid not the tender outflow of its sympathies, even though a merely careful prudence cries, 'Why this waste?'"

And in human nature itself, in its origin, its needs, and its destiny, we find this claim of the natural affections justified. These fountains of domestic and friendly love are in the deepest places of our being. They spring up at the very root of our natures, among those eternal forces amid which our special natures stand, and from which they have in some way been educed. They appear in us as instincts. They are vital, therefore, with the very life of that mysterious energy which is behind and anterior to our being, and pulsate with a power that comes throbbing from the central purpose and heart of the universe itself. These energies of wedded and parental love, of fraternal and domestic affection, whence come the ties of home and family, are so manifestly a pressure from the heart of nature, and are so essential to the ascending development of her life, that I know not why we may not call them the very power of God in the human soul. They are put, indeed, somewhat for direction and control under reason and conscience, and are amenable to the law of justice and general benefit that is the basis of social morality; but to deny them, to repress their divine spontaneity, to smother and annihilate them, is to sin against the purpose and law of universal nature, and might well be defined as one form of the transgression which the New Testament calls the sin against the Holy Ghost. It is the very life of eternal Being, seeking ever some higher and more favoring form of manifestation, that has organized these natural affections and sympathies within us. The power of God is in them as the very bond of the union. The dying Bunsen spoke not in metaphor, but only simple truth, when he said to his wife, bending over him, "In thy face, I have seen the Eternal." Tread reverently; for here is holy ground, here are shrines for daily worship. In the pure loves of our hearts for wife, for husband, for child, for brother and sister, for father, mother, friend, the Infinite One is near us,— ay, *lives within us.* It is eternal love that binds us thus together in affectionate mutual service. Hold it sacred. Profane it not, deny it not, defile it not.

Kneel at the heart's shrines, and gratefully adore and serve.

This inner circle of affection is needed, too, in order that the great outer work of life may be most effectually done,— in order that even the universal charities and philanthropies may be the better accomplished. There are portions of life which can only be developed in this close intimacy of affection, — which are too sacred for public participation,— which, like some rare and delicate plants, only appear under certain conditions of privacy as to shelter and temperature. Yet these portions are also necessary to the completeness of our lives and to the full performance of our duties; and they are necessary, not merely for their own sake and the rounding of the life in that direction, but for the perfect rounding of the life in all other directions and the complete development and action of all its parts. The men who live solely in public, whether it be for ends of business, or philanthropy, or political or religious service, lose a certain refinement and tenderness of nature and a certain moral and spiritual aroma, which are found only in the enclosed and sheltered gardens of private affection; and by as much as this loss detracts from the full completeness of the life, by so much does it detract from its strength and usefulness in any public service. We touch here, indeed, upon a great general law,— the law of culture. There must be a certain amount of general culture of our whole being before the best fruit of any special faculty can be produced. No man is a great statesman who is only a statesman.

No man who is merely a business man has breadth enough for the greatest operations in business. A man who is so narrow as to be only a mechanician is too narrow — he lacks the necessary knowledge — for the highest achievements in mechanics; and the man who is only a public philanthropist is not broad enough to achieve the grandest successes in philanthropy. In accordance with this same law, the culture of the private and domestic affections is necessary to the fullest accomplishment of the public service that is required of us. These affections enlarge, elevate, and refine the whole nature, and better prepare it for its special work in any direction. There is no love of universal humanity that can take the place of the heart's private loves; and the broadest love of mankind may have a· kindlier flavor, if it yield its austere demands now and then to home affections and delights. The domestic affections are the inns along the rough highways of life, where Duty is refreshed and girds herself anew for the severe pilgrimage and stern tasks before her; and as, without seasons of refreshment, the traveller must perish in the way, so, without these resting-places of the heart, conscience may be overstrained, and Duty sink down exhausted in her own severely appointed path. The lives that have been spent in attempts to show that it is possible to put away all earthly love, till the soul, intense with individual piety, shall seem a clear flame of spiritual devotion ascending to heaven,— these very lives have proved, by the fruitlessness of the effort or by some monstrosity in the result, the absolute necessity and divineness of earthly love.

But not only are the natural claims of the heart to be acceded to for the perfect development of our present being, but also for the better accomplishment of our destiny as beings who may be immortal. I would speak of this point with caution, because it is a point on which positive knowledge fails us; and we can only draw inferences from premises which rest on the basis of the strongest rational probability. Not arguing this question now, but assuming that some kind of continuance of existence for human beings, after these few years of earthly life are over, is the more rational alternative, I wish to make and emphasize the point that the culture of the personal affections is not simply probationary, not merely educational in the sense of preparing our natures for some great *spiritual* service in the world hereafter, but the affections themselves are immortal: they go with us and remain a part of us in the world hereafter.

If we are to preserve our personal identity after death, I see not how we can come to any other belief than this: the heart, with all its real loves, attachments, and sympathies,— with all its still folded capacities, too,— remains with us. It is in this that the richest and best parts of our lives have been found here. It is this that is deepest in our being, this for which more than anything else we crave personal continuance. I cannot conceive, therefore, any individual human existence hereafter in which the personal and social affections are not to fill an important place and contribute in a most important degree to the heavenly service and felicity. Nay, I believe that these affections must enter much more into our lives there than they have ever entered, or can enter, into our lives here. I do not picture the future life as simply the unimpeded intellectual discovery and reverence of truth, however high the dignity and large the satisfactions of such a career. I do not picture it as only moral adherence to the line of divine rectitude, though of necessity including that. I do not picture it as merely a higher field for the rigid, self-sacrificing services of charity and philanthropy, but as that and more. Least of all do I picture it as a continuous discharge of technical religious duties,— a monotonous scene of adoration and worship, of praises and psalm-singing and shoutings of hosannas around a celestial throne. Nor can I accept the more mystical interpretation of this latter view, and say with religious stoicism that the heavenly life is the rapturous adoration and worship of Infinite Being alone,— that it is to live with Him in such a way that all other personal relations, all other personal longings and regrets, are swallowed up and lost in the personal relation to Him. Not thus, O friends, do I read man's future. Not thus do I read it from his past or from his present, from his history or from his capacities and his yearnings.

We may hope, indeed, in that world of more refined mentality, to gaze with ardor upon the new truth that will be revealed to us; we may hope to walk with fonder obedience the path of rectitude, and to live as devoted helpers and lovers of our race; we may hope to know and serve and live in more vital connection with the Eternal Power, in some higher and larger way than anything our imaginations can now conceive. But the crowning distinction and glory of the future world must be, I believe, the unfolding, ever more and more, of the life of the human heart in its finite personal relations; the disclosure, ever more and more, of the mysterious depths of the riches, beauty, and power of these relations; the development of our natures as *persons* into ever higher and more determinate, yet more complicated and co-related forms, as organisms of the infinite energy and life. This is nature's highway of development,— increasing forms of differentiation, and thereby constant ascent in individual intelligence and power, and not reabsorption into the original mass of being. I see not how we could be nearer to *God as a person* in the future world than we are in this; for "in him," even now, "we live and move and have our being." Indeed, I cannot conceive of God as *a* person,— as one whom we can approach and have relations with, as we approach and have relations with each other. That, to my thought, makes him finite. But, if we are to attribute personality to him at all, he is Person of persons; or that which is the substratum in which finite personalities inhere,— the vital power through which they have found being and by which they are bound together in social relations and ties. And hence I conceive that our heaven will be the larger and freer unfolding and enriching of our personal being and finite personal relations. We shall not be nearer, in any literal sense, to God,— we shall never look upon his face as the face of a man; but we shall enclose more of his being in our being, and *in him* we shall draw nearer to each other, and look with clearer vision into each other's faces, and touch with fonder rapture and more blissful communion each other's hearts. We shall admire Truth and Goodness and Beauty,— the accorded attributes of Infinite Being; but we shall admire them mainly, and in ever-increasing measure, in their personal manifestations, and as they bind us by many a strong and sacred tie in social relationships. We shall worship,— less in form, but more in substance,— our worship becoming ever more and more the living "beauty of holiness,"— love, fidelity, affectionate, just, and helpful service to each other.

We know not, indeed, how these natural immortal affections are to build the heavenly homes, and circles and societies; but we know that they are strong enough to draw kindred hearts together here, and to build up homes, and to hold firmly the friendly circle. And so, with perfect assurance, we can trust them, in that freer and sincerer life, to rear the mansions of eternal love, and to draw into them, and into friendly neighborhood, the hearts that really belong together. The *mere* earthly relations may fall away,— they are but educational, preliminary; but the ties of the heart, the kinships of the soul,— these, if anything, must survive all changes of time and death and the grave.

We do not know all, my friends; but we know enough,— enough to cause us to put the culture of the domestic, personal, and social affections among the first of religious duties. Starve them not, suppress them not. Let them grow, and glow, and flame their genial warmth into all the cold places of life. And let them consume all the secret or tolerated impurities that usurp their sacred name. Guard all your true friendships faithfully, sacredly: the heart of your friend joins yours, because some portion of divine power possesses you in common at that point. Let your kindly word and deed be felt in all your neighborhood and through all your friendly circle,— elevating, purifying, enlivening with innocent joy. And in your homes,— oh for a tongue inspired to speak of the holy affections and obligations there! We have not yet half learned the worth of the home. We have not yet learned what depths of religion lie beneath the affections on which it is based. Not wealth, nor social ambition, nor fashion should build it; not prudence, nor convenience, nor even conscience alone, should build it. But love should build it; and love — wise love — should reign in it. Let it build it so pure and beautiful and sincere that it shall be a foretaste and type of the heavenly dwelling. Let it make its realities so attractive that no frivolities nor illusions can draw son or daughter, husband or wife, into temptation elsewhere. Let it fill it so full of pure service, irradiate it with such joy and peace, that no place in all the world shall seem so good, so divine. Let love — wise love — build it. Though it founds it on the earth, it will rear it to the heavens and open it into the celestial mansions; and, though the members of the household must one after another depart, they may still not be far away: they may have only gone

to some higher room, where Love, faithful housekeeper, shall find them, every one, and preside still
with patient fidelity over the one family on earth
and in heaven.

April 2, 1865.

VII.

ENDURANCE.

"Behold, we count them happy which endure." — EPISTLE OF JAMES.

IT is a well-known fact of physics that every result in nature is achieved through the operation of two sets of forces,— the forces of impulsion and the forces of resistance. Or, to speak more precisely, physical force manifests itself in two ways,— by direct action and by reflex action; and every movement, every growth, every evolution in nature, is the resultant of this double putting-forth of power. It is from the combination of these two exhibitions of force, harmoniously balanced, the first of which would impel in a direct line through endless space and the other bring to speedy rest, that the earth describes its symmetrical orbit, returning to it with precision every year. And thus, too, it is that all the heavenly bodies group themselves in families and systems, finding rest in their harmonious relations with each other, at the same time that they have infinite motion and variety in their endless circles. Science even allows us through the infinite vista opened by this law of forces to catch a glimpse of the process by which chaos first began to divide into worlds; and it is by this same balance of forces that all the physical phenomena of the worlds are continued. By this, stones get their structure, vegetation is produced, our feet walk the earth, and the nail clasps the wood so that our houses stand. It is from the impulsion of the wind and the resistance of the waves that our ships sail the sea; from the friction of the rail and the expansion of steam that the locomotive makes the circuit of the globe.

There is the same double manifestation of force in things moral and spiritual,—the force positive and the force negative, the force active and the force passive, the force direct and the force reflex, the force of impulsion and the force of resistance; and there must be the same harmonious combination and balance of these two elements, in order to produce efficiency and grace of character. There must be not only the impulse to do, but the capacity to bear; not only the incentive to move, but the ability to stand; not only the motive to act, but the power to endure; not only the will to say yes, but the will to say no; not only the supple, extended hand with ready generosity to offer help, but the firm, arched elbow and the knotted muscles prepared to resist and defend. These two manifestations of force are equally necessary, and in about the same degree, for the highest achievements of moral and spiritual character. It is, in fact, but one and the same force operating in different ways; and, where there is any real, original strength of character, it operates in both directions with equal efficiency : it shows itself, according to opportunity, both as strength to do and as strength to bear.

It is of this latter element of character — the strength to endure, to bear, to resist, to suffer — that I wish to speak this morning. And this needs, perhaps, the more to be enforced by speech than the other, since, in the very nature of the case, it is a more silent and undemonstrative kind of power in itself. The strength that is shown in direct and positive deeds, the strength to dare and to do, tells its own merits and carves its own fame; while the strength that simply endures and resists must of necessity remain very much in concealment, and, perchance, its achievements never be told to the public ear. One acts chiefly in public, but one must suffer in solitude. The heroic deed is done amid the cheers of crowding bystanders, and is lifted to the knowledge of the world upon the breath of their huzzas: the heroic suffering may be hidden in the sacred privacy of home, in the silence of some obscure chamber, or in the still deeper and more silent recess of some private heart, which bears a grief that no human being knoweth, and whose fame is carried only on the breath of that spirit which "bloweth where it listeth," but the sound of which comes to no human ear. Hence, to the majority of men there is more stimulus to do bravely than to bear bravely: the heroism of the former is seen and applauded, the heroism of the latter may be unrecognized and unknown.

Indeed, there are many persons who would at first question whether heroism of character can ever be shown through the passive qualities of endurance and defence. Their idea of the hero is of one who goes forth as an aggressor against the evils and ills of life ; who does not wait for the hour of defence, but averts the need of endurance by boldly advancing to annihilate the cause that threatens the necessity of such a resort. He is one who courts difficulties and hardships ; who delights in attacking wrong ; who seeks obstacles that he may overcome them ; who penetrates with a supreme disregard of self to the very front of danger, and flings his life with Herculean force into the deadly assault, determined, if he must die, to demand for the sacrifice the utmost possible price. Such a character as this is, indeed, admirable. It has our applause and our homage. The world will always need such heroes, and will gratefully find redemption and progress in following their footsteps. But is the whole of heroism here ? Are there no heroes save in the front ranks of battle ? Is it glorious to rush with open breast against danger, and not glorious, also, to stand in attitude of waiting, defiant composure to resist it ? The soldiers who stormed the forts of Vicksburg were not braver, nor did they do a more valorous deed for their country, than they who stood behind the ramparts of Gettysburg to receive unmoved the deadly fire, but who were not allowed to go out to assault their foes in return. The scout and the advance guard are needed ; but so is the soldier that defends the citadel in the rear, and to him may come as rare opportunities for bravery as to his more active brothers in the front. The man that runs up to the cannon's mouth, and seizes the flag from the hand of his enemy, and carries it in triumph from the field, is heroic. So is he that holds the flag secure against a hostile grasp; and he, too, who, far away from the noise and excitement of the fray, unseen perchance by mortal eye, bears with uncomplaining fortitude the pain of a shattered limb or the burden of a diseased and helpless body,— he, it may be, is the greatest hero of them all.

Strength of character cannot be measured by publicity of deed. There are perilous courses of business which seem to invite into them only the bravest blood; there are rare missions of philanthropy in which those who engage must needs have peculiar courage; there are sudden emergencies in life which sometimes call into public distinction that presence of mind, self-forgetfulness, and daring which specially mark the hero. And we are apt to think that it is only amid such surroundings that heroism can appear. But, perhaps, in your nearest neighbor's house you may find heroism just as true and triumphant,— in the silent submissiveness with which some great trial is borne; in the patient fidelity with which some secret, humble duty is performed; in the serene, cheerful resignation, telling no tale of disappointment and sacrifice, with which the heart has taken up some heavy cross, crushing its deepest impulses, at the command of conscience. Heroism? You shall find it in the patient, faithful life of the woman who has seen joy after joy depart from her side; who has buried the bright hopes of her youth; whose dream-castles filled with luxury and indulgence have vanished before the realities of hardship, poverty, and neglect; who pictures no longer any high mission or large place for the display of her powers; and who now gives her days with consecrated fidelity to some hard, obscure service of affection or of duty, finding the whole of life in domestic faithfulness and neighborly charity and kindness. Heroism? You shall find it in the man who sacrifices position, friendship, wealth, pleasure, and what are commonly regarded as the dearest objects of life, that he may live true to some one overmastering obligation of principle or of honor which the world knows nothing of. Heroism? You shall find it in the high resolve of youth to overcome passion, to defy temptation, to bear the ridicule and scoffing of companions, to struggle with unknown difficulties and obstacles, to let go the fondest personal desires, in order to keep with honor some private trust or to fulfil some pledge given to conscience, or given, perchance, to a mother's prayer. Heroism? You shall find it, perhaps, in the humble, scantily clad service-girl you have just passed unnoticed in the street, whose thin, poor dress covers a heart rich in patient endurance and self-forgetfulness, as she goes day after day to her wearing, half-paid toil to get the bread that shall keep her bedridden, widowed mother and her young brothers and sisters from the disgrace of the almshouse. No human eye has read her story; yet, if it could be written in a book as Heaven's eye reads it, even the world of fashion would read it with admiration and homage, and count her among its heroines. But she, perchance, cannot write; and so she only *lives* her heroism, and the great world knows nothing of it.

And, if we are to judge character by the standard of the world's purest and greatest teachers, which is, also, the standard of our own secret hearts, shall we not place such examples of brave, silent endurance in the common paths of life higher even than the great deed of valor that is blazoned round the world? These are never seen of men. Their left hand knows not what their right hand does. They are encouraged by no applause. They are incited by no competition. They only whisper their secret in trust to God, and their only reward is the consciousness of his approval and their own faithfulness.

Wonderful almost to the miraculous is the power of endurance which a single-eyed devotion to duty sometimes gives. Even the body, animated by a strong and serenely heroic soul, becomes less sensitive to fatigue and danger, and more able to resist privation and disease. I shall never forget an incident, in illustration of this truth, that came to my knowledge from the career of a private soldier serving in the army of the Potomac. In a Pennsylvania regiment was a young man who enlisted in March, 1864. Two months afterward, he was carried to the hospital, wounded in three places, one of the wounds depriving him of his right eye. In August, he again joined his regiment, just before an engagement, in which he was again wounded and carried insensible from the field. After another two months in the hospital, he was again in the field for service, and very soon was one of a body of men sent to make a demonstration against a rebel fort. Placed on the picket line, he was left there, exposed to capture, by the sudden withdrawal of the national troops without warning. Discovering his perilous position, he crept unobserved into a small ravine, hoping to make his escape during the night. But, before night, a rebel vidette was thrown out a few feet from where he lay, so that he could not change his location or even lift his body without being perceived. For six days and nights, he remained in the ravine, — the enemy's sentinel posted close beside him,— exposed to winds and rains and frosts, without food or drink, chewing for sustenance the leaves and roots that chanced to be in reach of his arm, and fearing almost to sleep lest he should attract attention by some unconscious movement, but resolved not to surrender, though he might have done so with perfect personal safety at any moment. On the seventh night, the enemy having relaxed vigilance, he crawled on his hands and knees to our lines, bringing with him his musket and all his accoutrements. His feet and hands were frost-bitten, his stomach had almost lost its functions, and one day more of such narrow imprisonment and he must have surrendered to death. Yet he seemed not to think that he had done anything extraordinary, or more than any patriotic soldier would have done. For myself, I could not help repeating as I read the story,— and I believe I made no irreverent application of the words,— "He endured hardness as a good soldier of Jesus Christ." I do not know that he was a "Christian," as that word is commonly defined,— I do not know that he made any claims to religion,— but he certainly showed a fortitude which the highest martyrs and saints of the Church have not surpassed; and, whatever were his sins,— sins of weakness he could not have had,— they were surely forgiven him, since he was ready to give so much to his country.

But such fortitude, it is said, noble as it is, is yet somewhat physical. It is, to a considerable extent, a matter of natural temperament. Another person, equally patriotic and brave, but of a different physical organization, might not have been able to show this capacity of endurance. There are worse sufferings than those of physical pain. There are disappointments of the heart; there are bereavements of affection; there are wrongs of neglect, suspicion, and false accusation; there are heart agonies deeper than any caused by Death's sharp blade. And to bear such trials with serenity is a higher test of strength than patient submissiveness to bodily torture. And here, too, my mind recurs to an example in a soldier's life that came under my own knowledge. In the "Deserters' Camp"— a camp for deserters from our own army — across the Potomac, a daily visit to which lay within the rounds of my duty during a part of the winter of 1864, I noticed, from day to day, a man whose strong, honest face, cleanly dress, and general manly appearance and bearing indicated a character quite different from most of those with whom he was there associated. Finally, after a direct question to him, I learned his story; for he never sought me to make known his complaints, as did the rest. He was a Maine farmer, and had served from the beginning of the war. He had fought in most of the battles of the Army of the Potomac, and bore then on his person the scar of a severe wound, proof of his valor at Gettysburg. In consequence of this, he had been transferred to the Invalid Corps; and, while going to the post to which he was assigned for duty, having neglected some technical military regulation, he was arrested as a deserter and sent to the military prison in Georgetown. Nominally, he was a deserter: really, he was no deserter; and his case could have been righted at once, if the circumstances had been known to the proper authorities. But the proper authorities could not know of every case in the Georgetown prison. And so the unfortunate man remained there for weeks in a small apartment crowded with prisoners, with no opportunity for a hearing or prospect of release. This was his reward for three years of faithful soldierly service. After a while, he was sent with others out to the "Deserters' Camp," there to be kept for weeks longer with the worst class of soldiers and the vilest of men. It was nearly three months from his arrest before his release came. Yet, when he related the affair to me, and told of the hardships he had suffered in prison, and of the difficulty of getting his case brought to trial, and of the worse hardship of being charged with desertion from an army which he had been proud to fight with for three years and from a cause which he would give his life willingly for rather than it should fail; and, though his eyes moistened when he said that his worst fear had been that he might die there, and his name then always stand on the war records with that stigma of cowardice or treason against it,— yet he showed no resentment and no bitterness, but, in the consciousness of his own fidelity, was lifted above all passion, and was as composed as if he had been promoted instead of being imprisoned. He knew, he said, it was all a mistake, no one *meant* to wrong him; and then he added, with a brave philosophy, " It matters not how much the United States government may punish me, or what charges they may bring against me, they can never make a traitor of me ; and, when they release me, I shall fight for them again all the same."

But does such fortitude as this seem too stoical, too coldly philosophical, to reach the religious standard? Does it have too little of the *joy* of sacrifice, too little of spiritual consolation and hope? Go with me, then, again to another scene, and see this silent heroism of endurance transfigured as if with the very light of the opening heavens. See a man lying in a hospital, worn with wounds, marches, and disease, nearing every day his death and knowing that death is already looking him in the face; see him there surrounded by no comforts, only with the rudest necessities of the sick-room, far away from home and friends, the fresh soldier hope, that pictured heroic adventure and romance and feats of brilliant contest and victory, turned into this pallor and feebleness, this emaciation and wasting corruption of disease,— see him there, simply suffering, enduring, and waiting to die; see death end the scene in peace, and his wasted body carried forth in its rude coffin to the soldier's burial,— and then turn back and read these verses on which the ink from his pen is still fresh : * —

"I lay me down to sleep,
  With little thought or care
  Whether my waking find
  Me here or There!

"A bowing, burdened head,
  That only asks to rest
  Unquestioning upon
  A loving breast.

"My good right hand forgets
  Its cunning now;
  To march the weary march
  I know not how.

"I am not eager, bold,
  Nor strong. All that is past.
  I am ready not to do,
  At last, at last.

"My half-day's work is done,
  And this is all my part:
  I give a patient God
  My patient heart,

"And grasp his banner still,
  Though all its blue be dim;
  These stripes, no less than stars,
  Lead after Him."

* This incident and the verses were found in William H. Reed's *Hospital Life*, then just published. The impression there given is that the verses were composed by the soldier just before his death. But the soldier may have only copied them; yet, though since published *anonymously* in many places, I am not aware that they have been claimed for any other author.

What one of the saints ever left a more exquisite memorial of trust, submissiveness, and peace! Here the deepest springs of life have been touched, and the eternal waters flow. If the imprisoned soldier, in his power to bear suffering and wrong, gave us only the type of a sublime stoicism, this dying soldier certainly, in the sweetness of his submission, shows us as fair a type as was ever claimed for Christian saintliness.

But do I seem to mock you, friends, with these examples of character drawn from scenes far off and from opportunities now happily past? Come with me, then, nearer home. Enter a dwelling in this city, which some in this congregation have entered many a time; and there may be some here who know well of what I am about to speak, but to most it is all unknown. Go into the servants' apartment of that house. There, a few months ago, you might have seen, in the person of a serving colored woman, an example of patient, heroic suffering, in which the very strength and tranquillity of heaven seemed so to mingle that an influence went out of her chamber, pervading the whole house and blessing all who saw her. She who had only engaged to serve with her physical strength for wages became at last the gratuitous teacher of the highest moral and spiritual truths; and, when her faithful hands failed in their office, she served even more truly than before, bringing gifts to her patrons on the wings of her spirit from the very gates of Paradise. And when, after months of pain thus bravely and cheerfully borne, it became expedient to try the last hope of recovery, and she went to the Massachusetts General Hospital to submit to a critical surgical operation, she showed there a fortitude and composure so extraordinary as to become a tradition of the place. So far from needing comfort, she seemed herself to be the sustainer and comforter. Virtue went out from her, to strengthen those around her better to do and to bear. They who went to wait upon her wants came away feeling that they had received more than they could give. Attendants, patients, surgeons, were awed by her marvellous strength, as if a supernatural presence were with her; and this humble serving-woman became the Christ-like teacher of professors and learned physicians, of men and women far above her in culture and social rank, and of all the humble, suffering poor, lying on their weary beds around. She died. But the power that went out from such a life, the beautiful, beatific influence of such virtue, can never die. It stays still upon the earth to help us be strong and to mould new life into its likeness.

These examples, then, of the strength and grace that may come to character from the simple quality of endurance are not far away; nor are the occasions past. Is there any person here whose position is lowlier, whose name obscurer, than the name and lot of those from whom these illustrations are drawn? And is there any here whose position is so high, or so well guarded by wealth and culture and all the facilities of external ease and comfort, that suffering and sorrow, infirmity and loss, cannot reach it? Such examples are all around us. No one of us is beyond the opportunities which call for this virtue

We admire it always in others: let us secure the possession of it for ourselves. Who of us does not love gentle Charles Lamb the more for his patient, long burdened, but unbroken and unmurmuring submissiveness to that fearful calamity which darkened his house, and for the heroic sacrifices he made because of it, all unknown at the time, to one tender obligation? I pray we may not be led away by any arguments for the rightfulness and sanctity of all natural human impulses into a philosophy of self-gratification and self-indulgence. I also would proclaim the purity and sanctity of all affections and sentiments that are genuinely natural to humanity. But, among these affections and sentiments, I find one which does pre-eminent homage to the virtue of self-denial and self-renunciation. I also would preach the doctrine of self-development as containing the fundamental principle of religious growth and progress. But I see that the way to self-development is often the way of the cross, and that the character that is perfected to the highest grace and beauty is most frequently moulded by suffering and sacrifice. In this aspect of things, the lot that seems hardest may be most blessed. There is no lot so hard, no dwelling so humble nor so afflicted, but that heaven lies next to it; and brave endurance no less than brave doing carries the key that will open the door to the highest of heaven's joys.

September 30, 1866.

VIII.

CHILDHOOD'S INSTINCT AND MANHOOD'S FAITH.

"Verily I say unto you, Except ye be converted, and become as little children, ye shall not enter into the kingdom of heaven."—MATT. xviii., 3.

THUS did Jesus rebuke the petty jealousies and ambitions of his disciples. Holding a little child before them, he contrasted their selfish strivings and vanity with its guileless unconsciousness of self; their anxiety about future emoluments and honors with its fulness of joy in its present life; their coldly scheming prudence and niggardliness of affection with its generous, instinctive trust and outgushing, uncalculating love. And, from this and one or two similar sayings of Jesus, it has come to be a common Christian inculcation that, to be religious, one must become like a little child. But, often as this sentiment is repeated, I apprehend there is a very vague understanding of what it is to become as a child in spiritual things. Paul said that when he became a man he put away childish things. And this is felt to be quite as important a truth as the saying of Jesus, and more in accord with the natural facts of individual progress. Yet the heart of Christendom has doubtless been right in holding on to this precept of Jesus as containing an illustration of some fine religious truth, though the understanding of Christendom may not always have rightly interpreted the illustration. He whose eye was quick to detect in the lilies and the clouds, in the sparrow and the grass, a religious lesson, saw in the simple spontaneous life of childhood a natural revelation of the truth he wished to teach concerning the spiritual faith of manhood. Perhaps it was only the simple spontaneity and docility of the early childhood nature that impressed him. But the comparison suggests a more interior analogy; and it is not impossible that it was to this that his thought penetrated,— an analogy between the trusting instinctive confidence of childhood and the serene faith and repose of true manhood. At least, it is to the development of this thought that I ask more specially your attention in this discourse,— *The Analogy between Childhood's Instinct and Manhood's Faith.*

The true point of the analogy lies deeper, I believe, than we ordinarily fathom. Indeed, as the comparison is commonly drawn, it is in many respects false. It is superficial, and contains more sentiment than sound common sense. We observe, with something of envy, the freshness, the simplicity, the unartificial ways, the joyous innocence of children; and the wish often utters itself,—" Oh that we could have our blotted, tattered natures given back to us in their infantile purity again!" The wish, of course, is all in vain; but, for other reasons, it is also irrational. It is but the old lamentation that ever puts the golden age in the past,— the crying for vanished pleasures when nobler are in hand or within reach. A man can no more return to the moral stature of his infancy than he can to the intellectual or the physical. He cannot have childhood's innocence again ; but he can have something higher,— manly integrity and strength, matured nobleness and power. Every stage of life has its appropriate virtues and graces ; and, while purity and kindness belong alike to all ages, maturity can no more put on those graces that are the peculiar charm of childhood than we can wear in adult years the clothes we wore as boys and girls. Besides, there is, I think we must confess, a good deal of romance in our talk of the children's innocence and happiness. They are innocent, Heaven be thanked, of our artificial, hollow ways of life. They speak their hearts right out, and with one true, keen word often prick the wind out of many a family sham. They have not yet learned to hold their tongues to silent lies, nor politely to speak the thing they know is false. Go back far enough, and we shall find innocence, it is true ; but who shall say when or how early it is lost? The moral nature seems to dawn simultaneously with the intellectual. And, with the unfolding of the moral nature, the dark side comes to the surface no less than the bright. The infant in arms displays anger and disobedience. The boy of four does wilful mischief, and attempts, perhaps, deceit. I was once present at the "christening" of a three-years-old child, from whom, just at the moment when the clergyman read, "For of such is the kingdom of heaven," there burst a violent ebullition of temper not commonly associated with that kingdom. These first manifestations of childish wilfulness and error may indeed be slight,— mere peccadilloes, which with wisdom may be controlled; but, none the less, they are not virtues that manhood needs to sigh for.

And there is often greater disorder, bringing positive and perilous wrong and unhappiness,— disorder that is inherited parentally, tendencies to vice born in the blood. As physical peculiarities, features, personal defects, are transmitted through long series of generations, so men and women of ages past — not more Adam than many a greater sinner since, nay, men and women living now — have sown the seeds of crimes which generations yet unborn shall reap. Your most pet and private weaknesses, secrets you think in your breast alone, may stand revealed upon your children, to publish your faults years after you are dead. They, indeed, the little ones, poor sufferers though they are, are innocent of it all; for we know not how many generations of sinning men and women have sent down the poison of their vices into these little frames. But innocence here is not purity, is not happiness. Though the accountability be in the past, the disorder is none the less real and present. We may give it a sweet name, but the thing is none the less foul. Such childish innocence may move our pity, but hardly our envy; and, though we may not adopt the hideous blasphemy of "total depravity,"— of mankind born desperately wicked and fit only for eternal perdition,— we may also avoid the deluded sentimentalism that talks of the moral graces of the cradle. The germs are there in the cradles,— germs of almost infinite moral possibilities; and even the germs by their tenderness and pliancy are adapted to appeal to all that is purest in our natures, and to put to shame that actual depravity into which the habits of our years may have hardened, by reminding us of what might have been. Yet, though infancy be thus lovely in its bud of possibilities, there must be germination and growth before the beauty of moral and spiritual life can appear. Such life is not born: it is character developing under the pressure of experience and of moral and social obligations. And, even if childish innocence were always inborn purity and joyousness,— as often, indeed, it is, even the flesh, as Emerson said, being "angels' flesh, all alive,"— yet it cannot present the moral stature which must be manhood's standard. No integrity is sure which has not met the seductions of avarice and ambition, and stood unmoved against them. There is no real chastity before the passions tempt; no temperance and simplicity which have not proved their ability to exist in spite of worldly wickedness. Childish *innocence* may be lovely and fragrant, but it is only the blossom. Manly *virtue* is the matured, life-sustaining fruit. And ripened grain can as well go back to the time of bloom, or the scarred and weather-beaten soldier leave unused his hard-earned victories and content himself again with the paper cap, wooden sword, and mimic battle-fields of his boyhood, as that the natural development of character can be reversed and manhood's virtue return to childhood's innocence.

Look, again, at another phase of childhood,— that alleged unconsciousness of self, which gives to the child its most exquisite charm, and for which, burdened with that intense self-consciousness they would be gladly rid of, men and women are so apt to long. Examining more closely, we shall see that this unconsciousness of self is only apparent. By physiological and psychological law, early childhood is really and necessarily confined to a circle of selfish aims. The life at first is wholly so, consisting of sensations and instinctive efforts that go only to self-nourishment and self-protection ; and for several years self predominates. Feeling, thought, play,— all aim at self-advantage. Life is somewhat advanced before the humanities and charities appear. Nature's first object is to develop and guard the new individuality that has been born, and that afterwards is to be a voluntary instrument of her aims. The appearance of unconsciousness in childhood, if the paradox may be pardoned, comes from the fact that young children are conscious of so little but themselves ; that is, they have not yet distinctly separated self from their environment, and so have not gained a distinct and well-defined individual existence. As this separation goes on under the experience of life, self-consciousness, indeed, for a time becomes more intense, though always diminishing its proportion to the whole momentum of life, till, by and by, self and the external universe come to be seen in their true relations. It is evident, therefore, that that forgetfulness of self which manhood yearns for and tends toward is not the unconsciousness of the child, who seems lost to self only because lost in his own joys; but the man, having discovered his relations to other beings and things, is to find his satisfaction largely in forgetting self in others' joys. And so self-denial, self-sacrifice, comes in,— the finding of life through losing it,— which is the very extreme of character-development from the first stage of childhood, and the highest reach of ethical life on earth.

Not, then, in the external condition or external graces of childhood do we find the point of the analogy which we seek. We are to become as little children in some other way than by trying to deck ourselves in the children's virtues. For, however beautiful these are in their time and upon the children, yet true manhood and womanhood have virtues all their own, and quite as noble. We must strike deeper into childhood, into its very constitution and essential relations, if we would find the analogy of the text justified.

Looking, then, at the very beginning of human life, what are its earliest phases ? What is the essential, peculiar nature of childhood ? We shall find the most distinguishing feature of infancy, whether we look at the subject metaphysically or as a simple matter of fact, to be instinctive trust in and reliance upon *what is*, with no questioning of its reality or of its ample capacity and purpose to meet all wants. The infantile life is divided between sensations and instincts. Through the instincts, it is connected with the external world; but only through its sensations are these instincts made known in the child's consciousness. The instincts and sensations are one to him. The infant, therefore, at first makes no separation between self and the external world. He is a perfect idealist. He knows of no world that is not found in his own consciousness. His wants are all supplied by some unerring power working through himself, and he is not conscious at first that this power is at all external to himself. The demand seems to bring the supply. His faculties of thought and of voluntary will-power all sleep as yet in embryo, and therefore in harmony. He has found, as yet, no contradiction as a gulf of separation between himself and outward things. He lies in the great lap of nature, peaceful, bound to her by the delicate but strong tie of woman's tenderness; in harmony as yet with the world into which he has come, and living on a mother's care and love in absolute, instinctive trust. And here in this perfect trust, this repose upon the power which has borne and still nourishes it, is the distinguishing feature of earliest childhood. We may call it a state of *instinctive, undeveloped unity with nature and its laws.*

Now, it is something corresponding to this instinctive trust of earliest childhood that manhood needs,— not just that, but something like it; and it remains to say what this corresponding condition of manhood is and how it comes.

This stage of implicit childish trust is very brief.

Indeed, no sooner does individual life begin its development than a separation begins between individual consciousness and the external world. The beginning of such a separation marks the genesis of personal life. The child's instinctive desires are thwarted; and so the sense of a separate existence and of conflicting aims is born, and nature's conative energy, which has been acting through instinct, begins to shape itself into personal volition. Mental perception awakes through the same cause; and by and by, through this new avenue, in gradual sequence, the external world, both of persons and things, is revealed. Other instincts also come in due order with the years,— tumultuous passions, appetites, ambitions, and all the practical desires and energies of the period of youth and of opening manhood. But not these alone: a higher world of thought and virtue also comes to light. It flashes in upon the soul through perceptions of truth, goodness, beauty; and conscience awakes to stand as sentinel at the opening ways of life, to declare the sovereignty of these higher ideas and aspirations over the self-seeking passions and ambitions. Thus, the human being becomes gradually equipped for all life's offices and work. And, through all these phases of development, the separation between self and the external world has become more distinctly marked. The object, indeed, at every step has been to develop a stronger and more powerful personality, — out of the vague and chaotic conditions of infantile existence to bring forth a concentrated, compact, sinewy individual organism which should be a new centre of beneficent activity and power in the universe. To this end, the struggles and conflicts, and all the fiery trials and baptisms of this earthly life, if rightly met, have been made subservient. The force and pressure of outward circumstances, the inevitable laws of nature, the infinite energies that both command and restrain the finite, have furnished the resisting medium which has solicited the efforts and developed the intelligent power and freedom of the individual soul.

But by and by, in natural sequence, there comes another stage in this process of life-development. The individuality, the selfhood, is established. The faculty and power of a free, self-centred personality are achieved. The *man* is ready, and stands in full armor prepared for the work of life. The question comes, What shall he do? Here, on one side, are the passions, the appetites, the ambitions, urgent and tumultuous, and all the self-sustaining and self-aggrandizing motives still actively pushing their claims. Shall this personal faculty, power, and freedom that have been achieved be put to the service of such masters? Shall self-aggrandizement and self-enjoyment be continued as the object of human life? Nay, that ideal of a higher, nobler life, which has been forming within the consciousness, starts up in protest and forbids such a consummation. Not for this has nature been intent on producing this new and wonderful organism of the human personality. Itself offspring of and in some way still vitally connected with Eternal Being, it must own allegiance to the law and purposes of this ancestral power, and live for them rather than for any transient objects and pleasures of its own. Not self-preservation, but the welfare of that which is infinitely greater than self, is the imperative command that is laid upon the human soul by the moral instinct. Hence, as man stands equipped for service at the opening ways of life, he is conscious of an obligation, above all others, to serve high objects of truth, right, and goodness; to exercise his power of personal sovereignty on the side of justice, integrity, beneficence; to so live that his life shall tell for all that is healthful, helpful, and beautiful in the manifold relations of human society, and be a perpetually nourishing factor in the commonwealth of mankind. The birth-time of this obligation is the genuine awakening of the religious consciousness. It is the hour for consecration, which is' youth's natural act. This may not come, however, at a definitely marked moment. It may advance by gradual increase of inward enlightenment, like the dawn of the morning. But it is a period which at some time, in some way, comes to every normally progressing soul. And whoever obediently follows this higher law of life becomes one of that happy company of souls who help to make a heaven on earth. Of such, in very truth, is the kingdom of heaven. They enter that kingdom not so much because heirs of its possessions as because ministers in its service.

And to this service, in behalf of the eternal laws and purposes faithfully followed, there comes finally, as its natural fruit and consummation, a state of mental confidence and repose corresponding to that implicit, instinctive trust which marks the earliest phases of childhood. This daily intimacy with and service of these divine laws beget reliance upon them. We come to rest in their embrace with the same unquestioning assurance which the child has in its mother's arms. As we lay then, ourselves helpless among forces that might in a moment have quenched our existence, yet secure against all hostility by the tie of motherhood, so we come to find a security as strong and as beneficent in the moral order of the universe. We lie restful in the lap of the infinite Bounty; and though hostile storms may beat round us, and our hopes and endeavors may be shattered, and our joys may lie stricken at our feet, nevertheless we are at peace; for, like the child, we then trust where we cannot see, and we still confide in the universal Bounty, arranged for the best welfare of all, though it deny this moment our special wish. Thus, at last, we find rest again,— rest even in the midst of life's struggles and conflicts, and solace for its woes. We return to that harmony with nature which was the first stage of our earthly existence, when there was no conscious separation between self and the not-self, and our very instincts were the direct impress of the divine energy. Only, that was an undeveloped, unconscious unity without personal character; while this is a *developed and conscious unity*, produced through the very organism of personal character,—the individual voluntarily accepting, trusting, and serving the Universal. In the place of instinct there is now moral intelligence and faith. The blind impulse of nature has blossomed into conscious volition; and what the child's instinct was as pledge of unquestioned security on its mother's bosom, that is manhood's perfect faith in the moral security of the world and in the rational acceptance of the facts and forces of the universe; or, to use the religious words, in Providence, in God.

And as, at first, the child makes no separation between himself and the external world, but finds himself led to the supplies for all his wants by some power working in and through his own desires, so the man or woman to whom this lofty mental and moral faith has come can no longer draw any line of demarcation between the human and the divine in the life of the soul. The idea of Deity as a distant, awe-enthroned sovereignty in the heavens has for them vanished. They know of no gulf of estrangement between God and man. *In* him, they live and move and have their being, and he in them. Their very prayers are the pulsings of his life in their consciousness; and the answer to them comes in a still loftier purpose and a larger measure of divine life in their own characters and acts. He worketh hitherto, and they work in and through his power. And when their action comes to the limit of human capacity, and their vision fails to fathom the inscrutable forces amid which they must needs live, they yet rest serenely on the all-controlling law of righteousness that is over all, and through all, and in us all.

January 27, 1867.

IX.

PURE RELIGION.

"Pure religion, and undefiled before God, the Father, is this, to visit the fatherless and widows in their affliction, and to keep one's self unspotted from the world."—EPISTLE OF JAMES.

SUCH is the definition of religion given by the Apostle James, brother of Jesus, first bishop of Jerusalem, head of the apostolic succession, and, after Jesus, official head of the Christian Church. And yet, notwithstanding this weight of official authority, this definition has generally been considered a very loose and heretical one in Christendom from an early date down to the present day. The Roman Catholic Church never did, and does not to-day, accept this as a sufficient statement of what religion is. It excommunicates, and in times past has tried literally to exterminate, persons whose belief concerning religion rests simply with this definition of the Apostle James. The Roman Catholic Church believes in works, in good works; and great credit is to be given to that Church for the various works of mercy and institutions of charity, which, both in its corporate capacity and through its individual members, it has inaugurated and cherished. But these are not what it specially calls *religious* works, and still less are they synonymous with its definition of religion.

In its view, "to fast" on certain prescribed days is a more specific religious service than to give bread to the hungry; to crawl up the "sacred stairs" at Rome on one's hands and knees a more religious act than to help the lame or the inebriate to walk on their feet; to make a pilgrimage of devotion to some holy shrine a better evidence of piety than to make a pilgrimage anywhere for the relief of suffering humanity. And to none of these works does it allow any religious merit without faith in the creed and traditions of the Holy Catholic Church.

And Protestantism, as a general rule, still more than Catholicism has departed from the Apostle James' definition of pure religion, and declared it heretical. Luther did not hesitate to say that the Epistle of James was an "epistle of straw," and to doubt its genuineness because it did not contain his doctrine of "justification by faith." None of the large, predominating sects of Protestant Christendom has ever thought James' definition of religion to be sufficient and sound. Most of them have said, "It isn't religion at all: it's mere morality; it's a snare to the soul rather than any security." Within the past year, I heard a learned doctor of divinity in a neighboring city declare from his pulpit that the merely moral men, those who are upright, pure, benevolent, full of kindness and good works, but who stop there, and make no doctrinal confession of religion,— that is, those who live precisely according to St. James' definition,— are a greater hindrance to Christianity, and do more harm to the world by their example, than do the openly wicked and criminal classes of society. And there are comparatively few Christian churches to-day that would be satisfied to admit new members to their fellowship on the simple statement of the Apostle James as an adequate conception of religious duty and covenant of belief. And the churches that would do this are commonly denied the Christian fellowship by the greater part of Christendom.

Now, which is right in this matter, the Apostle James or the prevailing sects and history of Christendom,— the first Christian bishop or all the bishops, popes, priests, and the great body of the Christian clergy and people since? The weight of authority numerically is certainly against the first bishop. But, then, it is also a Christian tradition that the opinion of a single original apostle must outweigh any number of later authorities; that the *quality* of a witness is here of more account than numbers. And so there seems to be but one course open to those who hold to the view of the majority of Christendom in this matter; and that is the course taken by Luther,— namely, to discredit the quality of the witness by questioning the apostolic genuineness of his testimony.

But this question is of comparatively little importance to us here, where we are accustomed to consider not so much who made this or that declaration as what was declared. Possibly, the Apostle James did not make this definition of religion;— though, from what we know of him through other channels, there seems to be no reason why he should not have made it. Yet, possibly, he did not. Possibly, Luther and others were right in denying the apostolic origin of the Epistle. Still, the vastly more important question remains, Is this definition of religion true? Is it complete? Is it sufficient? And this is the question to which our attention is specially called.

It must be admitted that the definition is somewhat lax in its terms. To those, especially, who are accustomed to the ordinary forms of church covenants, it must seem very latitudinarian. It does not require any confession of belief whatever, *says* nothing of belief in Christ or even in God: it speaks only of something to be done. It defines what "God, the Father," will accept as religion; but, among the things required, even belief in his existence is not named. If this definition is to be accepted, religious fellowship does not stop at Christian limits, much less at the boundaries that separate one Christian sect from another. The definition includes in its limits the devout, moral, and benevolent non-Christian people of the world no less than the same class of people in Christendom. It includes Epictetus and Socrates and Antonine no less than Paul and Augustine and Bernard, and would entitle the former saints as readily as the latter. It comprehends the true and good in all religions; presents the same test to the disciples of Christ and to the disciples of Buddha, and draws, without reference to any dividing lines of belief or forms of worship, all loving and truth-living souls into one religious fellowship. It says alike to Christians, to Mohammedans, to Jews, to Buddhists, "It is not anything which gives these distinctive names that makes religion." You may be called Christian or Jew or Mohammedan or a disciple of Buddha, and yet not have a particle of religion. There may be a vast deal of difference in the respective merits of the religious systems which these names represent, yet it is not adherence to one name rather than another that gives you a right to be called a religious person. Religion is deeper and older than all these systems, — something below them all and more comprehensive than any of them. Find that, and the particular religious name by which you shall be called is of little importance. Fail to find that, and the religious name by which you are known has no efficacy, though it be in itself the highest and best.

Thus broad and comprehensive is this definition of religion made by the Apostle James: so lax in respect to doctrine that theological belief is not once hinted at ; so loose on the matter of a special revelation and of one chosen people of God that Paul and Socrates may be equally included in its terms, and may stand together as fellow-servants of God and fellow-members of one Church.

But it is said that the definition is also unphilosophical,— that not only is it lax, judged by the common standard of Christendom, but that it is incomplete, insufficient, as a statement of the religious aspects of human nature, aside from any peculiar Christian beliefs or claims. It does not cover, it has been complained, all the spiritual facts, experiences, and relations to which, in the development of the human mind, the name of religion has been given. It says nothing of the religious sentiment *per se*, only of the moral and benevolent sentiment. One might, it is said, do all that this definition requires on the principle of seeking the greatest happiness for one's self, with no purely religious emotion or aspiration, with no prayer or belief in prayer, with no recognition even of God or belief in a God, with no element whatever in his conduct springing distinctively from the religious sentiment; and yet, according to the terms of the definition, he must be called religious. If he be only kind and just and virtuous, no matter from what motive, and even though he deny the very existence of God and declare religion to be nothing but a mass of superstition, this definition would nevertheless call him a religious man. The definition, therefore, it is argued, is insufficient, absurd. It is a definition, not of religion, but of morality.

And, if we were to consider the subject from a purely metaphysical stand-point, which was not the custom of the New Testament writers, it might be admitted that there is some justice in this criticism. As a strict philosophical statement, this definition may be faulty. To give it literal and logical completeness, it should include the expressed recognition of universal or divine law as the source of the conduct it commends. Making a free interpretation, it might be said, perhaps, that this recognition passes over from the first part of the sentence to the definition itself. But for all practical purposes, which were the only purposes had in view by the writer, the definition is complete enough as it stands.

And I am ready even to go farther than this, and to say, so inseparable are true religion and true morality, that whoever lives according to this definition, even though it be strictly speaking only a definition of morality, will yet live, in the best sense, a religious life, and will have a religious nature. The morality, if any will have it so, of the life will disclose the religiousness of the nature. I do not believe it is possible for a person to live consistently and thoroughly by this rule on the selfish principle that from such virtue the greatest happiness will accrue to his own life. No mere externally prescribed code of conduct for producing self-satisfaction, even though that satisfaction were of a moral order, could generate the spirit of the acts which this definition describes ; and it is the spirit which determines the real quality and efficiency of deeds. Two persons may perform what is outwardly the same deed of kindness,— may be equally generous of money, or time, or labor for some object of charity, may do literally what the text speaks of, visit and help the afflicted with equal assiduity ; yet, if one goes and does only from a sense of duty, especially if he undertakes the part of benevolence looking to a reward coming to himself, while the other does the same things, but in the spirit of a heartfelt love and sympathy which cannot help doing them, what a world-wide difference between the quality of their acts ! And how quickly is that difference detected by the persons who are the objects of them ! Who cannot tell, with regard to an act outwardly kind done toward himself, whether real kindness of feeling was at the bottom of it or whether only conscience or custom or still other motive was the producing cause? The very brute knows whether the hand that feeds it has love behind it or not. Much more does man know the spirit of the deed that succors him. And, in considering this definition of religion, it is rightly to be assumed that the conduct described has its origin in the highest possible motive; that it is real, inward benevolence and integrity and purity. And, this being the assumption, I am ready to say that no person can live thoroughly and consistently according to the spirit of this rule, whatever his lips may profess of belief or other lips may assert of his non-belief, without being religious in his heart.

For what are the essential elements in this definition of religion? They are plain and easily stated. First, is good will, benevolence, sympathy, charity, love. The definition says, "To visit the widows and fatherless in their affliction,"—putting, for greater practical effect, an illustration or single specimen of the principle in place of the principle itself. But the principle is plain. It is to have a heart and will ever ready to alleviate, help, comfort, restore, and bless mankind, in any of the manifold forms of misfortune and suffering to which they are subject. In other words, it is the entire spirit of that love which takes us out of self and merely selfish objects and relations, however pleasing and satisfying these may be, and bids us feel, think, and labor for others' welfare and happiness. It is that entire principle and law of our natures which puts us under obligation to serve others' needs; which breaks up our selfish strivings, our merely selfish aims and ambitions; which teaches disinterested devotion to human welfare, self-consecration to home and neighborly duty, self-denial and self-sacrifice; which brings the thousand little daily acts of affectionate remembrance and voluntary, unrequitable service that lift human life up above the plane of a mere traffic and barter, where each is seeking to get the highest price for all he gives, into a real communion and fellowship of heart and spirit; which brings, therefore, to the human race the bond of brotherhood, and makes the rational tie of society possible in place of the gregarious instinct and savage conflicts of animal tribes.

And what is this principle but the very genius of religion,— the important and chief thing which the great teachers of all the principal religions have emphasized, the thing especially which Jesus emphasized? And, as it is one of my aims to-day to show how far historical Christianity has departed from Jesus' teachings, I confine myself to him as an illustration. What is the most prominent feature of religion, according to Jesus' teaching and practice, but this very love and service toward others,— the helping the blind to see, the deaf to hear, the lame to walk, the sick to health, the hungry to food, the imprisoned to liberty, the suffering to comfort, the erring to truth, the ignorant to knowledge, the vicious to virtue, the degraded and miserable to light and usefulness and peace? What but this very kind of work filled his days and made the fruit of his religion? What else did he mean by the coming of the kingdom of God but the advancement of these objects of human love and service on the earth? And, when he told the parable of the Good Samaritan, it is plain that he not only meant to inculcate that benevolence and pity are moral sentiments, but that they are religious also, and produce the very highest fruits of religion, when brought into exercise. The priest and the Levite, representing the formal, punctilious, ceremonial, much-professing religion of the Pharisaic Jews, went by on the other side. They were hastening perhaps to their formal worship, and had no word of cheer nor act of help for a suffering fellow-being. It was the despised, heretical, and, from the Jewish stand-point, *irreligious* Samaritan, that turned aside to proffer the needed sympathy and relief. And so, all through Jesus' life and teaching, it is not the outward deed, whether it be called religious or not, nor the profession of the lips, that he places foremost; but it is this quality of love toward one's neighbor. And who is thy neighbor? The reply comes, Whomsoever thou canst help. "By this shall all men know that ye are my disciples, if ye have love one to another."

The second element of religion, according to the definition of the Apostle James, is signified in the words, "keep one's self unspotted from the world"; that is, integrity, purity, sincerity, incorruptibility, successful resistance to all snares and influences of evil. It is not to keep one's self aloof from the world; for that would be to violate the first principle, just discussed, of sympathy and fraternal help fulness. It is to live in the world to serve and aid it, and yet not to be stained by its vices, not to be swayed from the line of rectitude by its flatteries nor by its frowns. "To keep one's self unspotted from the world!" Call it simple morality, if you will; yet what a breadth and height of virtue, unattainable to how few, do the words include! Though it be simple morality, it is no easy task, no every day phenomenon, thus to keep the native integrity, the mental and moral independence, of one's being,— to be drawn from the true and the right by no promise of favors, by no fear or threat of evil. To keep sincerity amid the hypocrisies of the world; to keep healthful simplicity amid the enervating extravagances and luxuries of the world; to keep purity of thought and chastity of act amid the world's moral uncleanness and licentiousness; to keep honest in the midst of the world's knaveries; to keep truthful in the midst of the world's falsehoods; to keep temperate in the midst of the world's intemperance and debauchery; to keep humility in the midst of empty, worldly ambitions; to keep contentment with slow and honest gains in the midst of feverish haste of worldly men after riches at any cost; to keep self-respect and self-reliance in the midst of cringing conformity to fashion everywhere found in the world; to keep independence of thought and action in the midst of fawning subserviency to popular opinion; to keep one's convictions of truth and justice, if need be, even to the bitter end of dying for them, in the midst of tempting bribes of all kinds offered by the world; to keep one's soul loyal to its divine law and destiny, though the whole world and all the kingdoms thereof be offered in exchange for it,—all this and more is comprehended in that phrase, "to keep one's self unspotted from the world." "Unspotted,"—without speck or stain or fleck of evil to mar the infinite beauty of the soul, as we might conceive it to exist in a condition of perfect purity. "Mere morality!" Yet it holds up before us a standard of perfection which none of us will dare to say he has yet reached, and which, like the horizon, goes before us as we advance; ever before and upward, because it is a standard embodied in the conception of a Being who is infinitely perfect.

And this second element of the apostle's definition of religion is another of the essential elements of religion, according to the original teaching of Jesus. What is the one burden of the Sermon on the Mount but that of sincerity, intellectual and moral integrity, the necessity of inward rectitude and purity, the uselessness of a mere religion of conformity to fashion and tradition, into which the heart does not go? If there is one thing that Jesus teaches more than another, it is this: that men will be judged, not for what they believe, nor for what they say, nor even for what they do, but for what they really are in the dispositions and affections of their hearts. There is a *mere religion*, which, however showy in its forms, however brilliant and costly in its appointments of worship, and however eloquent in its professions of belief, is yet as empty and, for anything it will carry out of this world, as unsubstantial, as the breath after it has pronounced the words. And, on the other hand, there is a *mere morality*, which, though it makes no pious confessions, though it goes to duty oftener than to prayer, and seldom takes the name of God on its lips, and does not dare to call itself religious, yet grows year by year in strength and beauty, ascending from beatitude to beatitude, until it reaches the very holy of holies of the Divine Nature, and lives the eternal life.

We decide, then, for this ancient definition of religion by the first bishop of Jerusalem against all the definitions made by bishops and popes, theologians and church covenants since. It seems to us to cover the whole of human nature; comprehending, on the one hand, the duties each individual soul owes to itself, its obligation to keep its own integrity, purity, and independence, and, on the other, the obligations and duties that connect each individual soul abroad to other souls,— to home and family, to neighborhood, to society, to one's country, to the whole brotherhood of man. On the one hand, we have the virtues of self-reliance, of moral courage, of loyalty to convictions of truth, of obedience to the inspirations of one's own soul; on the other, we have the mutual kindness, good will, and regard for right that hold communities together, the affections of home and friendship, the sweet charities that carry relief to every form of deprivation and suffering, the multiform humanities that seek to establish justice and love between man and man, and to improve and elevate the condition of the human race.

If it be still questioned whether all this is religious work or an evidence of religion, I reply, in conclusion, that I know not what religion is, if it be not the practical allegiance of the human heart and life to the divine law of life; if it be not to keep one's own soul clean and truthful, pure and upright, according to the highest consciousness of duty which is made alive within it, and to help other souls to cleanness and purity, to truth, uprightness, and peace, according to the inspirations of that love which flows through us to bind us in one fraternity with our fellow-men. Say not that the soul thus living, even though it uses few religious forms and utters few religious words, gives no recognition of religion. This very integrity which it has is the energy with which it adheres to the law of eternal rectitude. This very love which inspires its acts, impelling it to constant kindness and beneficence, is an animating impulse from the very heart of Infinite Love. Let me have that integrity and that love, and I live day by day in serene communion with Eternal Being. My desires are prayers; my acts are worship; my kindnesses are sacraments; my natural advance in virtuous effort and achievement is growth in grace; and death, when it comes, is but a step, composedly and fearlessly taken, into the opening secrets of a life hidden with the spirit in God.

January 12, 1868.

X.
CHRISTMAS LEGEND AND FACT.

"Glory to God in the highest, and on earth peace, good will toward men."— LUKE ii., 14.

THE legend and poetry of religion are often as instructive and inspiring as its sober facts and actual history. Some of the most indestructible religious truths owe their preservation and influence upon the popular mind to the imaginative and dramatic form in which they have been clothed. And there is a large share of this poetic element intermingled with the early history of Christianity. It is only when it is claimed to be actual history that it offends our sense of truth. Regarded as poetry, we look for the truth beneath the imaginative dress; and our sense of truth is no more disturbed than when we read Milton's *Paradise Lost* or Goethe's *Faust.* With the eye of historical criticism, I read the Gospels, and see much that, as historical narrative, must be rejected; much that, if claimed for fact, is as puerile and unworthy of belief as many of the mythical stories in the old histories of Greece and Rome. But, when I read the same Gospels with the eye of religious imagination, which looks below form for substance, it reconstructs the dismembered narrative, and brings back, for their inner ethical or spiritual significance, those rejected portions which, when considered as literal facts, only stood in the way of truth. Because I deny, both from the antecedent improbability and from the defective credibility of the testimony, that there was ever a man in Judea who could summon by a word the buried dead alive from their graves, or who, once dead, reappeared in his natural body from his own grave, I do not therefore deny that there was a man in Judea whose life was a wonderful exhibition of the supremacy of all true spiritual life over the powers and terrors of death, and who gave such a mighty impulse to true life in his fellow-men as to confirm them in a desire for and a belief in an immortal existence. And because I reject the account that this man was born and developed in any other than the natural way, or had any other than natural means of communication with God, I do not therefore deny that his character was a most marked and precious illustration of the way in which Divinity may normally become manifest in humanity.

And, in like manner, though in common not merely with purely rationalistic critics, but with liberal critics generally (some of them believing in the miraculous elements in Jesus' career), I deny the historical authenticity of this narrative which purports to state things antecedent to and attending the birth of Jesus, I do not therefore throw the narrative away as worthless legend. Here, I see that the imaginative, poetic faculty of religion has been at work. But that faculty does not work upon *mere nothings*, in Judea more than in Greece or Egypt. It may have some germ of historical fact upon which to work; or, more likely, it has some vision of spiritual truth to express, and will take such shreds of history and tradition as it finds at hand for delineating and embodying the vision. In this legendary narrative of the birth of Jesus, I see the pious imagination of the early Christian Church endeavoring to construct for its already idealized Messiah a fitting dramatic entrance into the world.

In other words, those primitive Christians found the sober garb of prose entirely inadequate to clothe the emotions of the new life, which had been begotten in their own bosoms, and the ordinary methods of nature inadequate to account for that new life. Their very life was poetry, drama,— a sudden transition from the prosaic occupations of tax-gatherers and fishermen into discipleship to a wonderful religious teacher and prophet, whom they follow about, day after day and month after month, in town and country, over lake and hill, to catch his minutest words of instruction and learn of his loving wisdom; whom they accept as the looked-for Messiah, and expect constantly to see elevated with royal pomp and authority to the Messianic throne, and themselves raised to corresponding positions of comfort and dignity; whom, with bitter disappointment, they see, however, after two or three years, executed as a malefactor, and their Messianic expectations apparently brought to a tragic end; but then, in some strange way, they find these expectations revived, triumphant over the grave and the cross, and themselves lifted up by a mighty spirit and sent forth as missionaries, to proclaim the advent of the divine kingdom upon the earth. How is it possible that they should put the beliefs and emotions growing out of such life into logical propositions and historical chronicles? As the life was itself dramatic, so did it naturally take dramatic and poetic literary forms, in which to clothe its experiences; and, just as the childlike, spiritual hope of the age painted a vision of the second coming of the Messiah in the clouds of heaven, attended by the angelic host, to close the old dispensation and usher in the millennial era, so did the religious imagination, combined with that primitive faith, throw itself backward and around the infancy of Jesus, which was mainly free from historical data, picture scenes which were deemed befitting the advent of such a majestic and benignant life.

There were, probably, shepherds on the plains of Bethlehem, tending their flocks, when Jesus was born. That would have been a perfectly natural fact. Very likely, too, these shepherds shared the common belief of their time and race, that the Messiah was soon to come. That, too, would have been natural. But are we to believe that an angel literally articulated to them that the Messiah was that day born in a manger in Bethlehem? and that then the heavens opened, disclosing a multitude of the heavenly host, who literally sang in chorus, audible to the outward ear of the shepherds, "Glory to God in the highest, on earth peace, good will toward men"? Shall we take all the poetry out of this exquisite legend, and lose its fine spiritual truth, by thus translating it into a bald statement of outward facts, against which historical criticism and science will forever protest, and which the common sense of men will suspect and disbelieve? Let me read this as history, and I read it under continual protest from reason and the sense of historical veracity. Let me read it as religious poetry, as drama, and I see how the "opened heavens" were not the literal parting of the skies to the shepherds at Bethlehem, but the lifted and transfigured vision of the early Christian believers, a full generation and more after Jesus' birth. I see that the opened heavens were their own illuminated minds and hearts; that the angelic presence was the courage and faith, the hope, charity, and peace, which had somehow come to them from the life and teachings of Jesus; that the anthem, whose sublime notes still sound through the generations, " Glory to God in the highest, and peace on earth, good will toward men," was the echo from their own bosoms of the Beatitudes and the Parable of the Good Samaritan and the story of the Prodigal Son. This chorus was the song of rejoicing, which sung itself out of the new life and inspiration and power which had come to all their faculties. It was the utterance of the new religious faith, which had been begotten in their own souls, and which thus early stamped itself on the primitive consciousness of the Christian believers. But, since they were not metaphysicians tracing conditions of mind to their natural causes, nor rigid historians narrating events only for the sake of historical truth, but imaginative religious teachers, anxious to impress upon others in the most forcible way their own religious experience, the legendary and poetic faculty of the age readily seized upon this central truth of their experience, carried it back to the birth of Jesus as the most fitting time for its origin, and represented it, with all the dramatic accompaniments of the story now found in the New Testament, as proclaimed by angelic chorus from the skies.

By this poetic mode of interpretation of what in itself is essentially poetic, we may preserve the truth, while we reject the form, of the old legends, myths, and quaint beliefs in Hebrew and Christian as well as in other religions. Poetry and music have an inner significance entirely apart from the form in which they are clothed, and that lasts after the form has become obsolete. It is thus that poems like Homer's, Dante's, and Milton's keep their place in the world. That the form is felt to be false does not affect the truth below the form. The great oratorios, like the "Creation" and the "Messiah," can never lose their impressive sublimity, though we reject the theological doctrines that created them,— that created rather their *dress;* for the soul that is in them is older than they, and used temporary beliefs only to give itself a form. Their substance is something that speaks to the creative and redeeming spirit, everlasting in its nature, which exists in man himself. We may enjoy grand old tunes in familiar words which we no longer believe, because we are not listening for the sentiment of the words so much as for the sentiment of the tunes.

And so, when this Christmas season comes around, though no one now can tell just when Jesus was born (the festival, in the earliest ages of the Church, was a movable one), and though we may not believe with those who instituted the festival that it commemorates the advent of a miraculous personage upon the earth, still less the incarnation of the Supreme God in a single human form, yet the festival appeals to something within us, which never grows obsolete and never loses its power to stir and bless our hearts. And this is because it is not so much an historic as a poetic and dramatic commemoration of Jesus; not an attempt to revive his memory through some fixed ordinances and speeches on a set day so much as a putting, for a single day, of the kindness and good will, which are associated with his name, into the actual conduct and relations of people with each other. That is, the commemoration is through the actual emotions of the heart, and does not exist merely for its literal or historical significance; and the heart puts into it all that itself feels.

There is, certainly, an increasing disposition among all sects and all classes of people, religious or otherwise, to keep Christmas. This cannot be from an increasing sense of its being an actual historical commemoration, for historical investigation and criticism lead the other way; but it is because people of all sects, strict or liberal, and of all classes, religious or irreligious, are beginning to feel the poetic significance of the season, without regard to its literal and historical basis. It is enough that it is a season of mutual good wishes and good deeds, of friendly remembrance, of family enjoyment and the strengthening of family bonds, of the children's glee, of neighborly greeting and fraternity; enough that material and sordid enterprises for a moment remit their pressure, that the wrangling of parties, the strifes of politics, the selfish greed and ambitions of individual careers, are for a brief period laid aside, and that the hearts of people are open to gentle thoughts, tender affections, and gracious charities, while they' take each other more warmly by the hand, and try for a little time each to make every other blest by his presence. And all this is a most living commemoration of a religion whose nativity began with a song of "good will to men." For this is a vital part of that good will, keeping the religion alive because it is itself so fully alive with the essence of unconscious religion. These poetic associations of the Christmas season — its tender memories and joys, its fraternal congratulations and charities, its actual essays at living in the spirit of good will and peace — are to-day a stronger bulwark for Christianity than are all the creeds of the churches. Even the mythical St. Nicholas is, for children, a better introducer to Christianity than the historical and dogmatical St. Paul; and the loaded stocking on Christmas morning, which has been mysteriously filled during the night with the treasures that appeal to a child's heart, is a better teacher of religion than the catechism. As the little hands draw the bounty from those wondrous depths, a lesson is impressed of a religion of good will, of an exhaustless sheltering love and generosity, which not even the teaching of the catechisms and the false creeds and more wretchedly false practices of Christendom can ever quite obliterate. The child is actually living upon this religion of good will, though his consciousness is yet innocent of all theologies, and even of the word "religion"; and the glee that sings in his heart and utters itself all day long in his prattle and laughter is his rendering of that old anthem, "Peace on earth, good will toward men."

This anthem, indeed, which was sung out of the glorified heart of the first Christian century, and is revived by an actual re-creation of its spirit every Christmas morning, expresses the purest key-note of Christianity at its origin, and embodies what has always given that religion its best power; for, so long as we do not say that Christianity is the only religion that has the sentiment of love, which is the essence of this song, we do no injustice to previous religions, but only state a fact of history, when we say that Christianity particularly emphasized and put into specific form this sentiment both of divine and human love.

The Hebrews came to religion chiefly through the moral sense. Hence, their religion, to a great extent, became a mass of ethical laws and ceremonial precepts,— a list of commandments to do and not to do certain things. The Greeks came to religion chiefly through the intellect. Hence, their religion, in the main, among the cultivated was a philosophy, — the result of the rational faculty,— and among the mass of the people a mythology,— the result of the imaginative part of the intellect. Christianity, which mingled the Hebrew and the Greek streams of religious thought in its own, partook of the characteristics of both, but also developed the higher characteristic of love. It took a germ which we find in both of those religions, and cultivated and cherished that as the chief thing. It made the heart the source and centre of religious faith and works, and declared that what neither conscience nor reason had been able to accomplish by its commands through the Jewish law or the Greek philosophy,— *that* the heart, through its own instinctive love and faith, could bring to pass : that duty and inclination, reason and affection, could be atoned.

And it was this doctrine of love as the controlling principle of both divine and human government — this doctrine of love as "the fulfilling of the law" — which, put into the concrete and dramatic form that the Hebrew Messianic conception furnished, gave Christianity in its origin its great power to dissolve both Judaism and heathenism into itself. It was conscience and reason infusing themselves into the affections of the heart, and hence getting all the power of the heart for the accomplishment of their own ends. What a relief it must have been to people burdened with the ceremonials of a written commandment, and anxiously asking whether they had complied with all the perplexing details of a law which followed them into the minutest relations of daily life, or whether they were conforming their conduct to the highest demands of reason and philosophy, to find themselves the subjects of an inward life and inspiration which swept all these anxieties and perplexities into its current, and bore them along toward perfect blessedness by its own spontaneous impulse! What a joy to them to feel — not simply to know through their intellectual perception, but to feel in their inmost hearts — that God was not only the Law-giver, but the giver of every good and perfect gift; and that salvation was not something to be purchased through painstaking ceremonies and works to satisfy the conscience of the law, but the blessed boon of a life born of love and bringing forth the natural fruits of love as its saving works. What wonder if those to whom this inspiring faith had come felt that the millennial era was close at hand, and that the heavenly kingdom of divine peace and brotherhood was soon to be established on the earth! And what wonder if their childlike imaginations pictured the heavens themselves opening and angelic choirs giving voice to this divine sentiment which had been begotten in their hearts!

And, to-day, a new baptism in the spirit of love would atone for much that is irrational in the creeds, and cure much that is wrong in the practice of Christendom. Modern civilization has brought great opportunities both for individual and national aggrandizement. Its material inventions and enterprises, its manifold avenues to wealth, its wonderful development of all the physical arts and sciences, and of the outward resources of human comfort, refinement, and happiness,— all these bring not only great means for usefulness, but great temptations to selfishness. There is a corresponding urgent need, therefore, to arouse a spirit of benevolence, of devotion, of self-sacrifice,— a spirit that shall consecrate all these great opportunities, all this enterprise and comfort, wealth and knowledge, to the welfare of humanity,— to the service of a love that melts away all barriers between classes, nations, races, and religions, and seeks to bring humanity within the veritable bonds of one brotherhood. Most especially does this Christmas season fail to impress upon us its highest lesson, if it does not carry our thoughts and affections beyond the circles where self may still be predominant into those outlying regions of human want and woe, where the warmth, health, and cheer of social love are seldom felt. Not only must it bring refreshment and strength to the ties of family and friendship, but hospitality and impulse to all tender humanities and charities. It was an old belief among the Druids, from whom seems to have come the custom of decking dwellings and temples at this season with evergreens, that the gentle spirits of the groves and forests flocked to these green boughs in the houses, and so were preserved from the killing frosts and storms of winter, to resume with the coming of spring their re-creative offices in restoring life and beauty to the woods. So must we, if we would know the inner significance of this Christmas season, keep all the gentle charities alive in the hospitable warmth of our homes and by the glowing fire of our hearts, in order that we may send them out thence into the cold and desolate places of the world to help on the regeneration of human society, and bring in the era of peace and good will among men.

December 26, 1869.

XI.

THE EDEN OF THE SENSES AND THE EDEN OF THE SOUL.

"Therefore, the Lord God sent him forth from the garden of Eden, to till the ground from whence he was taken."—GEN. iii., 23.

THE religious philosophy of the Jews represented this expulsion from Eden as a curse. But history and reason agree in pronouncing it a blessing. Here was no fall of man, but a rise. The impulse that drove the first human pair out of that dreamy and sensuous Paradise,— admitting for illustration temporarily the truth of the tradition,— to make their way in the world through their own efforts and toil, was the first step in human civilization and progress; the first step in the long series of conquests by which mind has gradually asserted its power over matter, and the forces of nature have yielded themselves as aid and sustenance to man. Indeed, there is some intimation of this in the Hebrew story itself. Though the eating of the fruit of the tree of knowledge is represented as a sin which is punished by expulsion from the garden, yet the direct consequence of the partaking of that fruit is declared to be that the man and the woman have become *like unto the gods*, to know good and evil; that is, the act for which they were expelled from the garden is represented also as their first step *Godward*. And, again, it is said they were driven out, not only for what they had done, but from a fear on the part of Jehovah lest, having already, through eating of the fruit of the tree of knowledge, become as gods knowing good and evil, the next direct step would be to "take of the tree of life, and eat, and live forever," becoming therefore still more like Supreme Being. Now, of course, the motive attributed to Jehovah in this account — that of jealousy of the beings he is said to have created — is utterly unworthy of the infinite Being. According to later views of God, we should conceive it to be one of his supreme purposes and joys to create beings who, like himself, should live forever and grow forever into his likeness. But the Hebrews, at least in the early stage of their history represented by the Book of Genesis, and for some time afterward, had not risen to this conception. Their highest picture of human happiness and destiny was that of the Eden from which they believed the first parents of mankind had been driven. Their highest aim was to recover this primal condition of life. Their prophetic vision was of goodly lands, planted with stately trees, showering their fruits spontaneously for the sustenance of man,— lands filled with gold and precious stones, and all material things that the human heart can desire ; a land flowing with milk and honey, where everything that mankind could need should be given to their hands without labor or effort ; in short, a Paradise regained on earth,— a life of perfect material satisfaction and content.

Yet this Hebrew description of Eden, and of the causes which led to the expulsion of Adam and Eve from the garden, is instructive by reason of the very contradiction which it contains. It shows that, while man's first conception of his destiny is that of innocent and peaceful enjoyment of sensuous nature,— the finding all his wants, appetites, and instincts gratified and put to rest, without any murmuring or unsatiated cry for something more or something different; the living directly upon God's gifts, let down from the heavens or pushed up from the earth, day by day, without any thought or care of his own, and with no anxiety for the morrow; the existing with childlike content and happiness in a perfect material world, without toil, without trial, without pain, without any cloud of evil to interrupt the sunny days or check the warm, blissful flow of this serene atmosphere of material life,— while the traditional story of Eden shows this to have been the predominant primitive conception of human happiness and destiny, it shows, also, that, even in the earliest age, underneath this conception there lay the germ of another,— the dawning, namely, of a spirit that was not and could not be satisfied with these material conditions of life, however perfect and pleasant they might be to the material nature of man. This longing to taste of the fruit of the tree of knowledge, which all the sensuous delights of the garden could not satisfy or lull, though the Hebrew represented it as temptation and its gratification as sin, and which, when gratified, opened the understanding of the first parents to know between good and evil,— and to be, therefore, like the Creator himself,— what was this but the dawn of moral intelligence, the awakening of conscience, the springing to consciousness of a principle in man which was not taken from the dust, whence his body came, and which could not therefore be satisfied with mere material gratifications or find its destiny in the conditions of a material life, however perfect? What was it but just what the writer in primitive simplicity, regardless of the logical confusion and contradiction of thought, intimated,— the awakening of a power within that material framework of bones and flesh, which could discern the eternal difference between good and evil, between right and wrong, between truth and error,— a power which could discern and weigh *ideas*, which was capable not merely of sensation and enjoyment, like the body, but of thought and aspiration and will,— a power which made man like unto God, because it was the stirring of a spirit within him which was akin to Eternal Spirit itself — nay, identical with it — and which made man a living soul? And the author of this primitive description was again right, when he intimated that the eating of the tree of knowledge by man, which was the dawning of the moral intelligence, would lead him to put forth his hand and take of the tree of life, and eat of that, and live forever. For the awakening of the moral intelligence, being the birth in man of eternal spirit, brings longings, aspirations, and capacities, which only spiritual realities can nourish and feed, which only immortality can interpret and satisfy.

And the Hebrew was right, again, when he represented man as driven out of Eden, that paradise of the senses, *because* of this awakening within him of the ambitious desire to eat of the tree of life and be immortal like the gods; right, too, in saying that it was the Divine Spirit that drove him forth; only there was an illogical confusion, incident to the religious thought of the age, in respect to the reason and significance of the act. So far from being driven out of the garden as a punishment and curse upon them, these first ancestors of mankind went forth to be blessed, and to bless their race after them. The God that drove them out was no being in the heavens, ruling them as a retributive judge, but the God that had been awakened to consciousness within themselves. The impulse that led them forth from those scenes of enjoyment and peace into the world of toil and trial and care was the gesture of the Godlike spirit within their own souls; and, when the gate of that earthly paradise opened to send them on their journey into the rough wilderness of the world, and was barred against their return, then began the march of humanity heavenward and Godward.

Not a fall, then, but a rise, was the departure from Eden. It was the necessary result of man's coming to consciousness of his moral resources, of his spiritual relationship and destiny. It was simply impossible that a being created with mental and moral aspirations could remain content with the satisfactions that Eden afforded. Let it be,— though history and analogy will not confirm the proposition, — yet let it be admitted that man was first created in the happy serenity and childlike perfection of innocence which the tradition represents. Let it be that his dwelling-place was as full of beauty and delight as it is possible for a spot of earth to be,— that there, as the story says, grew "every tree that is pleasant to the sight, and good for food"; that "gold and bdellium and the onyx," and every precious stone, were to be found there, without search and without labor; that the garden was plentifully watered with the most beautiful of rivers; that it was stocked with every kind of animal for use or pleasure, all living together in harmony and mutual helpfulness; that it was darkened with no clouds, afflicted with no storms, marred by no noxious weed, absolutely impervious to any physical derangement or evil. What then? Would this be the residence that a soul of immortal aspirations would choose? These are all material delights, and nothing more. Had Adam remained content with these, he never would have been father of the human race, only of another, and perhaps a little higher, race of animals. Had Adam been content with these, his descendants, perhaps, might have remained in Eden and had Eden to this day. They would have had Eden, *but nothing more*. It was just that within him which made him man which made him also dissatisfied with Eden's limitations and with its serene, perfect life of material bliss. To the living soul, akin to infinite Soul, there can be no serenity, no satisfaction, no peace, no perfection, except in ascent toward infinite perfection. Any stationary condition of things, however perfect in itself, can never give peace to a being whose sense of perfection is only to be met by constant endeavor and movement upward. Vain, therefore, the expectation that a being, in whom a vital intellectual and moral nature has been born, can be kept content within any earthly Eden's walls. Put all the treasures of all earth's gardens into one, and still it will not be the garden that can keep a being in whom the power of immortal thought has dawned. It was not Adam's sin, but his and humanity's salvation, when he aspired to taste of the fruit growing on the tree of 'knowledge, whose branches reached over Eden's walls into the great universe outside, and whose top pointed heavenward, into the infinite spaces ; for, thereby, he parted company with the type of animal races that had existed before him, left behind mere material satisfactions as no longer sufficient to nourish his nature, and began the career of a moral being. He left Eden to enter heaven.

Does any one doubt this ? Shrink from accepting the world as it has been, with its roughness and hardness, with its physical and moral evils, with its struggles and failures, with its suffering, and its sorrow, its death and its graves, as better than that serene picture of life in Eden, where toil and struggle, death and suffering, were unknown ? Let him, then, compare the virtues which could flourish in the still atmosphere of that guarded enclosure with the virtues that he most admires in the history of mankind as it has actually been. Let him compare that passiveness with this constant activity; that calm content with what is with this intense joy of anticipating and seeking something better; that undisturbed, listless enjoyment of a good possessed with this heroic endeavor to possess something beyond present reach; that receptiveness of blessing with this effort to bless; that resting in the care of an external will with this wondrous putting forth of native strength and energy; that joy in each day's delight with this courage, faith, and hope that are ready to attempt all things; that serenity with this endurance; that bliss of having with this bliss of doing; that childhood's innocence and grace with this manhood's proved integrity and power; that satisfaction with a world complete with this noble struggle and progress in the endeavor to complete a world; that satisfaction with finite and material ends with these thoughts, aspirations, and purposes that only never rest, because drawn upward by a path that loses itself in the perfection of infinite intelligence. Humanity in Eden would have been scarcely above the "happy family" of animals which the showman has trained to live amicably together in his menagerie. But humanity driven out into the world, to live by the sweat of its brow in rough struggles with nature, has turned the wilderness into a garden, made a highway for its thought over mountain and sea, bended the elements to its service, and shaped the inhospitable earth to its needs; and thereby it has disclosed and developed a power that is verily Godlike in its quality and purpose.

So, too, the persons who have departed farthest from the conditions of life in Eden, who have had least rest and most service, who have even denied themselves all material and temporal satisfactions that they might eat the more freely of the pure knowledge of spiritual things, who have endured perils and tortures, and death even, in their conflict with the world, rather than go back to the Eden from which the divine discontent in their own souls had driven them,— these persons, the Socrates, the Pauls, the Buddhas, the Christs, are the heroes of this human march heavenward that most challenge our admiration and excite our enthusiasm to imitate. Yes: notwithstanding all the hardship, bitterness, and misery that burdened humanity has had to meet in its struggle with the rough conditions of existence, remembering even the fearful errors and sins into which it has fallen in the uncertain chances of the conflict, our secret hearts do yet declare for the heaven which is to be won through labor and sacrifice rather than for that which is given in the involuntary gratification of natural instincts.

And what is thus seen to be true with regard to the race historically is true also in individual experience. Nature's inexorable rule is,— Pay for all you get: take bountifully, unceasingly, of her stores, but give faithfully and unsparingly the labor of muscle or brain or heart for every atom of her wealth. Every human achievement or pleasure has its price. Even virtue is not given, but must be toiled for,— must be earned and purchased by constant resolution and sacrifice. And those possessions will soon slip from us — are hardly, indeed, worth the holding — for which we have not paid the cost. They are not really ours; and hence nature's laws, always honest and sagacious, contrive quickly to strip us of the false ownership. Even on the plane of material possessions, in spite of the apparent glaring exceptions, the law in general holds true. The proverbial saying, that a fortune which quickly comes quickly goes, attests the common belief in the necessity of labor to give a sure title to ownership in material wealth. There is not a father here who does not know, whatever his practice is likely to be, that it is vastly better for his sons to begin active life with only the wealth of strong hands, sound brains, and upright, courageous hearts, than, without an effort of their own, to have a millionnaire's fortune poured into their laps as capital. For strong hands, sound brains, and the pure, brave heart are not only able to buy the best estates of earth, but can purchase virtue, freedom, and heaven. Give your son wealth without the mental and moral qualities that can so use wealth as to pay back every cent of it into the treasury of the world's commonweal, and, though he ride in his carriage and revel in luxury, you curse him with a poverty worse than that which drives the beggar hungry and foot-sore through the streets. And the probability is that nature will soon set about to rectify your mistake, and will vindicate her law,— that there can be no ownership without paying for the title; will set about the task in paternal mercy, too, divesting the poor millionnaire of his unpaid goods, scattering his wealth, removing one by one his luxuries, and by and by driving him out of his Eden of rest and pleasure, to begin life empty-handed and to earn its blessings as he goes,— but thereby to save his soul.

And, if this is so in material things, much more is it true in respect to moral and spiritual possessions; for moral and spiritual possessions are not so much gifts or external acquirements as fruits,— fruits of steady endeavor and slowly accumulating experience. No knowledge, no achievement, no enjoyment, that can be given to any soul to-day, can be compared to the mental and moral power that grows, with the putting forth of effort, in the soul itself, and in which lie the germs of all future achievements and joys. And this power, which is the foundation of all human virtue and progress, can only be had at the price of toil and conflict with the world. It must be wrung out of the rough and stony conditions of this earthly existence,— out of its duties and obligations, its hardships and trials, its temptations and griefs. It is found in no Eden of dreamy rest: it must be paid for by resolute purpose and effort, just as fabled Hercules won Olympus and the company of the gods through toil and sacrifice and gigantic labors.

And the higher the virtue, the greater the price that it costs. Jesus paid his very life-blood for the virtue that is remembered to-day in hymn, discourse, and prayer all round the globe, and which is still a delicious spiritual fragrance in the worship of Christendom. The Grecian sage and moralist, after a life journey of brave toil and sacrifice, laid down his body, too, as the price of an integrity which the world delights still to honor. Read Plutarch's heroes; read the lives of saints and martyrs,— many a one, too, not canonized in any calendar of the Church; ay, read the deeds of America's latest martyrs and heroes, with whose glorious names the air has not yet ceased to vibrate, and whose lives shall yet immortalize some American Plutarch,— and what is it in these heroic careers that commands our admiration but just that which they paid for the achievements which have won their immortal fame, — the endurance, the toil, the courage, the patient effort and suffering, the precious blood, the talents, affection, and promise laid bravely on the altar of sacrifice to truth and duty? Such rare and enduring virtue can only be purchased at the costliest price.

But even joys, to be truly enjoyed, must be won by just desert. They must be wages for service rendered,— the wages of love, of sympathy, of healthy and helpful cheer. If there be any possession that would seem to be exempt from this law of payment, it is a gift from a friend. Yet have you not paid for that by your affection? It is your love, and only that, which gives the gift all its value to your eyes. Our commonest household joys, the children's love and presence, the daily domestic warmth and growing bond of intimacy and fellowship, and all the love, peace, mutual helpfulness, happiness, and sanctity we include under that word, *home*,— is there nothing to be paid for these? Shall we expect such possessions and joys without labor, without cost? Ah, friends, if so, they will not come. Generosity, kindness, helpfulness, disinterested love, self-forgetfulness, self-sacrifice,—only these, liberally and cheerfully paid, and with renewed payment every day, can buy the home. Only the recognition of constant obligations and the faithful performance of daily services can win so pure and holy a blessing. And so long as there is one atom of selfishness in our characters, kept back as a reserved fund for our own special enjoyment, there is to that extent a mortgage on our homes, which every day subtracts something from the income of our domestic wealth. Ay, the figure may be extended, to cover the whole breadth of the theme. As long as there is any *capacity* for a purely selfish enjoyment in our natures, which has not yielded to the solvent of the higher joy that comes from helpful service to others or for serving truth and right, so long there is a mortgage on our earthly estate, which must be paid to the last farthing before we are able to secure the full happiness of heaven.

But the divine law, though thus stern in its demands, is wise and merciful in its intent and benignant in its operation; and, if it exact strict payment for all the solid achievements and blessings of life, it does not do it without offering amply to our hands the means for meeting all its obligations. If it send us out into the world to purchase for ourselves the world's wealth of virtue and joy, it places at our feet, at every step of the way, the precious metal of opportunity, from which the coin is to come that will make the payment. We have but to stoop, and, by invention of brain, work of hands, and steady purpose of heart, take the rough ore from its bed and mould it into shapes for the commerce of truth, affection, and philanthropy, and we have the currency that will buy eternal possessions. Out of the very roughness and hardness of our earthly lot, out of the very difficulties and obstacles that perplex and sometimes close up our path, from the very tears of trial and sweat of toil that are wrung from us as we journey on over the dusty, burdensome way, do we coin the virtue which is to open the doors for us of a fairer garden than was ever closed behind Eden's gates. Let none therefore despair, none drop weary by the way. Let us take up the duties and burdens of life with fresh purpose, sure that thus we shall find its solid realities and everlasting delights. Its bitterest trials, its roughest and loneliest experiences, can be converted into the purest valor and fortitude and saintliness of character. Its temptations, successfully met and overcome, transfer their strength to the soul that has conquered them. Even its direst evil, sin, destroyed and with its corruption and rottenness ploughed into the soil of character, shall make it productive of a fairer virtue; and its direst sorrow, premature death, by removing the material and temporal veil from life, may teach the lessons and disclose the realities of life's eternal nature, so that the thickening graves may become mounts of vision from which our opened eyes see farther into heaven. Thus, everywhere, we win our heavenly paradise, not by evading this world's obligations, but by conquest of the difficulties, trials, and hardness of earth. Turning our backs upon the childish delights of sensuous Eden, we journey on to find the larger satisfactions of manhood and womanhood,— the Eden of the soul,— fed day by day with the fruit of that growing knowledge of mental and moral laws which is the sustenance of celestial beings; and thereby, in very truth, we become strong to "put forth our hands and take of the tree of life, and eat and live forever."

November 20, 1870.

XII.

THOUGHTS AND CONDUCT.

"All that we are is the result of what we have thought. it is founded on our thoughts, it is made up of our thoughts."— SAKYA MUNI.

THE Roman emperor, Marcus Aurelius, said, "Such as are thy habitual thoughts, such also will be the character of thy mind; for the soul is dyed by the thoughts." The more familiar Hebrew proverb, not far from the same purport, runs, "Keep thy heart with all diligence; for out of it are the issues of life." And Jesus, according to Luke, said substantially the same thing in the utterance: "A good man out of the good treasure of his heart bringeth forth that which is good; and an evil man out of the evil treasure of his heart bringeth forth that which is evil: for of the abundance of the heart his mouth speaketh."

These different utterances, including that from the founder of Buddhism, indicate my subject. They point to one of the universal and fundamental principles of practical ethics and religion,— the principle, namely, that the springs of character and life are in the inward affections and dispositions; that actions depend on motives, and motives have their origin in the feelings and thoughts of the mind; that the moral quality of a man's outward life will be determined therefore by the moral quality of his prevailing thoughts and sentiments.

But, as soon as it is said that the moral quality of conduct depends upon the thoughts and dispositions of the mind, a question of responsibility arises. How, it is asked, can one be held responsible for the thoughts that come into his mind or the affections that spring up in his heart? Are not the roots of them there by nature, and do they not originate spontaneously? Do they not come and go independent of any control by the human will? Since, indeed, the human will itself must be determined to action by motives, and these motives must have their origin in the sentiments and thoughts of the mind, would it not be a very patent instance of reasoning in a circle to say that the will may control these sentiments and thoughts? Is it not plain that the will is controlled by them, since it cannot act without their impulse, rather than that it has any control over them? The difficulty that suggests these questions has led to those philosophical theories which deny man's free agency, and declare him to be the creature of circumstances; and to those theological theories which also deny his freedom, and assert that he is absolutely dependent on a supernatural influence from Almighty Being to change his heart and make him capable of goodness and salvation. Now, I wish to show, if I may, that there is no necessity of resorting to these theories,— that we may hold to man's freedom and to the strictest sense of his moral responsibility, and yet maintain that the springs of character are in the inward thoughts and affections. I wish to show that these thoughts and affections are not beyond the range of human control, but rather that it is over these inner springs of conduct that the very centre of moral responsibility rests.

But, first, very much has to be conceded to the claim that, when we speak of the thoughts and dispositions of men's hearts, we must take into account those *predispositions* and those primal elements or germs of thought which are inherited, and over which, as a moral outfit, to begin with, the individual possessor, of course, has no control; and that we must also take into account the conditions and circumstances under which the first years, the educating years, of life are spent, since these, undoubtedly, though not determined by individual choice, are an important agency in moulding the mind and heart. I think no metaphysician or theologian will venture to maintain to-day that all human souls at birth are precisely alike in respect to moral quality, so that, if by any possibility all could be subjected alike to the same educational discipline and experiences, they would develop precisely the same type of moral character. They are all, of course, equally sinless,— equally innocent, so far as any moral responsibility of their own is concerned; but they are not all alike equally free from the inherited taint of moral evil, and do not start in the race of life all alike equipped with the same moral tendencies. While all are alike guiltless and cannot be held responsible for anything they inherit, it is yet true that some are born heavily laden with the woful burden of ancestral vices, which will surely incline them to positive moral transgression; while others may be predisposed, by a more fortunate moral inheritance, to paths of virtue; and others, still, may begin their career with more neutral characteristics. The idea that all human minds at birth are like a sheet of white paper, equally ready to receive any impression that may be made upon them, equally pure in color and fine in texture, may be said to be exploded. Physiology and psychology both deny it. Mental and moral features are doubtless inherited, as well as physical. The truth is, and the better it will be for mankind the sooner this truth is known and acted upon, the elements of character begin before birth. It is not to be claimed that *ideas* are innate, nor that any moral impulses and affections are at birth in a developed condition. But every infantile mind is full of the germs of ideas, dispositions, impulses; and these have all inherited some moral bias. Physiological science teaches that the very texture of the mind at birth, its quality of fineness or coarseness, its measure of strength, edge, power, its innermost substance and fibre, its capacity for one kind of accomplishment rather than another, are largely determined by ancestral antecedents. And, since the antecedents are very different, the stuff and texture of different minds at the outset are very different. Instead of all being like a sheet of white paper, they differ just as paper differs according to the material of which it is made. Some are pure white and of delicate fibre, others are coarse and dingy;

some are flexile, others fragile; some tractable, others obstinate. We shall concede then, I think, that characters do not all start alike; that there are innate differences of mental and moral tendency which must have much to do with determining the after thoughts and dispositions which are to furnish the motives of conduct.

So, too, it must be admitted that the surroundings after birth, during the early years of education especially,—surroundings for which the individual cannot be held responsible,—will necessarily have great influence in shaping the thoughts and dispositions which are to appear in the subsequent course of life. It is to speak in the face of the most open facts of society to say that circumstances have nothing to do with the creation of character, that all comes from within. The evident fact is that, for a certain period of human life, that which is within depends very much upon the character of that which is without. There are certain degraded classes of society, especially in large cities, where poverty, misery, filth, disease, vice, and crime prevail to such a degree that you know it would be next to impossible for a child who should be born and should grow up there, without knowing any other influences, to come to useful and virtuous manhood; or for one well-born, if taken into such scenes of life in infancy and kept there, to escape the contamination. The child of civilized parents, brought up from early life by savages, becomes degraded toward their condition. Yet the same child, if restored in youthful manhood to civilization again, would doubtless incline more readily to the habits of civilized society than would the child of a savage. The original inherited blood would assert itself, proving that it cannot be wholly neutralized by the power of circumstances. On the other hand, a child born in the midst of those dregs of misery, vice, and crime which ought to put our civilization to shame, if rescued in early life from the degradation and placed in a refined and virtuous home, will most likely grow up to lead a moral life; though it may be that the original bad blood, the inherited predispositions, will sometimes appear, and that, under a change of surroundings, they might reassert themselves with tremendous power. It does seem, however, that virtuous surroundings, *if persistently continued*, generally get the better of bad descent and birth,— as witness the successful results of Children's Aid societies. Contact with living virtuous character proves a stronger power than the evil which lurks in the blood from dead ancestors. But let us not think that hereby we have a right to boast much over our ancestors. For, probably, the converse of this proposition is also true,— that the immediate influence of vicious character, living, is a stronger power during the susceptible years of youth than the inherited virtue of ancestors who are dead. The rule works, unfortunately, both ways.

It will have to be conceded, then, that to birth and education, to inherited mental and moral tendencies, and to the outward conditions amid which the growing years of life are spent, the mind owes in a great degree the quality of its thoughts and dispositions. And hence, since the predominating thoughts and dispositions of the mind determine character, it must be allowed that character is largely dependent on birth and on circumstances.

But, because of this admission, is there no room left for individual responsibility and for individual effort? Because we do not create all the materials out of which our characters are formed, but have to take such as are provided by nature's laws or are given in a condition of things not of our appointing, does that destroy all our free agency in the matter? Because we do not originate outright within ourselves all the dispositions and thoughts whence spring the motives that determine conduct, have we, therefore, no accountability for our conduct? By no means does it follow from these facts that freedom and accountability are destroyed, and that there is no room for individual volition and culture in the development of character. On the contrary, from what has just been said of the power of circumstances and of the more direct appliances of education over the quality of the inner thoughts and impulses, we may see just where the responsibility lies, and to what point the aid of moral volition may be directed most successfully. We see that it is a fact that, to change the surroundings, to put virtuous influences in the place of vicious and careful culture in the place of neglect, is to change the current of the mind's thoughts, to transform the heart's impulses, and hence to develop good character where most inevitably bad character would have appeared, if things had been left to their own course. Whether, then, every individual is responsible or not for the thoughts and impulses that are most active within him, it may be rightly said that every generation of mature men and women in civilized society is responsible in no small degree for the thoughts and impulses that shall animate the rising generation and help to shape its character and conduct. Nay, we may go farther than this. Remembering how potent are inherited tendencies, we may say that every generation of mature men and women is to a large extent responsible for the moral quality of the generation that is yet unborn. There would be little need of what theologians have called "regeneration," or "being born again," if human beings only came into existence at first through right conditions of generation and natural birth.

Even then, if we were to assume that all the elements of character are included under the two terms, inheritance and education, we should not get rid of the doctrine of moral accountability. The seat of accountability might be shifted somewhat, but the pressure of moral obligation which the word covers would be none the less strong. Men might be inclined to blame themselves less for what they are, but they would feel more accountable than they now do for the condition of society in general and for the generation coming after them. Why, the very foundation of all theories of education is that the natural dispositions and thoughts of the mind may be changed and improved by culture; that they may be diverted from one channel into another; that they may be transferred from one object to another; that they may be elevated from low purposes to high; that minds may be trained to act from good motives rather than bad, and to spend their energies in noble pursuits rather than ignoble. And people of all classes, good and bad, are continually acting upon this theory in society. Though it be claimed that individuals have no free control over, and no responsibility for, their own thoughts and impulses, no fact is more patent than that society is constantly acknowledging its accountability for the thoughts, dispositions, and character of its coming members. Parents feel it toward their children, teachers toward their pupils, public speakers and writers toward their hearers and readers. Nay, the very individuals who may deny that they have any freedom in respect to their own dispositions and sentiments, or that they have any moral accountability for the character of those dispositions and sentiments, are continually trying to persuade other people into a change of sentiments and dispositions. Though professing that they are not free to control their own minds, they evidently believe in their power to mould the minds of others. How is this, then? Can it be that we have power over the thoughts and dispositions of our neighbors, and none over our own?

The answer to this question must certainly be in the negative; and it brings me to another point, and the culminating one, in our theme. That same kind of power which lies in education, in culture, in improved circumstances, in the presentment of higher ideals of action to change the dispositions and tendencies out of which character springs, we may exercise over ourselves. Character depends upon our habitual thoughts. The quality of the conduct and life will follow the quality of the prevailing dispositions of the heart, but our habitual thoughts and the prevailing dispositions of the heart are very much what we choose to make them. They are not forces rushing in upon us, and bearing us hither and thither, without any consent or action of our own. Man cannot, it is true, act without a motive. But he has power to choose between different motives or classes of motives. He can put himself under the sway of one set of motives rather than another. He can select the influences that mould his actions. He can change, to some extent, his circumstances, if he finds them unfavorable to the right development of his character. He can do with himself, in this respect, precisely what a wise educator would do with a pupil; that is, he can remove the conditions which excite the impulses and thoughts he would repress, and put in their place conditions that will stimulate the thoughts and impulses that need to be cultivated.

For instance, a man finds himself growing more and more engrossed in business. That which was originally taken up simply as a means of gaining a livelihood has come to occupy all his thoughts and energies. It absorbs him wholly. He lives in it all the hours of the day, and dreams it over at night. His affections are in danger of being dwarfed, his sympathies dried up, his interest in the great questions that concern human welfare destroyed. He has grown to love wealth, and to acquire it for its own sake, without thinking of its noble uses. Now, when a man finds himself coming to this stage in his business life, what can he do? He can resolutely stop and take new bearings. He can say: "I will take some hours every day out of my business for the culture of my mind and heart. I will devote more time to home intercourse. Here are books I will read. Here are art galleries I will visit. Here are charities and philanthropies, public and private, that need my interest and aid." Such a resolution resolutely made and pursued will work the change he desires. He is now a proof of the maxim of Aurelius that the mind will take color and character according to the habitual thoughts. His thoughts have been given habitually to business, until his whole mind, heart, and soul are there; and he is in danger of becoming a mere business machine. But he may give a different kind of proof of the same maxim, by habituating his thoughts to other interests and pursuits. His character will follow his new habits of thought.

Or suppose that one is addicted to sensual indulgence. He, too, is an illustration of the maxim. His character follows the thoughts which he indulges. Let him, then, enter the conflict there, *with his thoughts*. Let him put himself under influences that will lead his thoughts away from the intemperate demands of appetite. Let him avoid the places, scenes, companions, associations that excite these appetites, if he cannot otherwise keep his virtue. Let him hasten to strengthen the better desires and aspirations of his nature by re-enforcing them with the power that comes from virtuous companionship and from pure and cultivated circles of society. Let him put himself under the magic spell of a good book, which shall exorcise the demon of passion. Let him flee to the purifying influences of nature, which is often potent to cool the hot blood of animal desire. In some way, let him break up the train of his thoughts, and turn them in a pure direction. There is where the battle must be fought and won.

Or suppose that one is given to any form of self-indulgence,— to luxurious ease, or indolence, or undue love of pleasure, or excessive delight in social display and in the excitements of fashionable life. Here, again, it is a question of bringing the mind under a new set of influences, so that those impulses that lead to a merely frivolous and selfish life may be checked, and nobler desires may be aroused to activity in their place ; that is, it is a question of governing one's thoughts, of turning them from one object to another. Let such a person seek the society of the benevolent, read the biographies of self-sacrificing and philanthropic men and women,— good biographies are among the best inspirers,— actively participate in some good work of charity, and the better current of thought will surely begin ; and, by persistent and patient effort to keep in this current, nobler motives of conduct will in time become habitual. As the thoughts, so will the life become.

And, even without this aid from external influences, man has the power to break and turn the train of his thoughts, and so to call into exercise one

set of motives rather than another. With most of
us, perhaps, the easier and surer way to turn the current
of thought is to re-enforce the will with some
change of outer influence; yet it is man's prerogative
to be able by internal power to control the current
of his thought,— to set it by sheer will or by
voluntary mental effort in this direction rather than
that. And he has the healthiest and the sanest mind
who can do this best, or who keeps the mastery over
his own mental household. We all know in our own
experience, I think, something of this power, though
rare may be the instances of its complete possession.
Yet there are persons who, in a day, at the mere
bidding of reason and right, have broken up the
habits of years, and changed their whole after conduct;
and they are the manly and mighty persons who
have most of this power,— who are able to say, standing
up in the majesty of their moral nature, " Let
come what may of evil enticement from the influences
that surround me or from the appetites that
lurk in my brain, my will shall be swayed only by
the inner forces of reason and conscience, and that
love which seeks not its own." Such a one is not
so much the creature of circumstances as their creator.
And to this type of character we all aspire,— a
type of character wherein, though the texture of the
outward life will necessarily conform to the quality
of the inner thoughts, yet the thoughts will be servants
of the power of moral choice, which stands
supreme over all.

April 23, 1871.

XIII.

EASTER TRUTHS AND TRADITIONS.

"Through the tender mercy of our God, whereby the dayspring from on high hath visited us, to give light to them that sit in darkness and in the shadow of death, to guide our feet into the way of peace."
— LUKE i., 78, 79.

IN this affectionate and poetic phrase does some early Christian believer record his impressions of the mission of Jesus. It seemed to him like the dawn of a new day, like the glory of a sunrise, like the shining of a light in the midst of darkness, like the springing of life out of the shadow of death and the mould of the grave. We may appreciate the tender gratitude of his words, the fine ideality of his thought, though not interpreting him literally. We must allow to the element of imagination large room and influence in the shaping of religious beliefs and movements. And this sentence, as a prophetic description of the mission of Jesus,— represented as prophetic, though written after the event,— seems especially consonant with the sentiment of Easter Day, which has always been one of the poetic and dramatic days in the history of the Christian Church. To trace, indeed, the beliefs and practices that pertain to this day through the eighteen centuries of Christian history would almost give us the history of Christianity itself. I propose, in this discourse, to note some of the points in the historical associations of the day, which may serve to bring into clearer light the truths and traditions, the reality and the poetry, that have woven themselves into this Christian festival, known as Easter Sunday. We shall see, perhaps, that not in the literal, prosaic interpretation of the day are its finest meanings to be found, but that behind its alleged outward facts are ideal sources of belief and sentiment that are luminous with satisfying evidences of truth.

In the first place, let us look at the primary belief in which the celebration of the day began. Of course, to the large majority of the Christian Church Easter commemorates one event, and only one,— the resurrection of Jesus from the tomb. It was, we may say with truth, from the apostles' belief in the resurrection of Jesus that Christianity started as an organized specific religion. That was the one doctrine, more than any other, that was the burden of apostolic preaching. It is extremely doubtful, indeed, whether the disciples would have rallied from the bitter disappointment and grief into which they had been plunged by the crucifixion of Jesus,— whether they would have found any standing-ground for the proclaiming of the new faith,— had not this belief in the resurrection of their master somehow come to them. But, however this may be, it is certain — the New Testament and tradition both put the fact beyond question — that it was their belief in his resurrection that bridged the gulf between the actual life of Jesus and historical Christianity.

Yet, if we were asked to analyze that belief and state its cause, a rational, historical criticism would have to take issue, I think, with the popularly accepted answer of Christendom. A thorough examination of the evidence, noting its discrepancies, noting, too, the way in which the New Testament records were formed,— their undoubtedly late origin and gradual growth after the events to which they refer took place,— such an examination, I believe, will most certainly fail to establish the fact of a physical resurrection of Jesus, or even that the first apostles uniformly and definitely believed in the resurrection of his natural body. Paul's testimony, certainly the oldest and the most undisputed that we have to the fact that some kind of resurrection was believed in, favors the idea of a spiritual resurrection rather than that of the rising of the physical body. For he argues from the resurrection of Jesus to the resurrection of all mankind, and yet distinctly disclaims believing, with reference to mankind in general, that the same body is raised that is buried. "Thou sowest not," he says, "that body which shall be; ... but God giveth it a body"—that is, giveth to the soul a new body—"as it hath pleased him." The probability is that the more practical and matter-of-fact of the primitive Christians believed in the material resurrection of Jesus, for they could not otherwise grasp the fact of his resurrection at all, or of his continued existence; but that the more speculative and mystical among them, or the more intelligent we may say, those like Paul and Apollos (if he be the author of the Epistle to the Hebrews), believed simply in his spiritual resurrection, which had become manifest, as to Paul, in some vision. The testimony itself that is presented in the Gospels shows that those who gave it had no clear comprehension of the phenomena. The testimony is conclusive as to the existence of a belief in the resurrection of Jesus; but, considering the circumstances of the case and of the age in general, such a belief may easily have arisen without the fact of an actual bodily resurrection. To my mind, looking at the problem from every point of view, it seems infinitely easier to account for the belief in the resurrection from natural causes than to suppose such a stupendous miracle as would be the reappearing of a man who had been actually dead from the tomb. And since the positive evidence is not sufficient to establish so momentous an event, a rational judgment will withhold assent to it, even if all the natural causes of the belief in it cannot now be satisfactorily traced. In short, the New Testament story of Jesus' resurrection must be remanded to the realm of Christian mythology.

But because we may not believe in the physical resurrection of Jesus, because we read as uncertain tradition and poetical legend the accounts of the rolling away of the stone from the door of the sepulchre and of the coming forth of Jesus therefrom, and of the appearance of the angels and of the resurrection interviews with the devoted women and the disciples, do we for this reason say that there is nothing to commemorate, that nothing happened? By no means. Such a movement as historical Christianity did not begin in a mistake, in a delusion, in a fancy of two or three women who may have been beside themselves with disappointment and grief. Much less did it begin with a deliberate imposture. It began in a great fact, but the fact was mental rather than material; and the material form which it assumed in the legend of the physical resurrection was only the dress in which the fact clothed itself according to the fashion of the times, — the medium by which it became current with the common understanding of the age. And this fact was the mental and spiritual transformation, by which the disciples of Jesus passed from the crushing sorrow and despair into which his crucifixion had suddenly thrown them, to the faith, hope, and courage which enabled them to take up the cause which at first seemed to have been buried irrecoverably in his grave, and to carry it forward to triumph. They had fled from his cross; but, somehow, they had become strong now to face their own unflinchingly. They had slept when he met his agony in Gethsemane, apparently not believing it possible that he, their Messiah, could come to the ignominy of the crucifixion. Now, they were fully awake; and no burden was too heavy for them to take up. The cross itself, that had been their shame, had become their glory. So long as Jesus was with them, they had been dull of understanding and had misconceived continually what he had taught them of that heavenly kingdom which he had hoped to inaugurate. Now, in the sharpness of their pain at his departure, their vision seems to have been opened, so that they discerned more truly the nature of the work to which he had called them. So long as he was with them, they were children, looking to him for every slightest expression of command or wish to determine their conduct. Now, they were of age, strong men and brave women, with opinions and faith of their own, confident in their own powers, and prepared to act for themselves. Before, they were the flock, humbly following, but shrinking and timid. Now, they were the shepherds to collect larger flocks, and bold to lead. Here, in this mental transformation, was the great fact, the real resurrection. It would have been of little practical moment if Jesus had actually reappeared from the grave as recorded, coming so charily and vanishing again so soon. But it was of the utmost moment that the disciples should rise out of their despondency and grief to the faith and courage that comprehended and mastered the crisis.

But some one will argue that the physical resurrection of Jesus was needed to produce this transformation and was really the cause of it. But have you not witnessed similar experience in the common history of human careers? Why resort to an outward miracle, to an abnormal phenomenon of flesh and blood, to explain a spiritual process the elements of which are the common property of humanity? What a disappointment and dismay fell upon these Northern States after the first inglorious defeat at Bull Run! Yet in that defeat was the nation's ultimate victory. Out of it came the first substantial realization of the work to be done, as well as the heroic determination to do it. Had our army there triumphed and advanced to Richmond, and there, as was then hoped, put a quick end to the rebellion, slaves would have been still working under the lash in the South. Those first defeats of the war, bitter as they were to bear, were the cross by which the nation rose to the glory of the proclamation of freedom and of equal rights. You may see the same fact all through history. "The blood of the martyrs is the seed of the Church." You may see it also in private and personal experience. Who has not observed character developing unexpected strength and solidity, when outward props have been taken away, and it has been thrown back upon its own centre? Women, who have seemed weak, clinging, invalid, seldom thinking or doing for themselves, becoming clear-minded, self-reliant, and roused to heroic action, when some great exigency of bereavement has come upon them? Young men and young women, who have only been wont to lean on others, suddenly springing to maturity, and developing a power they were never suspected to possess, under the pressure of some severe external condition that has forced responsibility upon them? Soldiers in the crisis of battle, nerved up to almost more than mortal strength, as the contest goes hard against them and they feel the cause slipping from their grasp, which one more mighty effort may redeem? In all these and similar cases, the emergency seems naturally to develop the power that is required to meet it. The very need touches the springs of supply. And in harmony with this general law came the transformation of mental condition by which the disciples of Jesus passed out of the stage of helpless sorrow and despondency to the attitude of resolution and faith.

Moreover, to suppose that the miracle of an outward resurrection was necessary to effect in them this change is to disparage the influence of Jesus' life and teachings upon them. Can we suppose that the greatness of his character, the heroism of his career, had had so little power upon those with whom he had daily lived, that, as soon as he was gone, they would have forgotten and forsaken the cause to which he had called them, unless he appeared to them from the tomb? Is it not a more natural thought that the memory of what he had been to them, the recollection of his words, and the subtle influence of character that had passed from him to them, would be a strong incentive after he had left them not to let his cause fail in their hands? To suppose an apparition of his body after death to be necessary to convince them of his Messianic mission is to suppose that a physical wonder was of more moment than the truths he had uttered and the life he had lived; that a bodily manifestation was a fact of more weight than spiritual inspiration and moral fidelity.

Nor, again, was such an apparition required to enable them to believe in a future life. They believed that already; and they believed in the general resurrection of the dead, though whether material or spiritual may be a question. The Jews generally, before the time of Jesus, as the New

Testament itself bears witness, believed in these two doctrines. They had been familiar with these doctrines since the captivity in Babylon. Only the Sadducees, a cultivated but comparatively small sect, denied them. If we do not find them in the canon of the Old Testament, we find them explicitly stated in the Apocrypha. The resurrection of Jesus, therefore, was not needed to convince the disciples of his own or their continued existence after death. Yet the inestimable value of his life, the greatness of his virtue, the prophetic character that he possessed, the Messianic character that was attributed to him,— all this intensified and vitalized with new power the old belief in a life beyond the present. Such a man as this, they felt, could not die. Had it not been written, " Righteousness is immortal"; "The souls of the righteous are in the hand of God, and there shall no torment touch them; and, though they be punished in the sight of men, yet is their hope full of immortality"? How, then, should not such a righteous person as this survive, even though the cross had done its cruel work of destruction upon his body and the grave had claimed it for corruption? Thus must their grief have found refuge from its own despair. And since, because of his prophetic wisdom and nobility of character, they had accepted Jesus as Messiah, and since the Messiah they still believed him to be, this was an additional reason why they could not believe him to have utterly vanished with his body. His promises — so their bereaved but still hoping hearts assured them — must yet be fulfilled, his work must go on, his kingdom must be established; and he himself, not far away, would doubtless, in due time, reappear to claim the sceptre. It was natural that they should have thus reasoned. And out of such thoughts, beliefs, memories, and hopes, mingled very likely with some subjective vision on the part of some one or more of the primitive disciples, similar to that afterwards experienced by Paul, came, as it seems to me, the belief in the material resurrection and the various legends concerning it, that gradually took shape and were finally embodied in the New Testament record.

What, then, is it that Easter really celebrates? Not the rising of the crucified body of Jesus, but the rising of his crucified truth; not his physical resurrection, but his spiritual resurrection; not the superiority of his flesh to the laws of death, but the superiority of a noble soul to all torments of persecution, to all bonds of the grave. It commemorates the triumph of truth over error, of goodness over wrong, of light over darkness, of life springing up out of the corruption of death, and converting death itself into elements of sustenance and beauty.

That the early Christians themselves had no very definite data as to the phenomena of an outward resurrection is manifest from the fact that the churches very early fell apart concerning the time when they would celebrate it. The Eastern churches, following, as they claimed, a tradition from John, the disciple, adopted the fourteenth of the month called *Nisan* as the day of the crucifixion, and the third day after that as resurrection day, on whatever day of the week it might come. But the churches in Europe, following, as they claimed, a tradition from Paul, adopted for the celebration the Sunday nearest to the full moon of that month, without regard to the day of the crucifixion or the alleged day of resurrection. This dispute lasted for two centuries, at times becoming very serious and bitter; and it was not terminated until the time of Constantine and the Council of Nice, in the year 325, when the principle of the rule of the Western churches rather than the Eastern prevailed, and Easter was made a movable festival. It seems likely that the simultaneous occurrence of some pagan festival in Southern Europe, which could be transformed into the Christian, helped to determine the day, as well as to impart some marked features to the celebration after this time. Popular sports and curious superstitions of various sorts came to be mingled with the religious solemnities of the day. And these, probably of pagan ancestry, are still extant in countries where Catholicism has had most power. There arose very early, too, a difference of opinion on the very question we have been considering,— whether Jesus rose or not in the same physical body that had been buried. Some of the most learned of the Christian Fathers contended that he rose only in a spiritual body. Origen, Chrysostom, and Clement held this opinion. And this question never was settled by any decree of a council, so that it is maintained by some scholars that the orthodox theory in the Roman Catholic Church to-day is that the resurrection of Jesus was in his spiritual body, and not in the material.

If we trace the history of Easter celebration through the later centuries of Christianity, we shall find it taking shape according to sectarian views and characteristics. Among the Roman Catholics, and especially in Rome, it is still a great festival, celebrated with vast pomp and ceremony; the Pope, as Christ's vicegerent on the earth, receiving the homage considered to be due to the risen Lord. Where Puritanism and Quakerism have prevailed, the commemoration has been reduced to the very minimum of recognition or has been entirely abolished, because to these severe sects the hilarity and ceremonial display which had become connected with the festival in England seemed a scandal to the name of religion, that could only be removed by abolishing the festival itself. In recent years, this extreme Protestant condemnation of the observance of the day has been nearly obliterated; and Protestant churches now vie with the Catholic and Episcopalian in Easter celebrations.

But one of the most noteworthy events connected with the history of Easter Day is that which happened when Christianity came into Germany, and effected or received the conversion of the Teutonic nations. It found there a festival in the early spring, of ancient date, in honor of Eostre, or Ostera, the goddess of spring. This festival commemorated the return of the sun to Northern climes after its long contest with the genii of winter,— with frost, cloud, storm, and death. It commemorated the revival of the forces of nature, the fresh hopes that came to man and beast, the promise of a new seed-time and harvest. It was a thank-offering to the sun as the annual creator of the sustenance and beauty which the earth, at the touch of his fertilizing rays, produced for man. It was a festival, therefore, of grateful reverence and piety. It was religious, but it was also a day of popular joyousness. This festival of Teutonic paganism Christianity did not abolish, but adopted and transformed, in its primary feature, into a celebration in honor of the resurrection of Jesus. The two celebrations, in fact, came together and gradually adapted themselves to each other, until they coalesced finally into one, which retained some of the features of both. The very name of the pagan festival was retained,— Easter, from Eostre, — as were some of its popular out-door sports and traditions. The flowers — emblem of nature reviving from her winter of death — which have become such a feature of the day in modern Christian churches, also the eggs, traditionally associated with the day, and symbol of life, are a reminiscence of the old Teutonic celebration rather than of that which began in Judea. And yet they fit harmoniously to both. The two celebrations, before they coalesced, had so much in common that the conjunction was natural and easy. Both were on a day dedicated to the worship of the sun. The Christian festival had already imbibed some features of hilarity from paganism in Southern Europe. The fact, too, that Jesus was called the "Sun of Righteousness," "the Light," "the Dayspring from on high," that his religion came from the East, the home of the sun and the land of the sunrise, made the transition not difficult from the pagan to the Christian interpretation of the festival. And, for one, I like to think that there is this variety of sentiment and tradition which has come into the celebration of this day,—that in it heathen as well as Christian memories mingle. It is the same with the Christmas festival. I love to think that the roots of beliefs and practices in modern Christendom run down so deep into the past, not stopping eighteen centuries back, but threading all the ages and spreading out widely through the common soil of our humanity. I love to think that, in this Easter festival, kept in Europe and America to-day, there mingle traditions, though it may be unconsciously, of a time when our hardy Teuton fathers, independent but reverent, gathered, not in temples made with hands, but in the primeval woods and sacred groves built by nature's architect, and gave utterance to their grateful praise to the Power that every year re-creates the earth, clothes it with beauty, and fills it with manifold forms of life and joy. Say you that they worshipped the sun? Rather was it the Power within or behind the sun, the sustaining providence of the universe, bringing seed-time and harvest without fail in their season, and guiding this great orb of light, heat, and life for daily and yearly beneficence to man. There was trust and gratitude in their worship,— grateful reliance upon the order of nature. Though not in Jerusalem nor on Mount Gerizim, they yet, in these stately temples of nature, which Christianity has but faintly copied in its Gothic cathedrals, worshipped in spirit and in truth. To find these evidences of relationship among religions, to trace Christian ceremonies and ideas beyond Christian and Hebrew lines into the vast *common* of natural religion, so far from disturbing my faith, gives me a new and beautiful testimony to the solidarity of the human race and to the actual natural brotherhood of mankind. Instead of undermining my faith, these discoveries give it a broader and deeper foundation. Instead of a past of eighteen or nineteen hundred years merely, running up to a written record whose authenticity may be assailed, my feet stand upon a past that is coeval and coterminous with the entire history of man on this planet. I see the sects with hands raised every one against its neighbor,— the religions at war with the religions. I see that, in the growing light of reason, many of the doctrines and ceremonies that divide the warring zealots are vanishing away as superstitions. But, deep below all their differences, amid all vanishing of ancient doctrines, I trace the roots of the great beliefs, hopes, trusts, aspirations of mankind, down to certain primary impulses inherent in the very constitution of human nature, and which are what they are because they are vital with the creative energy which at that point passed over from the Supreme Source of all things to finite consciousness. And there they are safe. So long as human nature endures and keeps its identity, nothing can there disturb them. They are beyond the region of doubt; they are above the reach of literary and historical criticism. They may be reasoned about, but not reasoned away; for they are involved in the very nature of the reasoning intelligence itself. Their forms from age to age may change, but in substance they abide.

And, among these central trusts and beliefs of religion, it is not difficult to see what it is that the Easter festival has embodied and represented. It is man's inextinguishable hope and faith that *life is superior to death,*—that the vital and resuscitating power in nature is always stronger than the powers of decay and dissolution, and, after every apparent defeat, returns in triumph to the field; that there is also that in the life of man which is more than the body which disease corrupts and death dissolves, more than the dust which the grave can claim or hold. These two forms of humanity's confidence in the abiding power of Life, the Easter festival has clothed in symbol and poetry, addressed to the popular imagination.

Life is more than and superior to death,—that is the day's lesson; the old lesson and the ever new lesson. Science, even, is teaching now that death is only a phase, a stage, in the continuing and abiding process of life; that there is never any absolute cessation of power, of vitality, but only change in its direction and form. But, before science came, man was learning this lesson in the stern school of experience, and through the deep instincts of his heart, —feeling after the truth, if haply he might find it. He saw nature every year threatened with destruction. All the outward signs of life vanished from her. The winds and storms beat upon her, and her beauty fell. Farther and farther each day the warmth of the sun departed, and the world grew

cold, drear, and desolate. Nature seemed dead.
Snow and ice entombed her. And man must perish
with her. But anon he saw the sun return. The
old vital warmth was still there. Nature was not
dead: she was only sleeping. Day by day, her burial
shroud was loosened. The icy barrier was removed
from her sepulchre. And soon she reappeared in all
her old beauty, promise, and power. The Life-power
in nature stood revealed before his eyes stronger than
the Death-power. Man saw, too, his heart's affections threatened with destruction. One by one, his
friends and companions dropped from his side, and
he saw them no more. His house became to him
more cold, drear, and desolate than the winter of
nature. But by and by there awoke in his heart the
thought that, if the life of outward material nature
was so dear to the Creative Power that it was thus
carefully preserved through every semblance of death,
much more must it be the purpose of the Creative
Power to preserve this inward human nature, this life
of heart and mind, wherein man is superior to nature
and through which come his chiefest joys. And so
came the great hope and belief in immortality,— the
faith that to the soul's vitality there could be no
death. It is the most natural and axiomatic of all
thoughts that, *since Life is*, Life must be an object
to be cherished and preserved by the Creative Power
whence it came. Life, not death, must be the purpose and aim of the all-pervading energy.

But not material life alone, nor chiefly. Man has
learned that great lesson, too, and learned it through
the severe discipline of experience. It is not his

own material life that is dearest even to him. He will surrender his body to the powers of destruction rather than abandon a conviction of his mind. He will face fire and sword rather than forswear a moral principle. He will cast his own body into the jaws of death for the sake of an affection of his heart. There are grades of life, and it is clearly the providential intention that the lower grades should serve the higher. When man shall learn to co-operate perfectly with this intention, then physical death will come to him only as condition of resurrection to some higher form of life. Then he will live already in the domain of rational thought, in the wholesome atmosphere of a good conscience, in the purity of his heart's best affections; and so with him the corruptible will have already put on incorruption, and the mortal will have put on immortality.

March 31, 1872.

XIV.

OPTIMISM.

"We know that all things work together for good to them that love God."— ROM. viii., 28.

I SUPPOSE that all people who have any thoughts about the matter want to believe in the proposition announced in this sentence of Paul. Perhaps most people have moments and seasons when they do believe it. And yet, I suppose, to most people there come frequent times when they are compelled to doubt it,— times, at least, when "things" seem so adverse to good, when the apparently untoward and evil circumstances that beset human life press so heavily, that it does not look so certain that they "work together for good." Even if faith come to the rescue of the bewildered understanding with the assurance that, since infinite Goodness reigns, it *must be so*, nevertheless the question arises, and keeps urging itself, *how* it can be so. Though faith may be able to say, We believe that somehow, however dark and difficult the problem may look, all the ills of life are wrought over into good, yet if reason do not see at all into the process, if the logical understanding get no clew toward a satisfying solution, it is hard to keep back intruding questions and to hold that height of certainty wherein the mind with unshaken confidence can affirm that it *knows*. "We know that all things work together for good." *Do* we know it? To say that we believe it must be so, because we believe that the Sovereign of the universe is infinitely good, is rather to beg the question at issue than to answer it. This is the refuge of the baffled mind when, having come to the limits of its knowledge, it then throws into the scale for its beliefs the weight of its hopes, aspirations, and desires. And this refuge is legitimate, provided the limits of knowledge are not reached too soon. If we have proved the road over which we have been travelling to be safe, though many a passage-way at the time may have seemed perilous and many an ascent insurmountable, we learn to trust it to the end. It is natural and right, too, that we should accept the veracity of our better aspirations and hopes. Until proved the contrary, we may legitimately accept their testimony as evidence of the real drift and tendency of things in the universe. The writer of the Epistle to the Hebrews says, "Faith is the substance of things hoped for, the evidence of things not seen"; and there is a fine truth in this statement, a very full and satisfying truth. That ideal which the human soul possesses in its higher hopes and desires it instinctively trusts as the pledge of a future reality. And reason, where it has no adequate grounds for denial, may well accept this natural mental bias to trust the future for bringing something better than the past, as an indication that the immanent energy, which is the central life of nature and of man, is moving in the direction of good and is overruling evil for the promotion of good.

Still, there are few people who can in all circumstances keep this high ground of faith. Hope is not knowledge. Aspiration is not certainty. A vision of the future may be trustworthy, but it is not to ordinary people so palpable a reality as a present fact. Faith may be good evidence for things not seen, but the things seen are so close at hand and cover so fully the field of vision that they are apt to shut out all sight of this evidence. And these things that are seen are sometimes so inscrutably evil, so impenetrably dark, that, even though the soul may believe there is light beyond, yet it cannot trace one ray through the thicket,— cannot explain how all this evil is to be transmuted into the substance of virtue, how it is to be surmounted and put to use in the progress of the world. Optimism — the belief that the world is the best possible, and that every event in it at any particular time is the best possible in view of all the circumstances and in reference to the ultimate good of the whole — may perhaps be a true theory; and it may be a comforting theory to the theologian in his studies, to the philosopher in his speculations, to any person in moments of serenity, when individually free from the pressure of evil conditions. But I suspect that this belief does not generally come to comfort those who stand most in need of comfort. When the iron enters one's own soul, it is not so easy to be an optimist. I can hardly conceive it possible that those classes of society who are crushed under some great oppression, who are ground down by poverty, who are the victims of injustice and tyranny, who are forced to live in daily companionship with vice and misery; or those upon whose hopes and careers has fallen the blight of constant disappointment and failure, upon whose once fair auspices and happy home there has come, for instance, the wreck of fortune and love which persistent intemperance brings in its train; or those — and they may be in the most guarded and moral social circles — whose hearts are smitten by a sudden blow from some villany too black to name,— I can hardly conceive that any persons in such conditions can comfort themselves with the thought that "all things are the best possible," can look up out of their misery, out of their sense of humiliation and wrong, and say serenely, "Whatever is, is right." No: there are ills in our human lot too profound, too heavy, too bitter, for any who are under the burden of them to have the heart to say, "This is all as it should be; this is what I need; this is the best thing which could possibly have been arranged for me." Could such a sentiment find utterance, it would seem, indeed, but solemn mockery, and would betray a want of the very feeling from which must come the motive-power which is to resist the ills of life and triumph over them. If optimism is to be interpreted as meaning unconditionally, in the moral as in the material universe, that "whatever is, is right," as Pope put it in his oft-quoted aphorism, if it mean that everything in the world this moment is the best thing possible in the eye of infinite Goodness, and just as we might conceive infinite Goodness would approve and wish it to be, then, to my mind, optimism is most false both in theory and experience.

And, thus understood, optimism not only seems to me groundless in reason but dangerous to morals. I cannot bring myself to say that even all things are the best possible, considered with reference to the after and ultimate good of all persons; that infinite Goodness, though looking to the future, were it to keep full control of human conditions and actions, would arrange everything, will everything, just as we find it to-day. Such a doctrine of optimism appears to me to blaspheme infinite Goodness nearly as much as did the old dogma of predestinating a portion of the human race to eternal misery. To suppose that a Being of infinite purity could look with complacency upon the assassin's crime, the swindler's plot of lying and robbery, the profligate's infamous lust and treachery, the cruelties under which millions of human beings have been crushed by selfish power, because in the future his omniscient eye sees that good will be the issue,— much more, to suppose that he has by his own free purpose and will arranged all these individual acts as the best way of producing this after good,— this is to violate the very idea of goodness, and to confound all valid distinction between right and wrong. The only sense in which I can conceive optimism to be acceptable to a rational and morally earnest mind, is that the world, as a whole, is the best possible, considering that human beings are free, responsible actors in it, and help to make it what it at any moment is; that is, that the conditions of human existence with regard to physical and moral evil have progressed as far as could rationally be expected on the plan that man shall be a prime agent in improving his own condition.

Why man was made a responsible agent in arranging his own lot and destiny, why he was made subject to evil and suffering instead of being necessitated to a path of rectitude and happiness, is another question; and a question which it may be difficult to answer. We can only say that he is not thus necessitated,— that the human race, considered collectively or individually, has before it the tremendous task of working its own way up and out from evil conditions, and by a rational and virtuous use of its own powers achieving its own destiny. And we can say, besides, that this seems a higher order of being, even with all the liabilities and actualities of evil that attach to it, than would be a condition of existence in which there should be only a mechanical adherence to right. At any rate, so things are; and, however better it might seem, if we had all been made angels incapable of going astray, it is evident that, if we are ever to reach that state, it must be by our own effort and struggle. And very likely there can be no such thing as conscious *angelhood*, no such thing as the full development of a vital, organic, moral personality, without this effort, — without the rational perception and choice of truth and right rather than their opposites. In history, the fact that man by his own effort has been making his lot better, that human virtues have been continually blotting out the record of human crimes and woes, that truth and justice have triumphed over wrong, and right and love have been gradually winning supremacy over brute might and cruelty,— it is this fact that gives us a right to affirm that there is a supreme moral Order ruling in the affairs of men. Man has himself overruled his own evil doings. Whenever, therefore, it be said that "the world is the best possible," and that "all things in it are arranged in the best possible way for the ultimate good of all," we can justly use the optimistic assertion only in the sense that it was best that man should be left free, or should become responsible, to a great extent, for his own condition; and that being left free, though he will bring many evils upon himself, his moral intelligence can be trusted to overcome them, and ultimately to make "all things work together for good."

But Heaven forbid that we should suppose that, with reference to man's future good, all present things are alike available as material; that one act is as good as another; that a bad man is as good for the purpose as a good man; that wickedness is as serviceable as virtue; that all moral distinctions vanish in the presence of some supreme transforming spirit that takes all our human conditions,— the ill and the good, the bitter and the sweet, the vicious and the virtuous,— and, putting them all together into its crucible, straightway brings forth a product which has always the same wholesome qualities as a genuine elixir of life! Heaven forbid that, in any absolute, unconditioned sense, we should say, "Whatever is, is right," and that we should lose our horror of evil and crime, because, possibly, we may see some way in which they may, by and by, ages hence perhaps, be converted into good! All things do, indeed, work together for good. But they do so, because human beings keep clear in their minds the distinction between things as they are and things as they ought to be, and strive to make the "ought to be" actual. They do so, because man sees the difference between good and evil, and knows from daily observation and experience that there are many things in the world that are not right and that will not be likely to come right or be transmuted into any form of goodness, unless human beings take hold and help to do it. "All things work together for good,"—*but not without man as a worker.*

And, if we recur to Paul's words, from which we set out, we shall see that they also express essentially this condition. "All things work together for good *to them that love God*,"— in other words, to paraphrase the conditional clause, to them who look up rather than down ; to them who seek the truth, who espouse right, who strive to know and to do the good, who honor virtue, who love the ideal of infinite excellence, in which all truth, right, beauty, goodness, are conceived to harmonize as constituent parts, and who study constantly to copy that ideal into character and life. In a word, all things work together for good to those *who love and aim at the good.* The spirit of this aspiration and effort is the transmuting agency that converts the

base elements of human error and wickedness into
the pure coin of virtue. Those to whom this effort
and aspiration are wanting, those whose look is
downward, those whose career is only a yielding to
the cravings of selfish passions, those who find their
most alluring solicitations in the direction of sensual
appetite, those who are bound in the chains of
avarice and animalism, those who have given themselves up to false and vicious propensities, and are
making little or no struggle against them,— these
have no right to hope that things will in any
way work together for their good. The soliciting
spirit of the eternal Goodness must find some co-
operating response within the soul, or its effort is in
vain. Not until that desire for goodness, which
we cannot suppose is ever wholly crushed out even
of the worst of men, is somehow, somewhere,
aroused into a positive purpose and endeavor, so
that the soul looks and reaches up again, will a man
find himself possessed of the faculty of making even
the ills and sorrows of his lot steps in his ladder
heavenward.

If we apply these principles to the problems of
life's evils, we shall find them as true in practice as
in theory. Look at the history of the human race.
Humanity has progressed in proportion to the activity of its own rational and moral intelligence. The
work of progress has not been carried on by some
overruling Power outside and independent of the
power that resides in the human faculties. It is
through the human faculties themselves that the
divine purpose is unfolded, and the destiny designed

for man by the Creative Power is gradually achieved. Henry Ward Beecher once said, "The *elect* are those who *will*, the *non-elect* are those who *won't*." That is the modern interpretation of the Calvinistic doctrine of fore-ordination. And it is a true hint of the actual historical fact that the eternal Power works through human agency, and depends for its success, in no small measure, upon the co-operation of the human will. Humanity advances and achieves its grand triumphs, not through any spirit of fatalistic philosophy that would fold the hands and piously leave everything to God, but through its own prying, restless energies. The Hindu Brahmins have taught that men get nearest to God when they renounce the world and its activities, and indulge in retired meditation, cultivating an artificial spiritual clairvoyance; and this sentiment has reappeared to no little extent in the Christian Church. But nearer the truth was the old Greek legend which represented Hercules as mounting to Olympus and becoming a companion of the gods through his gigantic labors for the benefit of man on earth. It is true that, in the historical progress of the race, the doings of evil men are gradually overruled for good, and the pernicious result ultimately eliminated from the product that permanently remains. But this is because there are always some people, many people, who are seeking and striving for just that end; Herculean hearts and wills seeing clearly the demands of truth and right, and setting themselves to the task of meeting them. And if, as Count de Gasparin has well said, "there are moments when certain causes rule so absolutely that everything serves them, war as well as peace, defeats as well as victories, obstacles as well as means," it is because of the vast momentum which a moral truth may have acquired through the consenting and co-operating exertions of many rational wills to push it forward and give it supremacy. Without this, the great moments would never arrive.

And the same thing is true in our individual experience. We overcome personal trials and obstacles of every kind, we defeat evil both in its causes and in its results, when our hearts and wills lay hold upon goodness with their whole strength. In this alembic of a supreme moral purpose, all experiences are dissolved, however hard they may be to bear,— temptations, adversities, griefs, old transgressions,— and all are converted into materials of future character. We then mount by the very obstacles that would seem to hinder us. We get visions of heaven through the very tears that sorrow wrings from our eyes. This is the mood in which all things work together for good, the working spirit being in the human soul; and it is in this mood that we come to understand, with Paul, how "neither death nor life, principalities nor powers, height nor depth, things present nor things to come, shall be able to separate us from the love of God,"—which, to Paul, was specially manifest in Christ, but which is equally manifest now and throughout the universe. Through this human mood of aspiration after goodness and active receptivity to it, light streams into the darkest places of human experience. Often, we may see how the evil actually passes into good,— how, under the hammer of temptation and trial, the soul may be tempered to a finer virtue. • We see men and women pressed under great burdens of woe, who, instead of sinking thereby, rise under the burden to heights of wonderful strength and serenity. We see sometimes sweetness and purity of character growing right out of the midst of foul corruption, the ashes of sorrow converted into "beauty of holiness," the thorns which passion and wrong may have pressed upon the brows of their victims to torture them, blossoming into crowns of roses for their immortal glory.

And with these principles, which seem to be thus confirmed both in the aggregate history of the race and in individual experience, we may even venture to ascend to the larger and more metaphysical problem of the existence of evil in the general plan of creation. When we contemplate the universe as a whole, through all the ages and epochs of its marvellous history, whether we view it as believers in the theory of its gradual evolution or of its creation by special acts, what a scene do we behold! How everywhere into the web of existence are woven inextricably the opposing elements of good and evil! Not only in our human life, but in the great world-experience of which our human life is a part, the light and the shade are everywhere commingled. Light and darkness, virtue and vice, beauty and ugliness, joy and pain, right and might, hope and fear, order and violence, love and hate, creation and carnage, life and death, reason and passion, justice and wrong, spiritual aspiration and animal appetite, the attraction of a mental ideal and the clog and weight of physical circumstance,—thus everywhere are the world elements matched in fierce and persistent contention. Verily, from the very beginning of motion in the first plastic form that matter assumed in the primal origin of things to the latest struggle with calamity or temptation that may be going on this moment in any human breast, it is a "struggle for existence,"—a struggle for existence under that law which recent science, with a narrower application, has styled "the survival of the fittest." What wonder if, in viewing this struggle, theologians have felt themselves obliged to conceive of an incarnate principle of evil in some Satanic personage, or that philosophers have affirmed that the world is ruled by fate rather than by providence!

But science itself, even in this very phrase, "survival of the fittest," is beginning to show us the mistake of both theologian and philosopher. For what means this "survival of the fittest"? It means, finally, the survival of the *worthiest*. True, in the brute struggle for life, the word "fittest" has no moral import. Yet, even among brutes, it is not by any means always the strongest or the largest or the fiercest that survive. Whole species of animals, huger and mightier than any now existing on the earth, have become extinct. Intelligence comes in to help win the battle. And, among mankind, savage races, persistent, strong, and fierce in adhering to their savage ways, have yielded to the higher intelligence and milder manners of civilized men. And the cruelest individual passion or most degrading personal appetite, though it be the accumulated hereditary force of many generations of vicious indulgence, has succumbed again and again to the pleading voice of conscience and the refining influences of goodness. "Survival of the fittest" means then, in the end, the survival of the best. It means that, in this long struggle for existence among contending forces of which the universe is the scene, the victory is finally on the side of the true, the good, the beautiful. It means that right finally gets the better of might, justice triumphs over wrong, truth disarms error, roughness and uncouthness become moulded into beauty, and goodness is crowned, while vice is enslaved. It means, therefore, that the struggle is not merely a blind conflict of blind forces, but that in it is an aim; that it is not simply a battle, but a steady drift toward a goal; not a contest only, but a march. And this aim, this constant upward tendency and drift, this advance through the conflict, this progress in the process, must have been involved in the very first appliance of force from which all things have come, or in the primal substance which was the seed of the universe. In that first act of creation or first step in evolution, not only was motion, activity, life, involved, but in it was a power that determined the direction of the motion and the life. In other words, in that first organific impulse, the true and the right were weighted with a power (a power inherent in their very nature) sufficient to enable them to overcome all obstacles, and to survive all possible exigencies of the struggle. Evil may be the *condition* of development, the pain incident to growth and birth. But good is the substance of the developing power itself. More than condition or incident, it is that which gives to the process impulse, direction, and goal.

And what is this but to say that there is a Providence in the affairs of the world and in the affairs of men? Literally, a *pro-videns*,— a foreseeing of, and a general aiming toward, an end. Not a Providence merely vouched for by questionable tradition or resting on proof-texts that vanish before rational inquiry, but a Providence the existence of which is proved by the irrefragable testimony of science. Not the kind of Providence which is supposed to intervene in the affairs of life in special emergencies, and to come at every pleading desire that man may lift to the skies for personal relief from some pain or peril, but a Providence immovably established in the very order, law, and life of the universe itself; a Providence, through all the ages and epochs of the past as in the present, ever educing good out of ill, and in the human world doing this by the successful incarnation of its purpose in the hearts and wills of human beings; a Providence that this moment is soliciting every man and woman among us, through the knowledge that our minds may gather, through the pressure of conscience, and through all the gentle sentiments of human sympathy and helpfulness, to become willing instruments for working out its beneficent intent.

November 23, 1873.

XV.
MUTUAL SOCIAL RESPONSIBILITY.

"Am I my brother's keeper?"—GEN. iv., 9.

"The narrow-minded ask, Is this one of our tribe, or is he a stranger? But, to those who are of a noble disposition, the whole world is but one family."—ANCIENT HINDU.

A LEARNED author* says that "Cain, the first murderer, was also the first civilizer." And it is most probably true, as he and others maintain, that the traditional story of the contest between Cain and Abel, resulting in the slaughter of the latter, instead of being a narrative of a personal strife between two brothers, is a relic of a larger contest between two clans or classes of men, the shepherds and the husbandmen,—between a nomadic tribe, subsisting upon flocks and herds, and claiming an unlimited right of pasturage, and an agricultural tribe, who had begun to till the ground, and who claimed, as against the wandering herdsmen, the right of property in the soil they had taken to cultivate. Of these tribes, Abel is the representative of the herdsmen, Cain of the planters; and the conflict, which may have been long, bitter, and bloody, was really between primitive barbarism and the first impulse to civilization, since civilization

* Dr. F. H. Hedge, in the *Primeval World of Hebrew Tradition*.

begins with acquiring a right of possession to the soil. And, in this conflict, civilization, or the class of agriculturists represented by Cain, was the conqueror; and yet not wholly so, since Cain, though victorious in battle and putting Abel to death, is represented also as being compelled to flee into other lands to pursue his calling: which, it is claimed, signifies that the husbandmen, though worsting the herdsmen in battle, yet continued to be harassed by them, and finally emigrated beyond their reach to a new country.

This interpretation of the old tradition clearly turns the tables in favor of Cain. Though not necessarily absolving him from guilt, it represents him as standing for the interests of civilization and progress, and so far relieves him somewhat of the stigma of a mere criminal which the tradition has always fastened to his name. Yet Cain, though representing historically a better cause than Abel, may nevertheless have been guilty of gross injustice and cruelty in maintaining his cause, just as to-day the white settlers on the Western frontier of our country, though they are agents in promoting civilization and are pioneers of a higher mode of society and life than the Indian barbarism which they displace, are yet, in their encroachments on the nomadic Indian possessions and habits, guilty of the greatest wrongs and outrages, such as must forever disgrace the civilization which they represent. We may therefore easily enough accept the new rendering of this ancient story, with the new dignity it gives to the character of Cain, without doing away entirely with that feature of the story which is certainly most prominent in the Hebrew narrative,— the sense of Cain's guilt. If the story be a mythical representation of a primitive contest in society between the elements of barbarism and civilization, it none the less contains a strong protest from the dawning moral sense in man against passion, cruelty, and bloodshed. If it gives us a relic of a necessary and irrepressible conflict between two different systems of society in the early stages of human existence, it discloses also that the moral sense very early began to predominate in man, since, though Cain may have stood historically for the better as well as stronger cause, the Hebrew sympathy, nevertheless, went out toward Abel, his victim, and Cain, though the "first civilizer," was handed down to history, not for that glory, but as the first man whose hands were stained with his brother's blood.

We especially may find a double significance, a philosophical as well as moral, in that portion of this old legend which contains Cain's reply to Jehovah, who is represented as looking for Abel. Cain asks, as if in protest against the question, "Am I my brother's keeper?" If we look for it, we may find for this reply, in the light of history, a certain philosophical justification. We may conceive it to be an utterance of that primitive tendency to individual development — to self-assertion and self-maintenance and the exercise of personal faculty and power — which marks the first stage in the development of a race, just as a corresponding assertion of personal independence and will marks the first stage in the

unfolding of human character in a child. The child's
first instinct is to look out for self: to care for
others comes later. So, doubtless, the primitive instinct of the race was to provide for self,— to follow
individual desires and get individual power,— Abel
for himself, Cain for himself, each striving to the
best of his ability for what he individually represents.
And, looking at the matter from this point of view,
it may be said that the question put into the mouth
of Cain signifies this primitive individualism,— this
necessary *selfism*, which first sets society in motion.
It was as if Cain had said: " I am the keeper of my
own principle, not of Abel's. It is a struggle for
existence between two fundamental principles of
society; between different and irreconcilable modes
of living; between nomadic habits, on the one
hand, and the desire of a fixed habitation and recognized rights of property in the soil, on the other;
between barbarism and civilization. And the struggle must go on till one or the other principle conquers. If Abel's principle conquers, well: it will
bring its own consequences. If mine is victorious,
better, and better fruits. But the two principles cannot exchange places nor help each other." We may
conceive that the alleged answer of Cain in vindica-
tion of himself had some such philosophical basis as
this, when we consider the legend as traditionally
embodying clashing tribal tendencies, and not a mere
personal quarrel.

But this is not its deepest nor truest significance.
No philosophy at the time could reason away the
moral consciousness of guilt which the answer vainly

attempts to cover over and conceal. The words indicate that primitive man had already conceive l and was capable of acting upon another social principle than self-interest. That single word *brother* holds the germ of a new principle. It points to relations between man and man, which grow out of their kindred blood. It signifies common interests, sympathies, and aims. It is an index backward to a common origin and forward to a common destiny, and is a perpetual reminder of common obligations. From it, we may unfold all the varied links which bind human beings together in the social covenant. The impulse to individual activity for individual profit, though a mighty agent in civilization, would by itself alone never bring civilized society: the very bond of society would be unrecognized. It is when individual enterprise and welfare are turned to the common good, through the recognition of mutual and equal obligations between man and man, that society really begins. The central significance of the social compact is reciprocity, neighborly sympathy and equality, each for all and all for each,—the individual development and achievement harmonizing perfectly with the general advancement, and not capable of being separated from it. Humanity is so linked together that, if one member suffer, all must suffer with it, or, if one member rejoice, all must rejoice with it.

And this is the moral significance of this feature of the story of Cain which we are now considering. It discloses the principle of *brotherhood* as the most indispensable element of human society. Cain's philosophy was utterly helpless to drive away the remorse that fell upon his conscience because of the crime he had committed against his brother. All the time another voice within him was declaring: "I am my brother's keeper. We were sent into this world to live together, to work together. And my brother's blood cries against me from the ground till I make atonement for the wrong." The legend puts the assertion of brotherhood first into the mouth of Jehovah, but the God that spoke was the lordly voice of conscience in Cain's own breast If this old story contains under a mythical dress an historical relic of some primitive contest between barbarism and civilization, it surely contains no less the relic of a moral contest between the principle of selfish aggrandizement and passion and the dawning sentiments of justice and fraternity. Its grand lesson is that the principle of fraternity is at the foundation of human society, and that any violation of this principle, any injustice and sin of man against his fellow-man, tends to the disorganization and destruction of society. Other ancient records besides the Hebrew bring us the same sentiment as that which I quoted from India as a joint text, and which reads as a response to Cain's question.

But this lesson, though set so many thousands of years ago, the world has been very slow to learn ; and it needs to be reiterated as emphatically to-day as when it was first discovered. Let me repeat it. Fraternity, brotherhood, mutual justice and helpfulness between man and man, is the bond of society ; and any sin committed against this sentiment of fraternity is not merely a wrong to some individual, but tends at once to disorganize and destroy society itself.

The human race is joined together in a partnership from which there is no escape, and all the members of society are jointly and severally responsible for its moral condition. Wickedness may run a good deal farther back for its causes than to the will and passions of its individual doer, just as its consequences will not stop with his act. Yet the responsibility rests somewhere upon individual human hearts and wills, though it may be divided among many, and is not to be explained away by any philosophy that would shift the cause off from man to circumstances, to fate, or to God. We are, each and all, our brothers' keepers: upon our acts, our characters, our sentiments and purposes depends, not only our own welfare, but the well-being of all with whom our lives anywhere come in contact, and of countless others also whom we may never meet, and who are even yet unborn. The threads of our lives, whatever their texture, be they coarse or fine, strong or weak, beautiful or ugly, are taken up and woven into the character of the human race. Whatever grace, or purity, or moral firmness and fidelity we have, whatever good act we do or habit of heroic virtue we cultivate, it goes to enhance the strength and virtue of the whole. Whatever moral defect we have, whatever corruption, whatever vice, whatever untamed passion, whatever secret or open sin, it goes to make society poor, weak, flimsy, and introduces into it elements of disruption and decay. Every human being, therefore, is in some sense his brother's keeper. Upon the measure of integrity possessed by each person depend the average conscience and purity of the race.

And, now, I want to make these propositions clear by a few illustrations. Consider, first, the moral bearing of the physical unity of the race. The physical ties that bind mankind together are very subtile, far-reaching, and powerful. We can see them in their effects, though we may understand little of their method of operation. Very literally is it true, as the old Hebrew writer of Exodus said, that "the iniquity of the fathers is visited upon the children even unto the third and fourth generation." Into what wretched conditions of existence vast numbers of human beings are born! What disordered temperaments and passions, what disease and imbecility, what predispositions to vice and crime, are entailed in the blood! We are so connected by the physical tie of birth that we must necessarily suffer for one another, and not only for one another's sufferings, but for one another's sins. And, in the operation of this law, the innocent necessarily suffer with the guilty. The innocent babe, in whose little life is wrapped so many motherly hopes and joys, and in whom the moral consciousness has not yet dawned, may be cut off by an untimely death, because, through the laws of hereditary descent, it may have in its veins some drop of tainted blood, the virus of which has been handed down from the vices of some ancestor we know not how remote. Or, if it live and grow up to manhood, there may be suffering from weakness and disease, struggle with fierce temptations, and lapses into evil ways, because of a physical and mental constitution inherited from the same vicious source. A man, apparently well born, having fine abilities and a worthy ambition, finds himself, perhaps, in early manhood taken captive by the demon of intemperance, and all his fair prospects blighted for life, because some great-grandfather indulged overmuch his grovelling sensual appetite for alcoholic stimulus. So, again, the saintliest woman that walks the earth, dispensing charity, virtue, and moral healing wherever she goes, may die of dreadful disease generated in some haunt of filth and crime, of which her pure nature hardly dreams the existence. And thus it is throughout the world. The human race is imperfect, tainted, earthy, given largely to animalism, has a good deal of bad blood in its veins; and disease, vice, misery, physical and moral infirmity, premature death, mental atrophy and inertia — all the elements that tend to the dissolution of society — inhere in this general imperfection. What a terrible social fact — and a terribly damning fact against Christian civilization — is that which a physician in New York has recently brought to light from certain criminal statistics of the State,— the tragic story of a pauper girl who, some six generations ago, having been left unprotected to the mercies of society, and falling a victim to man's lust, became the ancestress of two hundred criminals and as many more idiots, drunkards, lunatics, and paupers! Verily, the iniquity of the fathers is visited upon the children with retributive usury; nor does it stop at "the third and fourth generation."

And, looking at considerations bearing on practical motives of conduct, what is there that should be more calculated to arouse conscience to a sense of the terrific evil of moral transgression, of its meanness as well as its wickedness, than the knowledge that, long after we have passed away from earth, our sins will live on in our posterity to corrupt the very fountains of life, and to spread devastation, death, and sorrow among the innocent? What father is there who, if he could certainly know that his vice is to slay his own son, would not by every moral effort in his power stay the malignant force? Yet his vice is most certainly to descend in retributive woe upon somebody's child as innocent as his. Some life is somewhere to suffer and have its days shortened for his guilt. For the vices which any man or woman may harbor, under however respectable an exterior, there must be somewhere at some time wretchedness, lamentation, disease, and death perhaps before the normal time. For every violation of the moral law there must be retribution, atonement,— not before it is committed (that were impossible), but afterwards. And, in this atoning retribution, the innocent necessarily suffer with the guilty; not by any arbitrary decree, but because, through the law of physical relationship, we are all of one race, of one blood, and are so closely and variously bound together that no man can either live or die to himself alone.

Yet, over against this dark picture, we can place

a brighter one. Virtue is just as accumulative by hereditary descent, just as self-generative, as vice. Man is not necessarily the slave of circumstance, not necessarily in hopeless bondage to hereditary evil. Again and again, by sheer inward moral power has that chain been broken, and the man, once bound, has declared his freedom from all ancestral demons, and taken possession of the domain of his own nature. Even persons far advanced in life — persons of fifty and sixty years — have sometimes broken the sway of confirmed evil habits, and stood up again in the dignity of manly power. This moral feat is difficult; it may be rare; but it is not impossible. And what may be done by the more hopeful process of early training and education in overcoming evil tendencies inherent in bad birth and surroundings is matter of record. The societies that are removing vagabond children from the streets into good homes furnish the proof. The law of "selection," of which we are hearing so much in the realm of nature, may assuredly be made available for the benefit of mankind through human volition. Bad blood may be improved. The virus of physical and moral disease may eventually be neutralized by generations of virtuous living, and pass out of the human stock. This is not conjecture, but a statement that rests on solid facts. And in the teaching of such facts is man's hope, here his unfailing incentive to effort. The law by which moral evil accumulates upon itself its own natural retribution by corrupting the race operates equally for the preservation and growth of virtue: with this important addendum, that we may believe the primal and eternal Power to be on the side of virtue.

Let us consider again this law of mutual social responsibility in another aspect more exclusively moral,— the joint responsibility of the individual members of society for the general moral condition and the moral public opinion of the community. We cannot justly visit the whole condemnation of vice and crime upon those who are publicly reprobated as vicious and criminal. The crime which breaks out upon the surface of society, in the low haunts of degradation and ignorance, is but the external appearance of a moral disease which extends far back and into very different grades of society. The poison shows itself at those weak spots which are unprotected by knowledge or unguarded by a sense of social respectability, and where the very atmosphere is foul with contagious vice; but it begins, and continues to be fed, from a very different source. It begins with vicious, ungoverned propensities, wherever found. It is nourished from homes and characters that are outwardly reputable. If you would read my meaning more clearly, look at that cancerous spot in modern society called "the social evil." See the women of the class on whom Jesus looked with tender compassion, but against whom Christian civilization has pronounced the awful anathema "abandoned"; and who are abandoned of all self-respect, of all true love, of all womanly grace and purity, and who are almost abandoned by society itself. But are they the sole sharers in this social guilt,— they, and the vile creatures, male or female, who help them to ply their infamous calling? Or is it, think you, the class of men who are socially low, poor, and degraded that support this vice? Alas, no! The accountability does not stop there: it hardly, indeed, begins with either of these classes. The poor and degraded have not the necessary financial means nor the arts of fascination that the vice requires. It is men who have money and can bestow gifts, men who have social position and who are outwardly decorous and reputable, that furnish the chief sustenance of this great evil; and it is because this class of men, men who help to make public opinion and may even be law-makers, are sharers in responsibility for the evil, that it is made so difficult for the civil law to reach the evil. No: it is not the poor creatures whom society calls "abandoned" who are the chief sinners in this sin. The evil has no such simple solution as that. But all that class of men whose ungoverned passions create and sustain these abandoned creatures are responsible sharers in the crime; and they may be men whom society, the "best society," is receiving with confidence to its bosom, and who are proud of their "good standing" in circles of culture and refinement. Well has it been called "the social evil," though the name seems to have been chosen delicately to veil the vice; for it is the evil which more than any other, perhaps, spreads its roots underneath, and overshadows with its baleful branches, all grades of social condition, and for which society itself is jointly responsible. Not infrequently does it break out into woful domestic tragedy and bloodshed. But think you that the wretched hands that may hold the murderous weapon are alone guilty? Ah! the blood cries out against other hands,— hands that may seem to be clean; hands that yours may take in the confidence of business every day, or that, kid-gloved, may be welcomed to your parlors. It cries out against the loose public opinion which permits to men, without great loss of repute, a license of passion for which it condemns woman to perpetual infamy. But, however lax be the law of public opinion, by the stern, unerring laws of nature, society is held accountable for this evil, and upon society falls the awful retribution for the guilt. One sex cannot suffer without the other sex suffering with it. No part of society can be victimized without other parts feeling the outrage and paying the penalty for it. And society never writes the word "abandoned" against the character of even one woman, but that nature's laws, and the Almighty Power that executes its will through them, brand the same word, or a still worse moral curse, upon some man's guilty brow.

This silent partnership in social responsibility may be illustrated again by considering the necessary conditions of any nation's progress. Look, for instance, at the history of our own country with reference to the institution of slavery and the condition of the negro race. It was shown by experience to be absolutely impossible for the country to develop its fundamental ideas of republican liberty and equal justice even for the white race, so long as these principles were violated in respect to the negro. The evil reacted upon the slave-owners, and made them irresponsible despots instead of republican citizens. It made itself felt throughout the whole country, and was an incubus upon the success of the republic to just the extent that it was a violation of republican principles. Finally, the righteous retribution culminated in the war of the rebellion, from which there was no safe escape for the nation except by granting to the negro the long-denied right to liberty, and making him a recognized partner in the struggle and in the victory. The same chain that bound his limbs as a slave fastened him as a millstone to the nation's neck; and the nation was forced to break that chain, in order to free itself from mortal peril. So it has been since the war, and so it must continue to be for years to come: the success, prosperity, peace of the country, are inextricably bound up with the negro's condition. However much any persons may wish it were not so, and may be inclined to rue, if not to curse, the day which brought the black man into the country, here he is, four or five millions strong, making an element that will not permit itself to be forgotten nor overlooked among the forces that are shaping the nation's destiny. In a hundred ways is the nation constantly warned that it cannot evade the responsibility of being the keeper of the black man's rights. His destiny is the country's destiny. Leave such a mass of population with only partial civil rights, uneducated, degraded, under the ban of social prejudice, with the ballot it may be, but with no knowledge how to use it, and the nation is maimed, burdened, and hindered in its progress to just the extent of their degradation. Nor is the evil confined to the South, but must be felt to some extent in every part of the body politic. The nation cannot go on, and leave any part of its citizenship behind. It will be held back to just the extent that it leaves any class with rights denied, with wrongs unatoned. It will be free for progress just in proportion as it guarantees justice, education, and a fair opportunity to all. The prosperity of the nation is the prosperity of its members.

Any of the old countries of Europe might furnish us the same example. Look at England. When we consider only her aristocratic and educated classes, of what prosperity and social progress does she not seem capable? All the resources of wealth, of culture, of science, of ancient national inheritance and noble blood, are in her hands to wield for social achievement and advance. But, clinging to her skirts and fastened by ties that cannot be severed, are millions of poverty-stricken laborers, an ignorant mass of degradation, pauperism, intemperance, animalism; and England, with all her riches, culture, and social refinement, finds herself confronting social problems the very presentation of which seems to threaten the stability of her social order and upon the successful solution of which the perpetuity of her institutions depends. It is clear that the nation has reached that point where it is decreed by the laws of social destiny that the aristocratic and educated class can advance no farther by itself, but can only progress by lifting up and carrying forward the mass of the people. All classes, however separated by artificial lines of distinction, are in reality welded together and to a common fate.

The present angry conflict between capital and labor presents another illustration, which I cannot, however, unfold at this time. Suffice it to say that there can be no solution of this problem except by a just practical recognition on both sides of the law of mutual responsibility in industrial enterprise.

And so it is throughout mankind. Across all lines of class separation — the lines that may be drawn by wealth, by culture, by occupation, by family pedigree and social rank, and even by vice and crime — stretch living links of natural kinship and those deeper laws of social organization which hold firmly all classes together, and bind them to one ultimate destiny. By these strong though unseen ties, the solidarity of the race is established, and every man is made to some extent the keeper of every other man's happiness and virtue.

Does it seem to inveigh against the goodness of providential law that there should be this general sharing of responsibility, and that ignorance, vice, and indolence should thus come as a burden upon the good, enlightened, and industrious, hindering their progress, and that the retribution of suffering for moral transgression should fall upon the innocent as well as the guilty? Rather, let me say, as the concluding point of the theme, this method discloses the very pathway through which the great providential purpose works to benefit mankind. By this law of mutual responsibility or of a common imputation of many of the consequences of wrongdoing to innocent and guilty alike,— this law by which all classes of society are so affiliated together that no man liveth and no man dieth to himself,— it is ordained and guaranteed that all parts of the human race shall hold together and advance together in the path of amelioration and progress; that no portion, however favored, shall get so far ahead as to be incapable of leading the rest; and that no portion, however degraded and criminal, shall be left so far behind as to be incapable of being led. Hereby, the light, knowledge, virtue, science, culture, refinement, power, achieved by the best portions of the race, are put under tribute to the advantage of the poorest and lowest. Nature's laws are set solidly against monopolies. Even the seemingly harsh laws of contagion and disease, implicating whole communities in torture and sorrow for one man's ignorance or vice, are ministers, stern but merciful, to awaken among those who have the knowledge and the power an active interest that shall set itself to the task of eradicating the error and the vice whence such miseries spring. Thus, it is irrevocably decreed by the very laws and forces of the social organism that the highest portions of the race shall raise up the lowest, the most advanced draw after them the weak and ignorant, and none be left hopelessly and helplessly in the rear to perish of their own imbecility. However high any may lift their heads into the light of mental and moral power and into the clear atmosphere of self-control, their feet are planted still on the old common earth whence the race has sprung, and where many individual souls and tribes are still grovelling in the degradation of ignorance and animal passion; and from all around sordid hands, which cannot be turned aside, are stretched up, clutching for support and help. "Give us," they pray, "in our darkness of your light, in our despair of your hope, in our helplessness of your strong leadership. Hold us by the hand, that we sink not, but be lifted up with you." And the Divine Providence of nature, through these organic ties of the social bond, has decreed that those outstretched hands shall be held.

And, if the hindrance and pain that thus ensue to the faithful seem hard, this fact is only the necessary reverse of the larger and brighter fact that the true and the strong are to give of their strength to the weak, and lead them along to the final blessing of all. Once, on a Western railroad, I saw a rapid passenger train, to which, for some temporary cause, a mixed train of emigrant and freight cars had been attached. There, in the advance, were the elegant palace cars, with their refined and comfortable company of wealthy travellers; then came a car or two of more ordinary pattern for the less luxuriously inclined; and then the miserable emigrant cars, with their freight of lowliness, poverty, and not a little squalor; while a number of dingy coal-cars brought up the rear. Yet all were running together on the same track, drawn by the same powerful engine, bound for the same goal. So it is with mankind in the great world-journey that we are making. All classes, grades, and conditions of society are fastened together in one train, only with this difference: that the coupling here is no accidental and transient circumstance, but is so insured in the very nature of the eternal laws that no part of the mixed train of humanity can ever be dissevered and left behind. And, if any of these life-travellers, complaining of the delays and accidents of the journey, shall presume to ask: "Why should my course be hindered and disturbed? Am I my brother's keeper?" the reply comes back from the providential purpose inherent in the eternal order of things, "Yes, O man, whosoever thou art, thou art thy brother's keeper; and wheresoever on this earth thou standest, and however proudly thou standest in thy power or in thy knowledge or in thy virtue, unless thou acknowledgest that primal obligation, the voice of thy brother's blood crieth against thee from the ground."

May 3, 1874.

XVI.

HEART IN NATURE.

"I look for the new Teacher, that shall see the world to be the mirror of the soul, shall see the identity of the law of gravitation with purity of heart; and shall show that the Ought, that Duty, is one thing with Science, with Beauty, and with Joy."— R. W. EMERSON.

A CHINESE priest of philosophical temperament, who lived in the sixteenth century, in discussing the old and ever new problem of the creation of the world, represented the beginning of things as a crude, chaotic mass of nebulous matter, which, through a principle of self-generation, gradually expanded into the countless beautiful varieties of nature and into an infinite system of worlds; but all these forms of nature and this whole infinite series of worlds he described as being included within one universally diffused and all-pervading, ethereal essence which he said was hard to name, but which might best be called "Heart." This man was a believer in the Buddhist religion; a religion which, more than any other perhaps, has perceived and emphasized the evils of human existence, and which has been characterized by some theological critics — critics, however, who have little appreciated the depth of its thought or the practical benignity of its mission — as the organization of human despair. And yet this man, confronting this traditional picture of the lot of mankind which was the common property of his religious faith, and confronting the actual miseries of the men and women in the populous communities around him, could not complete his conception of the creative and sustaining forces of the universe without adding something which he could express only by using a word that covers the tenderest facts and relations of human life. Face to face with the whole vast catalogue of human woes, face to face with his beliefs as to the necessary and inherent evil attending all finite existence, he yet could say that the universe had a heart, and that this quality of heart was the subtile essence or spirit of the whole, embracing, surrounding, intimately pervading all the parts.

This attitude of the Chinese philosopher is not exceptional. It represents the common attitude of humanity in the presence of humanity's ills; and it is for this reason that I bring it here to indicate the subject of my discourse this morning,— *Heart in Nature*. Has the universe in the midst of its laws and forces any heart? This is a question which many individual minds are asking of themselves openly or silently to-day. It is a question which humanity has hitherto answered in the affirmative. Whatever speculative theologians may have said, whatever doubts may have been raised by philosophy or by science, and however sceptical individual observers may have grown as they have watched the stern and often afflicting processes of nature, humanity as a whole, and through all the varying epochs of its history, has said confidently and said emphatically: "The universe has a heart. Somewhere within it, in spite of all existing evils and woes, are the elements of tenderness, of compassion, of good will, of love."

And I know of no more pathetic picture in human history than the persistency with which this belief in the good intentions of the universe has asserted itself against all the pressing facts of evil to which man has been subject. See by what ills human beings have been buffeted! They have been assailed by floods, by storms, by pestilence, by famine, by earthquake, by destructive insects and venomous beasts, by every type of disease, by every form and hue of suffering. They have been assailed in respect to their possessions, their lives, their affections, their dearest hopes and endeavors. They have won their achievements by a dire struggle against conflicting and opposing forces: nay, only by constant and bitter struggle have they maintained existence itself. They seem, indeed, to have been brought into existence just to contend for life and its possessions amid the rough and clashing forces of nature, which travel on their ways irrespective of human desires, and deaf and pitiless to human entreaties. For more than half of mankind, the struggle is terminated by death before even the period of manhood is reached; and over life at every age death ever hovers threatening, sparing no household, no heart. Yet surrounded by this host of natural and inevitable evils, and amid numerous others of personal wrong and wretchedness, arising from

man's weakness or inability to cope successfully
with the conditions of his existence, human nature
has persisted in believing that all these ills are
encompassed, penetrated, and overruled by elements
of sympathy and goodness. Though again and
again hope and desire may be disappointed, and
again and again the cry for mercy find no answer,
and though the inquiry that searches in the dark for
the clew to the beneficent purpose continues to be
baffled, yet the persistent faith remains that somewhere that purpose clearly runs, to bring in some
way fruition to all good hopes and desires. Even
when man's heart has been wounded, he has pressed
the gaping wound against the force that has aimed
the blow, in mute appeals for sympathy, and has
continued to comfort himself with the belief that
behind the hand that struck was a heart that felt.
My own wounded heart, he says, bleeding and suffering, bears witness to Heart within the universe.

Examples of the persistency of this belief in the
goodness of the universe press upon us from all
sides. The Hebrews, in their captivity in Babylon,
suffering persecution, and almost despairing of res-
toration to their country and to the ancient purity of
their faith, could yet sing of the "loving-kindness"
and the "tender mercies" of Jehovah. Year after
year was their hope deferred, until their heart was
made sick. Their God did not lead them out of
their bondage, and yet they steadfastly believed that
he would; and no postponement of the grand event
could shake their confidence in his promise. The
early Christians were in poverty and distress. They

were despised and maltreated, and could reckon little success for their cause; yet they talked of the near coming of the kingdom of heaven, and called God their father. Their kingdom of heaven did not come; no God, the Father, descended to dwell among them on a renovated earth; no Christ reappeared in the clouds to bring them deliverance. Yet they continued to believe and to hope. The beliefs and hopes changed their forms to suit successive disappointments, but the substance of them remained. If the good was not to be found here and now, it was to be found in heaven and hereafter. The hope of it was good against all failures as to time and place. The Asiatic Buddhists regarded life in all finite forms as necessarily evil; yet never was there a more vigorous or more humane faith in the existence of an ultimate good to be attained by human endeavor than these same Buddhists possessed. Over against the fact of finite ill, they placed the fact of infinite felicity, when the finite and the Infinite should become reconciled and be at peace. Epictetus — and he may be taken as a type of the Greek and Roman moralists — had suffered slavery, was infirm and poor, knew little of life's outward joys, and possessed few of what are ordinarily called the bounties and blessings of heaven. Yet could he say to his God: "Whatever post or rank Thou shalt assign me, I will die a thousand times rather than desert it.... If Thou shalt send me where I cannot live conformably to nature, I will not depart unbidden, but upon a recall, as it were sounded by Thee. Even then, I do not desert Thee.... Though

Zeus set me before mankind poor, powerless, sick; banish me, lead me to prison,— shall I think that he hates me? Heaven forbid! . . . Nor that he neglects me, for he neglects not one of the smallest things; but to exercise me and to make use of me as a witness to others." Was there ever a finer ideal interpretation of evil facts? Our old German ancestors believed in a perpetual conflict between good and evil powers, not only on this earth, but extending throughout the universe and beyond the veil of death; yet their hearts cherished the vision of the final victory of good over evil, and of a new earth that should be the fair abode of virtue and peace. The Persians and other nations who have believed in a dualistic division of the powers of the universe into divine and satanic have clung to the same hope in the ultimate supremacy of the principle of goodness. Even the Christian sects that have believed in the eternal perdition of the incorrigibly wicked have never put Satan on the supreme throne of the universe, and have deftly explained their dogma of eternal perdition as a manifestation, not of the wrath, not of the vengeance, but of the exceeding righteousness of God. None more than they, even with that dreadful belief in a bottomless pit of torments opening at their feet, have been wont to praise the mercy of the Almighty. And, however shocking this belief might be to our sense of justice, there was, on another side, something sublime in it, when it rose to the height of a willingness to be forever damned so only God's ineffable justice and glory could be maintained. Here was the spirit of old Epictetus again: "I will never forsake Thee, never cease to believe in Thee and in Thy goodness, even though Thou sendest me far from Thee into exile and suffering." "Though Thou slay me, yet will I trust Thee."

People who are even far lower in the scale of civilization than any I have thus far named, people barbarous and degraded and idolatrous, people that seem almost helpless amid the forces of nature and are on the plane of fetichism in religion,—even such people, however crushed they may seem under nature's inexorable sway and play of forces, yet manifest a faith that, against all appearances, there is a power in nature that is protective and benign. They believe it is there, if they can only reach it! And so by supplications, sacrifices, and gifts they hope to coax it out into light and activity,— turning to it after every disappointment and after every new blow from nature's malignant powers, with a faith that is doomed again probably to disappointment, and yet is so pathetically superior to all surface-evidence, to the facts of experience even, that it looks right away from these, though pressing so close upon it, and reaches out wistfully and still believingly for that which is "the substance of things hoped for and the evidence of things not seen."

Thus, everywhere and in all conditions has man asserted his belief in the essential goodness of the universe. He has kissed the rods that have scourged him, in faith that they would blossom into blessings. He has met every kind of misfortune; and yet he has believed that the ruling powers meant to be kind, and would bring him good fortune at last. He has prayed for help in life's emergencies; and, though the help he asked for has not been given, he nevertheless continues to pray, and to believe that the help would be sent, if it were best that it should be. He has put up his appeal for mercy; and, though the mercy has been delayed or has not come at all, he affirms his trust in it still, generously believing that it has been withheld for good reason. He has seen communities swept away by flood or earthquake or pestilence, and devout people, in all the agony of despair, on bended knees, beseeching heaven that the peril might be averted. The peril was not averted, the suffering and the destruction came; and yet the afflicted and desolated survivors have not ceased to believe in the over-governing Goodness, — not ceased to believe in its pity or its power, nor to put up their prayers for its aid. He has seen the great fact of death, present everywhere on earth, among all nations, through all ages, from the beginning of human existence, mingling its shadows with the fact of life, breaking up at some time every home, desolating at some time every heart. He has seen human beings shrink and crouch before the coming terror with eager supplications that it be stayed. But it cannot be stayed. It is part of the universe of things, part of the drama of existence. But do they, therefore, say the universe has no pity, no heart? Rather does this fact of death seem to have touched springs of tenderness as no other fact in human experience has done. It has drawn people together in common sympathy, and driven man to rely on an infinite Love that shall flow into every vacancy where the fair form of a human love has been removed.

Whence, then, this apparent solecism in human experience? — these hard facts of ill and the unanswered desires and prayers that go with them? these hard facts of calamity, of struggle, of suffering, frustrating the highest aims and wishes of human hearts, while human hearts, through all, cling with unfaltering faith to a Power in the universe greater than our hearts, and still believed to be inspired with tenderness and compassion?

The solution of this problem that depends upon the recognition of a miraculous revelation of Divine Goodness, overbalancing all possible forms of evil, I leave aside. The religious faith that rests on miracle has little standing-room in modern days. The miracle presents to the inquirer a greater obstacle than the faith itself. Nor shall we find the solution completely in outward, material nature,— at least not in outward nature considered by itself. The old arguments of natural theology to prove the benevolence of the creating Deity from the objects and operations of nature have very much less force than they once had. Modern science allows little to the argument from design. The great phrase of modern science to express the history of nature is "struggle for existence, with survival of the fittest"; and, to fit this formula, the argument from design must be stated entirely anew. The "design" is now seen to be general, not specific,— a broad, general drift and purpose, inclusive of broad and general results, and not the personal adaptation of force for the working out of this or that special end. And against nature, on any hypothesis, it is not difficult to marshal the facts in the light of modern science, so that they shall seem anything but evidence of benevolence. John Stuart Mill in his essays on Religion, posthumously published, brings against nature a most formidable indictment. He says: "Next to the greatness of these cosmic forces, the quality which most forcibly strikes every one who does not avert his eyes from it is their perfect and absolute recklessness. They go straight to their end, without regarding what or whom they crush on the road.... In sober truth, nearly all the things which men are hanged or imprisoned for doing to one another are nature's performances every day. Killing, the most criminal act recognized by human laws, nature does once to every being that lives; and, in a large proportion of cases, after protracted tortures such as only the greatest monsters whom we read of ever purposely inflicted on their living fellow-creatures. ... Nature impales men, breaks them as if on the wheel, casts them to be devoured by wild beasts, burns them to death, crushes them with stones like the first Christian martyr, starves them with hunger, freezes them with cold, poisons them by the quick or slow venom of her exhalations, and has a hundred of other hideous deaths in reserve, such as the ingenious cruelty of a Nabis or a Domitian never surpassed. ... She mows down those on whose existence hangs the well-being of a whole people, perhaps the prospects of the human race for generations to come, with as little compunction as those whose death is a relief to themselves or a blessing to others. . . . A single hurricane destroys the hopes of a season; a flight of locusts or an inundation desolates a district; a trifling chemical change in an edible root starves a million of people. The waves of the sea, like banditti, seize and appropriate the wealth of the rich and the little all of the poor, with the same accompaniments of stripping, wounding, and killing as their human antitypes. Everything, in short, which the worst men commit either against life or property is perpetrated on a larger scale by natural agents."

We hold our breath at this bold and eloquent indictment, while we ask, Where is the Heart in such facts? And the worst of it is, all of the alleged facts, taken by themselves, we must admit to be true. But this is literally and exactly the worst of it: that the facts, *taken by themselves*, are true. But this is worse than the case of actual nature; for there such facts do not stand by themselves, but are everywhere mingled with facts brighter and better. Such marshalling of the evil facts of nature may be legitimate in argument against the old school of theologians, who culled the good facts to prove benevolent design; but it gives no truer picture of nature than did the more amiable theologians. The scientific truth lies somewhere between the two. Nature does not show herself all heart, but she shows at least the germs of heart. We find in her no complete system of benevolence, and benevolence only; but we find her forces moving toward benevolence, and benevolence all along mingling in their operations. Nature manifests, besides Mr. Mill's dark list of evil facts, facts of felicity, of delight, of satisfaction, of sunshine, growth, and blossoming, facts of successful fruition, of harmony, beauty, and gladness. And wherever exist gladness, beauty, harmony, healthful growth, successful achievement, and happiness, there must exist in the heart of them some elements of goodness. Moreover, the history of nature, traced in the gradually unfolding activity of the vast cosmic forces which seem so reckless and which are so inexorable to human entreaty, presents proofs that, amid all conflicts, struggles, and retrograding periods, there is a steady tendency and aim toward good; and whence this tendency and aim but from the fact that the element of heart, or of goodness as well as intelligence, is inherently mixed in the very substance and essence of things from the beginning? But, more than this, nature — outward, material nature — does not show.

Whence, then, we have to ask again, does man get his faith, not merely in an *element* of heart mingling its threads with the dark facts of human woe, but in a whole heart, all-comprehending and all-pervading,— in a goodness stronger than all the powers of evil, shining above all shadows, and infusing into all forms of decay, destruction, and death the mightier forces of life?

Whence does man get this faith in universal heart but from his own heart, from the human heart? The testimony from nature must be supplemented with the testimony from man, when we ask the question, What does the universe teach? Outward, material nature is only a part, and not the highest part, of universal nature. In a large sense and in a strictly scientific sense, nature includes man. The cosmic forces have evolved him no less than the earth upon which he dwells and the plants and animals that help to sustain his existence. He is the culmination and crown of nature. Nature's tendencies and aims complete themselves in him. Her meanings in him stand revealed. By his own heart, man discovers that nature has a heart,— a heart that must be at least as large as his own, as large as the heart of all humanity,— nay, as large as the heart of all possible finite races of beings in all worlds. There can be nothing in the parts which is not in the whole, nothing in the heart of man which is not in the heart of Universal Nature. And so, when man reckons up the affections, the sympathies, the pities, the tendernesses, the charities, the loves, the philanthropies, all the emotions which make up that moral organ and function of his being which is called the Heart, he justly credits them all to the aim of Universal Nature. Because he finds them in himself, he knows that they must have been in the womb of nature before him, and must belong to that power which is the living essence and soul of nature, in-soul and over-soul of the world,— which escapes all analysis, all search, hovers always just beyond our finding out, but which we know must carry in itself the promise and potentiality of all that is.

In fine, on the principle that whatever is in the

effect must be potentially in the cause, that whatever is in the stream must be somewhere in the fountains and sources whence the stream has come, it is by looking into his own heart that man attains and maintains his faith that there is heart among the forces, powers, and movements of Universal Nature. If there is heart here, there must be heart out there, and everywhere where life is. The colored sibyl, Sojourner Truth, put the whole logic of this thought into her simple, quaint prayer as she escaped from bondage: "O God, help me! If I were you, I would help any one in distress." Man finds tenderness within. So he says and believes it must also be without, in the life of the universe. Has he compassion for weakness, sympathies for distresses and sorrows, pity for human frailties and sins? Then he knows there must be founts of pity, sympathy, compassion, in that life-power, whence stream these qualities of mercy into and through his nature. Has he the spirit of helpfulness, generosity, charity, toward misfortune? Then, by that token, he knows there must be a helpful activity in nature, which is working for his welfare and that of all mankind. Does he find human sympathy, when it is at its best, patient, unwearying, inexhaustible, going out on errands of healing to all places of need, and going at the cost of self-denial and self-renunciation, that it may carry, if possible, redemption and comfort? Then, behold, he says, a higher than mere human love that is pouring itself through these channels of philanthropy. Does he know something of the watchful love of human fatherhood and motherhood? Whence comes it, he says, but from the fact that there are fatherly and motherly attributes in the essence of infinite Life?

It is clear, then, why the Hebrews in their captivity, why the early Christians in their distresses, why the Buddhists in their keen sense of the evils of existence, why our Teutonic forefathers in their beliefs in a deathly struggle between good and evil powers, why Epictetus and the Stoics in their face-to-face conflict with life's ills, why barbarian tribes, even when seemingly crushed as helpless victims under the reckless blows of nature's forces, why people everywhere and in all times, under the burden of the manifold ills that flesh is heir to, have yet looked up out of the ills, out of their distresses, and from beneath the weight of their burdens, and have caught glimpses, or freer vision, of a Power able and willing to protect and to save from them all, and have sung in faith of his loving-kindness and tender mercies, and have clung to him in trust, even when scourgings came instead of the hoped-for bounties, and have believed, in spite of all, in a coming felicity, virtue, and peace. The faith, the vision, the trust, the song, have come from the Divine Heart within their human hearts.

And man's own effort to cherish the vision, and his faith and joy in following it, help to make the vision real. By faithful adherence to the unseen ideal, man gradually translates it into visible and tangible certainty. By his intelligence, he catches the clew to nature's intention, and by his skill can mitigate and even prevent many of the dire results of her blind activity. Man lends to nature eyes that she may see her goal, and in his thought and heart her own ideal aim is completed and fulfilled.

> " Life loveth life and good: then trust
> What most the spirit would, it must;
> Deep wishes, in the heart that be,
> Are blossoms of Necessity.
>
> " A thread of Law runs through thy prayer,
> Stronger than iron cables are;
> And Love and Longing toward her goal
> Are pilots sweet to guide the Soul."

November 28, 1875.

XVII.

WAITING FOR ONE'S SELF.

"It is a long time that I have been waiting for myself."

So said a Persian poet of the tenth century, and the sentence comes down to us freighted with the pathos of human disappointments and human hopes. Like all true poets, the writer spoke not so much for his own personal feeling as for a sentiment common to human souls. Or, speaking for himself, he spoke also for thousands of other souls, of his own and every time, and indicated an experience which has lost none of the keenness of its edge by the lapse of the centuries since he wrote. His words do not fail to touch responsive chords of mutual understanding as they greet our ears to-day. Some of us, doubtless, will find a deeper meaning in them than others do; but to no one of us can they be, I think, without significance. They will recall to us, from our own experience or observation, pictures of successive disappointments and failures, of a good aimed at just lost, of procrastinating purposes, of self-reproaches and self-dissatisfaction verging toward despair, and yet companion pictures, also, of a patient and persistent self-confidence, hope, and courage, a pathetic trust still in often broken resolutions and defeated purposes, which are ever returning to the field of defeat, and are finally more than a match for all failures and despair. An anecdote is told of General Grant at the important battle of Pittsburg Landing, to this effect. The first day was very disastrous to the national army. General (then Colonel) McPherson, Grant's chief of staff, had been reporting all day one calamity after another; and at the close of the day, in summing up the condition of things to the commanding general, — how our troops had been driven back several miles from the positions occupied in the morning, and our lines were everywhere broken and in confusion, and two-thirds of our artillery and great numbers of our infantry had been captured, and our dead and wounded were left on the field in the hands of the enemy,— McPherson could not conceal his impatience at his chief's undisturbed serenity, expecting some orders for saving the rest of the army by a prudent retreat; and, as he turned away from the unbroken silence, he threw back the excited question, "And what do you propose to do about it, sir?" "I propose to re-form my lines, and attack the enemy at daybreak; and will he not be astonished to find us doing it?" was General Grant's answer. And that night the lines were re-formed. At daybreak, the attack was made; and the enemy was astonished. Our troops went forward to triumph, and not only regained all that had been lost the previous day, but won one of the most important victories of the war.

There are many experiences in our human lives of which this anecdote may serve as a rough illustration,— experiences of waiting through long seasons of discouraging disappointment, failure, and loss, until, by some happy combination of personal power and circumstances, the higher self is evoked and takes the leadership, and the long-desired and long-sought-for object is gained. We often have to wait a very long time for ourselves; but, if we patiently wait and faithfully wait, and keep our trust and hope in the coming and do well our own part toward the coming, the trusted self will surely come at last.

The poet's doctrine, we may observe at first, points to an encumbered and divided self,— to a self that is compelled to wait and to a self that is waited for; to a self, therefore, that can be hindered, bewildered, burdened, fettered, drawn away from its true aim, drawn down from the higher light that reveals its possible pathway, and to a self that is able to surmount all obstacles, thread successfully bewildering thickets, cast off burdens or grow the stronger and more erect for bearing them, break confining fetters, conquer all temptations, and in time reach the height of personal attainment the shining glory of which, however far off and long waited for, no cloud of discouragement has ever been dense enough wholly to hide. We may say, indeed, it is one self, but with two dominant impulses or attractions,— a higher and a lower, an upward and a downward, a spiritual and a carnal, a mental and a material; one self, but two centres of variant forces acting upon it and determining its orbit. Yet it is significant that, though man, so long as he has had a history, seems to have been cognizant of this duality of tendency in his own nature, he has yet been nearly unanimous in calling that part of his nature which is responsive to the higher attraction — that part of his nature which subordinates material appetite and passion to a mental aim and law — his real and true self. The other part,— the seat of temptation, hindrance, and failure, the source of scores of besetting sins that becloud his vision and drag back with such fatal energy upon his steps,— though he has been miserably conscious of its supremacy in his actual experience, he has yet, in characterizing his own nature, proudly put under his feet, and said, "Not this which holds me down to earth, but that toward which I lift my eyes, is my real self." It is there, in the best conception of self of which any individual man is capable, and not in the poorest and lowest, that he places his goal. There is his aim, his standard, the enthronement of the law he owns as binding upon his conduct, the hope of what he means to be,— and there he confidently waits his own coming; waits, though the iron of some bitter present experience may be pressing into his soul; waits, perhaps, through years of weariness and hope deferred, through many wanderings in bypaths of illusions, through many stumblings and fallings and blinding storms, yet waits still in faithful expectancy.

And this is essentially the same doctrine that the Apostle Paul teaches in those strong and memorable passages where he depicts the inner conflict between the two forces,— the force of good and the force of evil. Though he finds "the evil" always "present with him," so that even "the good that he would, he does not, but the evil that he would not, that he does," yet he takes the high ground that this evil bias and impulse make no part of his true self. "I delight," he says, "in the law of God after the inward man; but I see another law in my members, warring against the law of my mind, and bringing me into captivity to the law of sin which is in my members.... So then with the mind I myself serve the law of God, but with the flesh the law of sin." And hence the great apostle, though the conflict was by no means over, though many harassed years were still before him, though disappointments and obstacles were still to be met and conquered, yet seemed not to count nor to see any of these things, but to look right through and beyond them to the time when he could cry, "I have fought a good fight, I have finished my course, I have kept the faith: henceforth there is laid up for me a crown of righteousness." And *this* Paul, singing this song of triumph at the goal reached, was the real Paul. He felt all the possibilities of achievement alive and throbbing in his being while yet he was toiling on the way. And so the song kept singing itself by anticipation in his heart, when he was down in the valleys, and under the clouds, and within prison walls. At the end of the long, devious, burdensome way, the battles over between the two laws,— the law of his mind and the law of the flesh,— he sees himself waiting for himself in triumph, here a struggling soldier on the field, there a conqueror crowned.

The same kind of experience manifests itself in various ways in the manifold phases of human life. All faithful toilers for truth know what it is to wait long for the realization of their highest thought. Truth does not flash upon the world full mid-day at once; but it comes by slow gradation of light, building itself up ray by ray, like the glory of a sunrise upon the gradually displaced darkness. How long the great discoverers and inventors, the great scholars, poets, artists, have had to wait and toil, and toil and wait again at their tasks, before they have been able to reap the fruit of their toil! At first there comes to them a little gleam of light,— an idea, a thought, a kind of vision of some truth,— which at first may be very slight, and yet, impinges upon the mind with an intensity that so startles and holds attention that it will not move from its lodgement in the brain. By its very insistence, it creates belief in its genuineness,— as if it must needs be that what so urgently claims the recognition of an observing mind should be a part of the actual forces and relations that make the universe what it is. Thus, such an idea, thought, or vision of a truth becomes a part of the mental life of the person to whom it has come,— something to be cherished, cultivated, followed. It becomes grafted upon the nature like a new self, and yet may be only a natural unfolding of the old self; and, if it be large and grand enough, it will draw all the faculties and gifts of its possessor to its service, and shape for him a career and make a destiny. Yet there is hardly one who leaps to that destiny at a bound, or travels to the goal of a career without severe toil and many disappointments on the way. Even if truth has flashed upon some minds in an instant, it may have required long and arduous effort to find an adequate expression for revealing it clearly to the world. Kepler seized in a sudden flash of thought the law of the planetary orbits, but had to wait years before he could work out a mathematical demonstration of it.

The example of the men who make the great discoveries in the sciences and arts furnishes many moral and religious lessons. If we seek illustrations of enthusiasm, faith, persistency, patient labor, disinterested love of truth, heroic conquest of obstacles, splendid constancy to an ideal, we cannot find better specimens than are presented in this class of men. Here, we find many of the men who are the most trusting and patient waiters for self; men who believe so thoroughly in a thought that has come to them or a beneficent fact they have discovered, and in their power ultimately to make such thought or fact popularly accepted, that no difficulties can daunt them nor ridicule discourage nor opposition terrify. They may have to wait long, but they wait in faith that their claim shall yet be vindicated. When Columbus found America, he found the self he had long waited for at the same time. Bernard Palissy gave his whole life for sixteen years to the discovery of the decorative enamelling that made his name illustrious. In spite of cost, hardship, repeated failure, scoffing from unbelievers, he toiled on. He reduced himself and family to poverty, came almost to the last crust of bread, and finally had to tear up the floor of his cottage to get fuel for his all-devouring furnace. But this last desperate step of sacrifice was the one that brought him to his expected discovery and to his long waiting self. So every ardent toiler for truth, believing in the reality of the truth sought as thoroughly as he believes in his own existence, comes so to identify truth with his own existence that, when he cries with Archimedes, "I have found it! I have found it!" he might also cry, "I have found myself."

For the same thing may be said, substantially, of those whose interests and labors are directed more particularly to other spheres of truth,— philosophical, æsthetic, moral, and religious. Immanuel Kant was nearly sixty years old before he wrote the famous book, the *Critique of Pure Reason*, which gave such a powerful stimulus to thought and made a new era in the world of philosophy. For eleven years he was writing and rewriting that work, hardly knowing during the earlier part of the time where he was coming out or at what he was aiming, but pressed by a dissatisfaction with all existing philosophical systems and feeling within him a power to clear a way through their labyrinth of errors, if he could only succeed in faithfully unfolding and following that clew of thought which had vaguely but deeply impressed itself upon his consciousness as holding the mystery. And so through all these years he studied and worked at this thought, wrote and rewrote it, went round and through it and into all its consequences, and thus felt his way slowly and patiently along, but ever more confidently and clearly, until the New Philosophy stood in his mind and before the world in all its logical completeness, symmetry, and strength. Nor, previous to this time, had he shown any marked metaphysical ability, but only, as it were, the germ, struggling to unfold into the light but never quite succeeding, of metaphysical aspiration. He had tried theology, preaching, the physical sciences, mathematics, lectured in his university on anthropology, the theory of teaching, natural law, physical geography, and various other themes, showing the versatility of his mind and the breadth of his knowledge, and except in preaching, where he failed, meeting with a reasonable and constantly growing success; yet, in all this work and through all these years, that which was his deepest thought and yearning was not satisfied, was indeed hardly touched, and he did not show himself for the great man he was. He had not yet found his real self. For that supreme hour he waited — waited at hard work and small pay, never going in all his life more than forty miles away from his native town — for nearly sixty years; waited till the yearning within him grew into a passion, and the passion cleared the way for thought, and the thought clothed itself in masterly forms of logic and went forth to the world in books,— in books that revolutionized the philosophical thinking of Germany and will live in the mental life of mankind till the latest time. He waited long; but the deep, trustworthy, genuine self came at last.

Men of a different stamp of mind — poets, painters, sculptors, musical composers — are quite generally thought to do their work and to rise to their full measure of greatness by a sudden influx of power, by inspiration; and this is sometimes the case. Yet how often the moment of inspiration may have to be long waited for! The soul that is gifted with artistic genius has many a dream before the thoughts that aspire and burn within are able to shape themselves into solid artistic form. Not till the moment comes when the conditions of the sensitive inner organism and the conditions of outward circumstance are both attuned in rhythmic unity with the striving creative spirit within is that spirit able to manifest itself in the reality of art. And this is a moment that may be long deferred, — a moment that does not occur in every hour nor even in every year, and that to some souls of even the finest gifts only comes in perfection once, twice, or thrice perhaps in a lifetime. Such souls, therefore, though conscious of the artist's power within them, may have to wait through long, arid, and laborious years for the hour when the inner chaos of aspiration, impulse, and thought can shape itself cosmically into "a thing of beauty." Milton proved himself to have a poet's genius in his early years, and even then had thoughts of some high epic theme which should fully test his strength. But the civil commotions, the revolutions and wars in England, intervened; and for twenty years he was forced "to lay aside his singing robes," and appear as a champion of human liberty in political and social polemics and in practical offices for the State. He, too, was almost sixty years old before he found the poetic self so long waited for. Not till after many bitter experiences of calamity and pain, of political revolution and counter-revolution, of disappointment and blight to his affections, of assiduous and heroic labors in a hopeless cause,— not till after he had lived to see the political principles he had so openly and bravely espoused thoroughly defeated and repudiated in England, and he himself was pursued with obloquy and no public service was permitted him, and blindness had closed his vision to all outward light,— not till then did the inward poetic vision of his earlier years come back and shape itself into the poem that has given him an immortality of fame. Michel Angelo left, perhaps, at death more unrivalled products of his genius than any other artist the world has known. Yet his unfinished works were more than his finished; and some of the former show conceptions with which his mind had labored and which had come to him, doubtless, in the highest moments of his thought, but which his hand had not found itself adequate to put into color or stone. Magnificent as were his achievements and crowded with labor as was his long life, death found him at eighty-eight with a power still within him seemingly conscious that it had not yet fully uttered itself and must wait for more facile organs for executing its behests.

Or look at a very different kind of career,— at the life of any of the great religious teachers and reformers; at that of Jesus, for instance, as most familiar to us. It is evident that we have in the New Testament but a small part of the real biography of Jesus. We have a sketch — somewhat confused, and mixed, without doubt, to a considerable extent with legend, but more or less authentic — of the two or three years that constituted the public part of his life. Of all the thirty years that preceded the brief time of his public mission, we have only the fewest possible hints. But these hints indicate what we might naturally suppose would have been the case : that Jesus did not step at once, by the light of a sudden outburst of revelation, upon his great public career, but that through many years the thought, the summons, had been lying hidden in his mind and he had been brooding upon it,— in the closet, at his carpenter's bench, in the synagogue, and by his mother's side at home. It was there, in his young soul, when the boy drew apart from his father and mother and went back to ask questions of the rabbis in the temple. It was there,— this brooding question of his destiny, this haunting vision of what he might become and do for the good of his people, this consciousness of a possible spiritual messiahship which might in his person fulfil the expectations and yearnings of his race,— it was there when he went to be taught of John the Baptist and to be baptized by him ; there, too, when he went into the desert, apart from all human kind, after the manner of a hermit,— for self-communion, for it was the impulse that drove him thither ; and it was there through all the doubts, darkness, and tempting suggestions of that season of solitude, confidently abiding its time and awaiting its triumph. It was not till after all these years of waiting, these trials and self-searchings, that even Jesus found himself and his mission.

Now, the lives of these great workers — these prophets, seers, artists, sages, who make so large a part of human history — only present in larger and finer picture, in more effective grouping and richer beauty, elements of mental and moral life which are to some degree the possession of all of us. There is one law of growth, of progress, of accomplishment and power, that runs through the whole family of mankind. "First the blade, then the ear, then the full corn in the ear,"— that is the law for man as well as nature. And between the time when the blade first appears, a little streak of living green, above the ground, and the time when the full sheaves, ripened, are borne home, there may be long seasons of drouth or wet, of burning heat or killing frost, when the powers of life are tested to the utmost, and even hope is only kept alive by faith in the great law which brings seed-time and harvest in their order and never fails. Whether a man possess one talent or ten, the law for use and increase is the same. There is the same slow process of unfolding, the same liableness to disappointed hopes, the same subjection to hindering conditions, the same waiting expectancy that the heart's deepest and most consecrated purpose shall yet emerge from all impediments, free and triumphant. We may even say that the highest thought or purpose of the universe itself did not reveal itself at once full-grown and full fruit, but ripened slowly. When we see through what incalculably long processes of preparation the material world, with its vast variety of creatures, was passing, to make ready for the advent of man on this planet,— by what a devious pathway of struggle, of tentative efforts, of conflicts of force against force, nature passed before man emerged as the consummate product of the whole,— we may say indeed, and say it with all reverence, that even infinite Being waited long for himself; waited long and wrought patiently for the coming of a finite form so organized that his own attributes and purpose might be self-manifest therein.

And we are offspring of that Being; and as he worketh and waiteth for himself, reacheth not his sublimest forms of revelation at once, but weaveth by degrees the garment of glory by which he is seen, so must we work and wait for the highest revelation of ourselves,— expecting to see our cherished hope often deferred, but never to see it conquered; doing our best with present conditions and opportunities, but — or *therefore* we might rather say — looking confidently to the future to bring us to something better than any past or present has ever afforded. In one form or another, it is the destined lot of every human being to wait for himself. Our duty is *here*, at the post of present responsibility, of present joy, sorrow, temptation, or trial; and here, with various degrees of faithfulness or unfaithfulness, we are doing or neglecting to do the requirement of the hour. But, whether doing or neglecting to do, there is no one of us whose heart's ideal is not *yonder*, away ahead of us, awaiting our tardy coming.

The waiting ideal perhaps is mental, or perhaps it is moral. It may be a career of which we have had some youthful vision, but which, from outward circumstance or inward infirmity of purpose, we have hitherto failed to attain. It may be some form of unsatisfied affections, leaving a vacancy and a yearning not yet filled in the heart. It may be some beckoning path of philanthropy, once enchanting our eyes, but not yet offering the looked-for opportunity or summoning the needed self-consecration which makes opportunity. Or it may be some high attainment of character, some inward self-conquest, some decisive triumph over a strong and degrading temptation, — a triumph which will set our faculties free for the good service of which we are conscious they are capable, but a triumph which is yet delayed by our own halting purposes and treacherous passions. In whatever form the waiting, unattained ideal appear, it presents the same pathos of contrast between a self that has failed and a self that still hopes; between purposes, visions, and aspirations which have hitherto been checked and frustrated and an inner sanctuary of faith, yearning, and courage which will not yield to despair nor death, but which look across the grave of every worsted and down-stricken resolution with eyes that behold another self, and that the real self, in the resurrection robes of victory. Even the most degraded victim of vicious courses does not lose all hope in a better fortune to come. He, too, has moments of some purer aspiration and thought, — moments when down into his darkness and wretchedness there streams a ray of the great

Light which fills the heavens and overspreads the world, and toward which he can but lift his eyes in earnest longing. In that moment, "he comes to himself"; and, in coming to himself, he turns again toward father and mother and home. In the very act of lifting his eyes to the Light, he greets his better self, and in the radiance of that upper glory sees himself as he yet may be.

So with us all. Whatever may be our lot, whatever the form of our longed-for ideal, whatever hindrances and delays may beset our course, and however long and burdensome may still seem the unfinished way before us, if we are but faithful to present light, to to-day's opportunity and duty, there is a better self waiting for us in triumph at the end. In that which waits there is a Divinity that appeals invincibly to a divine purpose and hope in that which is waited for, and there is no power in the universe that can prevent the coming together of this cause and this consequence. The waiting may be long, the earthly pilgrimage may not end it; but by and by, if not on earth, then in some celestial morning, the soul may wake to a surprise of felicity,— perhaps not that dreamed of, but something greater and better than that, like a clear, calm sunrise after a starless and tempestuous night.

December 10, 1876.

XVIII.

THE SILENT REVELATION.

"Does heaven speak? The four seasons pursue their courses, and all things are being continually produced; but does heaven say anything?"—CONFUCIUS.

"They have no speech nor language, and their voice is not heard; yet their line is gone out through all the earth, and their words to the end of the world."—HEBREW PSALM.

THESE fine words, in their different ways, from Hebrew and Chinese Scripture, utter essentially the same thought, *the Silentness of Nature's Revelations;* and it is to this thought and its lessons that I wish to call attention this morning.

Nature is ever active, ever at work, ever producing the grandest results; yet she never utters a syllable of her purpose, never whispers in advance her intent to any curious ear. In silence are her tasks achieved. All her activities have a profound significance, yet not until those activities have brought forth their completed results is their meaning disclosed. She reveals herself, not in speech, but in deeds; tells what she means to do only by what she has done; assures us by the character of her achievements, not by the eloquence of her promises. True, her work goes on not in absolute silence. Sound of all kinds accompanies it. She shouts, she sings, she sighs. She thunders in the tempest, roars and moans in the ocean, whistles in the wind, chirps in the insect, becomes musical in the throat of the bird and the voice of man. She shrieks from pain and makes melody for joy. Yet she articulates nothing. She is dumb and silent, so far as revealing her thought and purpose by intelligible language is concerned. Though her sound has gone out to the ends of the world, yet she has no speech nor language, and her voice is not heard. The sounds are incidents of her work, but not conditions of revelation. They are themselves a part of the mystery to be revealed, and are only understood when the whole intent is made evident in the finished product. The inanimate forces make their various noise, the brutes cry, man speaks; but heaven is silent. The finite forms of earthly force utter their voice as if striving to phrase their meaning; but heaven, the infinite Power, says nothing. In silence it does its work, and leaves its work to speak for itself.

The thing done is Nature's revelation, and its significance is disclosed only by the interpreting mind that has observed the process. The morning stars never sang together to reveal the harmonies of their movements; but the song came from the musical soul of man, who watched these silent orbs of heaven until the order and rhythm of their movements were translated for him into melody. The seasons, as they come and go, say nothing of what they mean to do. It is only by what they have done, for years and generations and ages past, that we know what is in their heart to do this coming year. Look at the forces which, in any year, build up the glory of the summer. Not a word do they utter of their intent, not a syllable lisp of the mighty things they mean to do. The invisible powers, as they began to stir around us again last spring, did not go to loudly boasting: " Now see what great things we will do! We will carpet the earth through all these northern zones with green ; we will dress the trees in gorgeous robes ; we will bring flowers, rich with all hues, to plant and shrub ; and fruit that shall follow in its turn, to bless man and beast." But in silence and patience and little by little, the minute, unseen forces went to their work, not uttering a boast or a word of what they were doing, until the glory and the beauty were spread all around us in a living revelation to eye and heart. No voice, no language, yet has their line, indeed, gone out to all the earth. Had that been the first time that any human eyes had gazed on such a phenomenon, it would have been to us a miracle. We should not have had the slightest idea of its purport or intended result, and in vain should we have pleaded with heaven to utter any word for interpreting the meaning of the miracle. Heaven would have been as silent as the forces themselves. But, though no miracle, the wonder of the phenomenon is none the less ; and the meaning of it has been revealed only by the silent faithfulness of the forces to their appointed tasks through many generations and ages of human experience. Only by what again and again they have done, do we have faith in what they are doing and will do at any present season.

Or look back farther into Nature's laboratories. When the heavens were forming into firmaments and worlds; when the chaotic masses of vapor were concentrating into fluids, and the fluids into solids; when the processes were going on by which life gradually appeared on these worlds, and the life diverged into manifold species, and these species on our earth prefigured and prepared the way for man,— through all the vast processes, extending through periods of time which no mathematics can compute nor imagination grasp,— Nature uttered no prophetic voice to disclose her purpose. Her forces labored in silence at their great secret. ' Could any listening ear have been there, it would have detected not the faintest whisper of her meaning. Not from the heaven above or the earth beneath was anything *said*. There was only something *doing*. And it was not until the thing was done, not until man appeared, and not until he had been on the earth a hundred thousand years or more,— not, in truth, until this century in which we are living, when man has turned up the strata of the earth and learned the science of its creation, and studied the forces of the heavens through his telescope and the life of lands and seas through his microscope,— not until now has it been discovered that these silent forces all along carried the secret in their bosom. They carried the secret, but did not tell it. All along they meant something, and meant probably just that which has come to pass. But they did not tell what they meant until the thing appeared to speak for itself.

But it is to be noted next that, though Nature has no voice and utters no articulate prophecies concerning her intentions, she yet does disclose her character, does reveal herself. As has already been said, she reveals herself in doing. Silent, she yet speaks. Could we suppose ourselves to meet her for the first time, to our bewildered and even agonizing petitions for some word of light as to her future relations to us, she would be dumb. Only by a silent gesture would she bid us wait and see. But knowing her as we do by our own familiar experience of her actions, and by the aggregate inherited experience of unnumbered generations of our ancestors, she speaks to us through all that gathered knowledge. All her past actions, so dumb while they were in process of performance, now have tongues that speak to us clearly of her present intentions and her future results. We know her, and can trust her almost better than ourselves. No life-long friend, beloved, leaned upon at our side, is more thoroughly known or a surer reliance. Even the dependence on impartial parental love is not more sure than the confidence with which we cling to the hand of our silent mother Nature,— the mother who never spoke one word of promise to our ears, but whom we know by her faithfulness to all the generations of men. Through this accumulating experience, this aggregate knowledge of the human race, drawn from daily life with her, is Nature revealed. By what she did yesterday and the day before, and through all the yesterdays, do we read her intentions for to-day and to-morrow and the days and years thereafter. And, thus knowing her, we know her not only as power, but as power that works toward order, method, harmony, beauty, use. We know that her forces work with such constancy and with such regularity of tension toward a definite result that we call her operations laws. To them, we know that human law must bend and human power be subservient. And, if by any means any of her methods which we name laws can be evaded or abrogated, it is only by calling into service some other of her forces that is for that time and place superior, or setting into operation another law. Nothing is more clearly known in the universe than that Nature is a law-abiding power,— that she is moved by an impulse that is not reckless, not chance, not whim, not caprice, but an impulse that aims in a definite direction and for a definite result. Whatever apparent exceptions there may be, human experience has yet learned that her aims may be trusted, her forces confided in. The whole stability of society depends upon this trust,— that what Nature has been and done she will continue to be and do. All this common experience teaches.

But science shows more. Science shows that, along with this law-abidingness, this constancy, there is an order that means progress, advance, unity of plan, unfoldment of purpose, growth into ever finer symmetry of proportion and beauty of form. Deep within the beauty which all eyes see there is advance to a higher idea of beauty. Deep within the movement of forces which all minds can comprehend there is the harmonious unfoldment of a vast cosmic plan which has become revealed only to the eye of scientific intelligence, by which these forces are seen to be self-improving and self-regenerating forces: so that Nature, when we look upon her mighty periods of activity, has been advancing upon her own work, making the bad good and the good better, as if aiming at a best. Thus, though working in silence, does Nature make her revelations and win our trust.

And now I want to draw into some simple and brief shape some of the moral and spiritual lessons of the theme.

The first lesson that would naturally suggest itself lies in the parallelism which might be drawn between this history of Nature and the history of the human race, illustrating how the great human exhibitions of power, how the great epochs that have actually stood in history for the revelation of new principles, and how even those epochs that have been called special eras of religious revelation, have rather advanced by the unseen strength of silently operating forces than by any sudden intervention of marvellous power from the heavens or even noisy demonstration of human speech. Not until the epochs have come and actually made their mark is humanity able to read their full meaning.

Jesus and his disciples little thought, I suppose, what was in the bosom of that one idea which they preached with such persistency, "the coming of the kingdom of God." Their business was to plant the idea. But, concerning the forces by which it was to grow and spread and assimilate to itself other ideas and unfold from itself things which they never dreamed of being in it, they had no responsibility nor obligation. The speech was small, considering the result that came, and does not account for it. The important sentences of the Sermon on the Mount can be found piecemeal in the sayings of Hebrew rabbis before Jesus. The doctrine of love to God and Man was the sum and substance of the Jewish religion. Jew and Persian alike had looked for a Messiah. Neo-Platonists and Platonizing Jews were inculcating a doctrine of the *Logos*, or Divine Word, seed of a new dogma of incarnation, the development of which had such a mighty influence in shaping Christian theology. Thus, silently, in many directions and under many soils, were the seeds of the new era germinating; and the era had come and passed before people knew that it had come enough to name and to reckon back to it. The new revelation was rather the aggregate character of all that had been done than any special speech. It was the new growth, the new life, of the manifold silent forces that were operating in the human communities that made up the Roman Empire eighteen and nineteen centuries ago.

So, again, the first movers in the Protestant Reformation little dreamed of all that their acts meant. It is hard, indeed, to find the first movers, so inextinguishably does the religious movement shade off into an intellectual and political one. But not even did Luther and his brave compeers foresee all that was to come from their doctrine of private judgment as against the voice of the priest and the Church. Perhaps they would have shrunk from it, if they had. But it was not theirs to foresee nor to proclaim the result. It was theirs only to do the duty of their own hour. Within their duty, concealed in the heart of their deeds, other forces were working in silence, with other meaning and for greater results. With the results, the revelation of the meaning of the Protestant reform has come; but this revelation could not be made nor understood then. It was not even outwardly prophesied, though Luther and his helpers were of the type of prophets. The genuine prophet, perhaps, never knows that he prophesies. The prophecy is uttered through him more by his entire character and attitude than by his spoken message, and only when the fulfilment of it comes is its meaning revealed. Thus it was also in the birth and growth of our own nation. The processes that finally ultimated in a national consciousness and power among the American colonies were of long duration, and were silently operating through many minds that spoke no public word and little dreamed whither they were tending. Separation from Great Britain was a thought at first too daring to be broached.

And so, in general, in human history as in the history of Nature: it is by the faithfulness of the unseen and silent forces to certain appointed tasks of the hour that the great advances are made, and the inner meaning of the forces that thus work through nature and through man is revealed. Not so much by any uttered words in behalf of righteousness, though spoken never so eloquently by prophet or martyr, as by the silent grip with which the masses of civilized mankind adhere to truth and virtue, is the stability of society assured. There are principles of mental and moral intelligence which have come to have the same constancy in the world of mankind as the laws of physical force in the world of matter, and upon which we rely with the same security. They may never have been spoken from the heavens, they may not even have been intuitive endowments of the human mind when man first made his appearance on the earth; but, as now seems most likely, they may have been gradually and slowly evolved through the various discipline of human and ante-human experience, and may be mingled with human infirmity and error; yet deeper than aught else in man's nature they declare the purport and destiny of his being. They are the silent witnesses, which, growing clearer and clearer with man's historic advance, interpret for him all other revelations, and

> " Which, be they what they may,
> Are yet the fountain light of all our day,
> Are yet a master light of all our seeing."

One is tempted to inculcate as another lesson of the theme more reliance on the silent working of moral forces in the amelioration of human society. Certainly, when we regard the incessant speech-making that is going on among men, the immeasurable quantity of words that, through the living voice or the printed page, one portion of mankind is uttering for the benefit or entertainment of another portion, and when we regard the tumult, tug, and tussle of it all, one may be pardoned if he sometimes longs for the mythical half-hour of silence that is said to have occurred in heaven at the opening of creation's drama. And, seriously, it may be asked whether, in schemes of education and of social reform and philanthropy, we are not in danger of relying too much on talk, while we lose sight of the silent influence of character and the potency of quiet deeds. Whatever may be said of the power of words and of the influence exerted by a great master of speech, the men who do rather than the men who say are yet humanity's leaders. The resolute act is stronger than the eloquent speech. This, of course, is not to say that speech has not its proper place and service, nor that any great social work is likely to be done without great and earnest words being somewhere spoken in its behalf. Much less is it to inculcate any fatal listlessness to calls for moral and philanthropic service, and a passive trust that the work will somehow be done without our aid. I have no sympathy with that merely dilettante interest in reform which professes to believe that things will somehow come right of themselves, while human beings lie back at ease, and look on. Rather is it to appeal for more aid by acts that I cast suspicion upon the easy mood of talk. Talk that has not originated in silent thought, and will not bear the test of silent thought, is worse than weak. And so I think that public talkers (and private, too) need often to recur to silent meditation to recruit their strength. If some of us never came out of the silence with public discourse, the world might be no loser. But in the silence of private meditation have the great thoughts been born that have moved the world. A master speaker may stir a listening mind to some heroic resolution. But the heroic resolution that is made under the mastering silence of a noble thought that has taken possession of the mind is more likely to remain as an abiding power in the life. "While I was musing," says the Hebrew Psalm, "the fire burned." Meditation no less than speech may kindle zeal, and is necessary for sustenance to moral strength. Channing once said, "There is no eloquence like the deep silence of a crowd." I used to prize the silence of the Quaker meeting as often better than the speech that broke it. There may indeed be an empty silence as there is empty speech; but the empty silence, at least, does not invade others' rights, as the inane speaking does. Better the empty silence than the hollow words. But there is a silence that is felt like an inspiration. It is the silence that is alive with emotion and thought. Such silence is vital with the seeds of mighty actions. It holds the secrets of many hearts, which shall one day be revealed in deeds.

But I must hasten on to speak of one or two other lessons which may come closer to the individual experience of us all. It is the lot of our humanity that we are, not infrequently, cast into perplexing and painful straits of life, where we long for a word of revelation, which is not vouchsafed, to lead us out of our difficulties and show us our future. We often say, If we only knew what the future is to bring to pass, how much more content we might be, and how much more wisely act in the present! What, we anxiously ask, is to be the consequence of our taking this course or that? What is to be the coming career of our children and of others we love? The young themselves are often troubled with anxieties about their future course in life. If they only knew what they are best fitted for, what they can best succeed in, how easy would seem present duties! To-day, perhaps, nothing seems to open: what, then, will it be to-morrow? Sometimes we may be watching by a sick-bed, or watching with painful uncertainty our own health. Or, harder still, we may in dread suspense be watching the uncertain moral steps of one we love better than our own life. Oh, if we only knew! we say. And sometimes the questions so press upon us that in our helplessness and despair we are tempted to cry out for the heavens to be opened and a special revealing message to be sent to our aid. But to all these entreaties the heavens say nothing. To all such pleadings there only comes the answer of silence. Is heaven, then, dumb? Does it deny all revelation? No: not more surely does its shining canopy of blue embrace to-day the gladsome earth and nurse its waiting life than it broods with silent care over the human soul, and has given to it all the revelation that it needs. It is a fallacy to suppose

that to know with certainty the future is to reveal
present duty. For our duty is not so much concerned with consequences as with motives. Consequences may depend on many wills, on many concurrent forces entirely beyond our control. But our
duty concerns our present act alone. Moreover, to
ask to know our future, or any future with which
we have concern, is to ask an impossibility. That
future is to depend to some extent upon what we
do at this present time; and it rightly so depends,
by the great law of moral responsibility. And to
ask that we may know the future so as to determine
present action by it is to reverse this primal law of
human development. We must ourselves, by our
present faithfulness, help to make that future. And
it is seldom that the duty of the present moment,
the duty that is the very next to be done, is not
revealed. The necessary revelation has been vouchsafed in the silent working of our own reason, in the
light of conscience, in the natural influx of a love
that binds us in ties of sympathy to our kind and
makes us both strong and tender toward all human
wants. In the faithful activity of these great faculties,— Reason, Conscience, disinterested Love,—
the law of life is revealed. And if, even with these
silent revealers of duty's path, the present opening
for that path may seem to us closed and we see not
where to apply our hand; if, having done all within
our power, we seem to be called only to the post of
passive submission and endurance,— let us remember still that "they also serve who only stand and
wait."

And there is another silent waiting imposed upon us, and wisely, by the necessary conditions of our knowledge, another waiting for a revelation which is made only in silence to the waiting heart,—the revelation of the kind of life that is to be after this life of earth. If human entreaties from the time mankind began their existence could have brought a disclosure of the futurity after death, all the mysteries of heaven would now be open to our gaze. But not a syllable of the great mystery has yet been articulated that can permanently satisfy or that is worthy of the quest. The curtain hangs there, drawn by a silent hand; and it hangs there wisely. Let us not profane its sanctity by hands that with too curious eagerness would lift it aside. Infinitely better is it to wait in the quietude of a patient hope. Yet is there no revelation made? The revelation of all future life is silently made in the life that now is, — in those deep qualities of life that draw their sustenance from eternal fountains, and so proclaim their own immortality; in the wisdom and goodness which are adequate to all emergencies of our earthly life, and which we may trust to provide what is worthiest and best for the life hereafter.

December 16, 1877.

XIX.

THE RELIGION OF HUMANITY.

"No man is so great as mankind."—THEODORE PARKER.

I PROPOSE to speak to you this morning on the topic suggested by the phrase "The Religion of Humanity." It is a phrase that has come into use somewhat in these latter years to indicate a type of religion that is growing up, mainly, outside of ecclesiastical lines and independent of the old claims of religious authority. In the history of religious thought, the phrase was first adopted by the French philosopher, Auguste Comte, who turned it to a certain philosophical use, to signify, in his hierarchy of the intellectual and social sciences, the place and service of religion. In his system of positive knowledge, or of science as based only on phenomena and their generalized laws, theology had no place. He declared that theology represented the obsolete and obsolescent child-mood of the human mind; that it grew out of the disposition to refer to supernatural agencies things which the human understanding could not account for by natural causes. But, though theology was not recognized by Comte as having any valid basis, and though he believed in no Deity as a first cause, nor in personal immortality, nor in any special religious revelation as having a claim to authority over the human mind, yet he conceded the vast power and service of the religious sentiment; and upon it, newly directed, he mentally constructed and endeavored to put into practical operation a new system of religion, with a complete *cultus* and all the officers and equipments of an organized church. He called religion the crown of all the social sciences, the goal of sociology. He defined it as "the complete harmony of human existence, individual and collective, or the universal unity of all existence in one Great Being," whom he calls Humanity. Emancipated from the crude primitive forms of polytheistic worship and from the vague metaphysical conception of a single Deity in the skies, the religious sentiment, he claimed, would finally ripen into the personal devotion and self-sacrifice of individual being for the welfare of universal humanity. Hence the name, "Religion of Humanity," which the stringent disciples of Comte still use as a title for their special religious beliefs.

In this usage, however, the phrase has a somewhat technical, if not sectarian meaning. It must at least be said that Comte's plan of an organized church, however revolutionary his ideas, was modelled too closely after the Roman Catholic Church to gain much headway in the modern world. He adopted very much of the old ecclesiastical machinery and not a little of the papal idea of ecclesiastical authority, from which he thought the common people were not ripe for release. The saints' days and festivals he changed into days of homage to the world's great religious and moral teachers of all faiths,— as Moses, Socrates, Zoroaster, Jesus, Mohammed, etc. He even projected a reform of the calendar, so as to name the months and days of the week after the names of distinguished benefactors of the human race. But, with all his wealth of learning and his wide grasp of intellect, Comte apparently does not seem to have perceived that the people who were ready for emancipation from the old ecclesiastical authority, the people who were prepared to understand and welcome his revolutionary thought, would not be easily marshalled under the sway of a new external authority in matters of faith. And so his grand plan of a new church remains only a model — on paper. He made the mistake of thinking that a religion, instead of being a natural growth, was an architectural structure to be artificially built.

But the phrase "Religion of Humanity" is suggestive; and it suggests something more important for our notice than the French philosopher's elaborate scheme of a new form of worship and a new church. It suggests certain tendencies and forces in modern society, certain lines and methods of thought, certain drifts of opinion and belief, by which old religious ideas and usages are being revolutionized, and, inside of churches and outside of churches, in the midst of dissolving creeds and worships, an essentially new form of religion is growing up. And it is chiefly these tendencies and movements that I have in mind in bringing the subject here. They are observable not only in

Christendom, but in other religions,— in Judaism, in Buddhism, in Brahmanism, in Mohammedanism, in the little remnant of the Parsee faith that still survives. In every religion which has a constituency respectably civilized there is a progressive party, a section that feels the influence of modern ideas and is astir with the mental and moral life of modern times. This party, which is following the authority of reason rather than that of old ecclesiastical faiths, may still keep, perhaps, the old religious names, only modifying them, it may be, by the prefix *liberal*, as Liberal Christian, Liberal Hebrew, Liberal Mohammedan. But the tendency, wherever found, is in the same direction; the movement, whatever its starting-point, is toward a common goal And, when the movement becomes more self-conscious and self-centred, it will most likely find some new and common name for its now separate branches.

In the first place, the phrase "Religion of Humanity" suggests an antithesis to the religion of supernaturalism. The prevailing idea concerning religion — of all religion commonly regarded as true and efficacious — is that it is of supernatural origin and is preserved by supernatural agencies. Its light is not believed to be the light of the common human reason, of natural conscience, of the aspiring human spirit, but a light miraculously revealed from the heavens. Its first promulgators are claimed to have been specially commissioned by the Almighty for their work, endowed with the power to perform miracles to attest their authority. Its Bibles were written, it is alleged, by supernaturally inspired men.

Its doctrines could have never been discovered by the unassisted human mind, but were sent into the human mind directly from heaven. Its church was organized under specific divine commands, and has been directed by a special outpouring of the divine Spirit in no wise natural to humanity. The kind of faith that it inculcates may harmonize with human reason or it may conflict with it; but, in any event, it is superior to human reason, being the direct gift of God. The kind of prayer that it inculcates is the asking of God for spiritual or temporal favors, in the belief that effectual prayer will bring from the Being addressed, by some supernatural process, the needed answer. Such are some of the main characteristics of supernatural religion. They are not specially Christian or Hebrew. They belong quite as much to other religions. The devotees of all the great religions of mankind have believed in the supernatural origin and protection of their own special faith.

To all these beliefs, the Religion of Humanity is opposed. Its primary principle is that religion is the natural product of the human mind, of the human race,— of the human mind aspiring indeed toward infinite Mind, searching after a First Cause, seeking to come into practical relations with that which gives life and law to all finite existences, but still the human mind. When ecclesiastical religion says, "Religious truth came by revelation," the Religion of Humanity replies, Revelation is natural. It is the human mind unfolding by natural impulse to truth as a flower to the sun. When ecclesiastical religion says, "Special divine inspiration is necessary to bring religion upon the earth," the Religion of Humanity answers, Inspiration is by natural law: it is "the light that lighteth every man that cometh into the world." The Religion of Humanity knows no miracle greater than the laws of nature. It believes that the human mind, by natural relationship, is connected with the source of all that is, and by natural processes draws its life from that inexhaustible fountain. But, since the religions have their origins on the human side of this relationship, and since they necessarily have their historical development within human conditions, the Religion of Humanity affirms that they are all subject to human limitations, to human error and infirmity; that they partake of the race-characteristics of the people holding them, and correspond to their phase of mental enlightenment and culture; and that none of them can legitimately claim infallibility.

The Religion of Humanity consequently asserts that the special religions are progressive; that they are evolutions, not outright creations; that none of them was given fully matured, with ritual and doctrine and precept complete, but that all have grown and been shaped by the natural exigencies of all historical development; that their doctrines have been wrought and rewrought in the chemistry of human thought; that their rituals have been gradually moulded into form by the spiritual imagination of the people adopting them; that even their moral impulses have taken direction, their very virtues been modified, and their character been transformed, by the conditions of the changing epochs through which they have passed. There is found no such fixity in religion, no such unchangeableness of doctrine or spirit or method in religious history, as the claim to supernatural origin and supernatural preservation would imply. The process of religious development is traced in the ordinary grooves of human history. It is closely allied with the natural development of human intelligence, of language, of literature, of nationalities, and is as easily accounted for on natural grounds as is any of these. To whatever spheres of truth, to whatever forces of vital power, beyond and above humanity, religion may be linked,— and that it is connected with such there is no denial,— this connection is by laws and processes perfectly natural. The outreaching, all-embracing sphere of truth comes naturally within human cognizance. The circle, however high it may arch, dips down to the natural vision of the human mind; and the human mind, by natural attraction, follows the circle upward. Wherever the vital forces that sustain the universe may have their primal source, the well-springs by which humanity is to live and do its work are within the natural domain of the human mind, close to its daily tasks, and do not have to be opened by any miracle to be of avail. Therefore it is that this view of religion may be called the Religion of Humanity,— that is, it is religion conceived as having its historical beginning in the human mind, its development in the natural limits of human history, its vital power all along as associated by the natural relationships of human faculty with whatever may be the ultimate Source and Unity of all power,— in contradistinction from that view which refers the original existence of religion to supernatural revelation, and its continuance to supernatural preservation.

From this primary principle, it follows, secondly, that to the Religion of Humanity the special religions are so many different sects. Just as Christendom is divided into numerous sects, Baptists, Episcopalians, Catholics, Unitarians, Quakers, and the like, just as Judaism and Buddhism and Mohammedanism have also had their conflicting sects, so these various religions, Judaism, Buddhism, Christianity, Mohammedanism, etc., make the larger sects into which the religion of mankind is divided. And as each sect of a special religion thinks that it has the true faith or form of that religion, and that all the others are at some point or points in error, so the devotees of each of the world's great religions think that they have the true faith, and that all other forms of religion are erroneous. And hence between the religions, just as between the sects of a particular religion, the sectarian spirit prevails, and sectarian controversies and conflicts exist. No controversies are so bitter as those which spring from sectarian animosities. No wars were ever so fierce or so bloody as those which have been declared in the name of religion. No armies were ever led against each other with such relentless and destructive collision as those which have been marshalled under antagonistic banners of religious faith, each claimed to be the standard of the true God, and therefore pledged to conquer. To the Religion of Humanity, this sectarian spirit between the religions, as between the smaller sects of the same religion, is all wrong. From it has come not only enormous and cruel destruction of human life, but immense waste of human power,—waste of intellectual energy, disastrous misdirection of moral and spiritual enthusiasm, self-consecrations arrayed against each other in fatal combat, and neutralizing each other's aims, instead of combining their might for the welfare of mankind. There is no sadder sight in history than this sight, so common, of religious enthusiasm battling against religious enthusiasm; than the spiritual consecration of one portion of mankind—this highest demonstration of power of which man is capable—in deadly conflict with the spiritual consecration of another portion of mankind. Yet, so long as the religions of the world, in a sectarian spirit, lay exclusive claims to supernatural communications with divine truth, each arrogating to itself the privilege of having the only saving knowledge of God, this wasting, ruinous antagonism is inevitable. To the Religion of Humanity, it is morally and mentally wrong. Since, in its view, no religion is infallible, none supernaturally authenticated, none miraculously guaranteed to contain the truth, the whole truth, and nothing but the truth, so this sectarian dispute and warfare among them are as irrational in logic as they are bitter in spirit and destructive in practice.

This rational theory of religion does not affirm,

indeed, that all of the special religions are alike in value. It does not claim that their contents are equal. It does not say that they are all equally enlightened or equally spiritual or equally adapted to serve the needs of all nations alike to-day. All that it asserts is that the religions originated and grew by the same natural process; that no one of them can assume supremacy over the rest by reason of any difference in respect to birth or family. But that the religions should differ in the relative value of their contents is as natural as that literatures should differ, or that languages should differ, or that nations should differ in respect to civilization and culture, or that individual persons, born of the same parents, should differ in intelligence and character. The Religion of Humanity, however, is not so much concerned to display these natural and readily conceded differences, nor so eager to prove by detailed comparisons that this particular religion is superior to that, as it is desirous to discover and disclose the things that are good and true in all the religions, and to acknowledge that, in their time and place, they have all rendered some good service to mankind. It finds in them all a moral standard better than the prevailing moral practice and a spiritual aspiration that shames the average grossness of daily living. It will not commit what has well been called the flagrant injustice of comparing the low-water mark of one religion with the high-water mark of a neighboring faith,— the present practical moral condition of India, for instance, with the ethical standard of the Sermon on the Mount; for this is a mode of comparison that might be turned end for end, and be made to strike quite as effectively in another direction. Christendom has had, for example, the Sermon on the Mount for eighteen hundred years; and yet the average practical morality of the most enlightened Christian country to-day might be put to the blush by the side of many a chapter of moral precepts from the Scriptures of Asiatic Brahmanism and Buddhism. Nor, even comparing practice with practice, can Christendom boast very loudly over non-Christian countries. Keshub Chunder Sen, the native reformer of the Brahmanistic faith in British India, on his visit to England a few years since, was astonished and grieved at the moral condition of this leading nation of Christendom,— at the prevailing grossness in eating and drinking, the intemperance, the costly entertainments, and material extravagance of all sorts, the struggle after and worship of wealth, the inequality between the rich and the poor, the degradation and criminality of large sections of population, and the merciless recklessness with which the upper strata of society, with few exceptions, push their interests, roughshod, over the bodies and souls of the lower. This was a heathen judgment on Christian England.

But there is little profit in these comparisons, on the one side or the other, except as a means of rectifying partisan and sectarian judgments. More profitable is it for the devotees of the different religions to seek out their agreements and identities; to inquire how much ground they hold in common;

to compare ideas and theories in the spirit of truth-seeking; to meet each other half-way across the dismantled walls that have hitherto divided them into hostile camps, and to ask each other how they can best put their forces together for the amelioration of the human degradation and distress around them. To the Religion of Humanity, it is not so vital a point to decide with precision by just how much one religion may be theoretically better than another as it is to bring out and make practically applicable what is good in them all. The intellectual and spiritual rank of the religions may be left to the rational judgment of the historian, of the antiquarian investigator,— to the ultimate conscientious judgment of mankind. But, in every one of the great religions, even in those deemed the poorest, there is enough of pure moral truth to save all their professed adherents, if they would only live up to it. And the question with the Religion of Humanity that presses before all others is how to make this truth of avail, and turn it into practical benefit.

For, again, it is another characteristic of the Religion of Humanity that it is more eager to improve the present condition of mankind than to settle any disputed question of theology or to discuss the relative merits of the many forms of ecclesiasticism. This, indeed, is its main object,— the improvement of man's moral, mental, and physical condition here in this present world,— in a word, the enlightenment and elevation of mankind. This object, to be a *humanitarian* religion, dominates all others, and might well be regarded as giving to the rising modern faith its name. It would be a Religion of Humanity in deed as well as in word. Questions concerning man's origin and early history are not void of profit,— far from it. Not even are stories of Gardens of Eden, and of Golden Ages in the past, and of Deities visiting the earth, walking visibly among men, conversing with them, and writing books for the use of mankind, wholly without interest to historical investigation. But it is a higher proof of moral and religious purpose to strive to make a Garden of Eden and a Golden Age and a Divine Presence on earth to-day than to put faith in these traditions of bygone times. This rationalistic, humane religion does not deny that there is a life hereafter,— some future world for man; but it affirms that man's chief and all-controlling duty is here and now in this present world,— that to perform well his part on the globe and in the sphere to which he is now allotted, and thus to show that he is able to manage wisely and well the world he now possesses, will be the best possible preparation for any world that is to be given to him hereafter. This view of religion does, indeed, in contradistinction from what has been the prevailing teaching of the Christian Church, lay more emphasis on the life that now is than on the future life. It arraigns, in fact, the popular Christian theology for drawing man's thought too much away to the life hereafter, so that duties here are liable to be neglected in dreamings and visions of a future bliss. The Religion of Humanity says, Let the vision of the future remain a vision, a hope, a faith, if you can; but let it not entice moral interest and energy away from the pressing responsibilities and stern realities of the present time. *Here* is our place for the present, here our task, our charge, our mission. Let us insure the hoped-for felicity now, on earth, right in the spot where lies our daily task, by a faithful inquiry how we can best discharge our obligations to our fellow-men and to ourselves, and by a faithful obedience to our own highest ideals of duty. Mr. Ruskin somewhere says that that is the true mother church where every man takes the hand of every other man helpfully. And to bring in this era of fraternity, of brotherhood, of mutual helpfulness,— to remove as far as possible the burdens that oppress men, to enlighten ignorance, lessen misery, assuage suffering, prevent sin,— is the aim of the Religion of Humanity.

Some of the old ecclesiastical types of religion, in their efforts to imprison the human mind, in their attempts to stifle human thought and fetter personal liberty, in their contemptuous and even malignant treatment of the human body, in their persistent struggles to bandage and bondage the human soul, and to keep it in a condition of mental and spiritual childhood, and in their threats of infinite torture in an eternal future by way of enforcing their teachings, may rightly be styled religions of *Inhumanity*. From all such bondage, from all such cruel terrors, the Religion of Humanity endeavors to emancipate the human soul. Its teaching is: Give free room for growth, for development, for culture ; give opportunity, give liberty, give manhood, spread knowledge, inquire, gather facts, think. Human society cannot be harmed, but only benefited, by thought. Let us have more thought, and better and truer thought. The Religion of Humanity would awaken the human mind from the nightmare of old superstitions that press upon it. It would couch its vision, and bid it see the glories of the world which modern science reveals, instead of groping in the dim twilight of primeval faiths. It bids us be men and women, whole men, whole women,— not necessarily saints after the ecclesiastical pattern, not the cramped, lop-sided, long-faced, and bloodless specimens of humanity, expurgated editions of human kind, that passed for saints in mediæval times, but it urges us to attain the highest ideals of manhood and womanhood possible to our highest vision.

The Religion of Humanity gratefully accepts the work of prophets and apostles in olden time,— not those of one religion alone, but the sages and spokesmen of all faiths. Yet it does not believe that the spirit of wisdom and power that spoke through them has gone so far away that it cannot reach the human mind to-day. It affirms that, to the willing ear, to the open mind, the spirit of truth may yet come with all its ancient power. The Religion of Humanity has its Bibles,— not only the good words of one faith, but of all faiths,— the best words of all literatures, past and present. And it would use all these external helps, past and present,— the prophets, apostles, preachers, sacred words, illustrious examples of consecrated and noble living,— not to overawe and overpower with their authority the present mental and moral life of mankind, but rather to stimulate that life to a like self-reliance and to a nobler fidelity to those unseen inner laws that are stamped on each soul,— the law of Reason and the law of Duty.

If it be objected that this Religion of Humanity seems to have very little to say of a Supreme Being, very little to inculcate in respect to forms of worship, let me say, in conclusion, that it requires a subtler metaphysic than philosophy has yet given, a keener logical method than science has yet discovered, to draw the line in the human soul that shall separate there the divine elements from the human, and to say, On this side is man, on that, God. The Religion of Humanity, emphasizing chiefly the moral idea and aim, does not, it is true, put into the articles of a creed any speculations concerning an infinite and confessedly incomprehensible Being alleged to sit upon a throne in the upper heavens and to govern the universe from that distant seat of supreme sovereignty ; but it nevertheless recognizes the logical necessity of a Power more than commensurate with humanity — commensurate with all possible existence — in and through which all things have their law, their root of life, their present vitality and being : and special organizations and services may be of great use in practically strengthening and enlarging this sense of vital relationship. But when man lives by his highest sense of duty, when he lives a life of strict integrity, of purity, of kindness, of love, of self-devotion to truth and righteousness, though he may profess little faith in the conceptions of Deity presented to him in the creeds of the churches, yet such a one carries within him the very presence and power of the Eternal. He does not need to seek without to find Deity: Deity has found him. The infinite power, the divine life, is coursing this moment through the natural arteries of his own mind and conscience. God dwells within him. And, though he go to worship neither at Jerusalem nor on Mt. Gerizim, he carries ever within himself that daily worship which is in spirit and in truth.

March 24, 1878.

XX.

WHAT DO WE WORSHIP?

"This world is not for him who doth not worship."—ANCIENT HINDU.

I WOULD fain bring to you this morning, friends, some vital central thought, which should concern not only our service here, but the larger service of our daily lives. And how can I better indicate such thought than by the question which I have chosen for the subject of this discourse, *What do we worship?* It were well, certainly, if we should occasionally put this question to ourselves. If worship be anything more than a superstition, if it be anything that at all corresponds to the high claims which in all ages and nations have been made for it, then it is something of supreme moment, and, since it concerns man's highest interests, deserves his most serious attention.

I said, "If worship be anything more than a superstition." But perhaps I shall be reminded a the outset that there are intelligent minds who question whether it be anything more; that there are persons who affirm that all theology is mythology, and that all forms of worship are but modes of superstition, which, with the advance of reason, necessarily become obsolescent; and that, therefore, the first

question to be settled is whether worship has any
genuine and permanent reality, any rational and
abiding basis. To this, I reply that I regard what is
called worship as a specially organized expression
and aid of religion; and that I do not think that
religion can be rightly considered as synonymous
with, or necessarily dependent upon, any system of
theology which the human mind has ever framed or
believed. Rather does religion represent a faculty
or function inherent in the constitution of human
nature itself, and therefore necessarily existent so
long as human nature exists and keeps its identity.
It is the creator of theologies and worships, not
their product. What becomes obsolete and passes
away is theology; that is, human beliefs about
religion,—creeds, statements of faith, mental views
and convictions concerning Supreme Being and
man's relation thereto. These have been continually
changing from the beginning of human existence,
and are still subject to change as advances are made
in knowledge and in the application of reason to
matters of human experience. Many of these beliefs,
indeed, must now be classed with superstitions:
they belonged to man's childhood and immaturity,
and have passed away as a manlier knowledge
has been gained. And forms of worship that were
founded upon such beliefs or necessarily implied them
have passed away too, or are certainly doomed to
the same obsolescence and oblivion. But, amid all
such changes, religion itself has remained, surviving
numerous sects and systems of theology. Religion
is man's recognition — through the threefold form

of feeling, thought, and act — of his own vital relation to the infinite Power or powers of the universe; and it is difficult to see how any sane mind can fail to have some degree of such a recognition. And — so long as religion exists, changing its beliefs to suit the progress of human reason, modifying its conceptions concerning the nature of infinite Power — it is irrational to affirm that it may not institute and sustain forms of worship which shall not be amenable to the charge of superstition, but shall be in harmony with its own progressive character, and ever a fitting and helpful expression of itself.

And I wish specially to bring this question of worship to our attention here, at this resumption of our Sunday services after several weeks of separation, because we of this society profess to hold the most rational and liberal views of religion. We desire and seek to let in the light of the freest reason upon all religious doctrines and institutions; and hence some among us may be already asking whether such services as we hold here from Sunday to Sunday have any foundation in rational philosophy or in practical usefulness. The plain question is, — and it is a searching question as well as a plain one, — Can this free human reason, which we profess to take for our guidance, consistently engage in any form of worship? We must answer this question before we can answer intelligently that other question, What do we worship?

But, first of all, I want to say that we should not allow ourselves to come to this question with any prejudice against the institution of worship derived

from its irrational associations. If we think it
better, as many liberal thinkers do, in order to save
ourselves from being misunderstood, to abandon the
use of the word *worship*, because, like a good deal
of ecclesiastical phraseology, it has become damaged
by the superstitious practices and beliefs with which
it has been so commonly connected, why, well and
good. I, for one, do not insist on the word. Only
let us not fall into the error of thinking also that
that disposes of the essential thing which the word
at its root signifies. The word in itself, in its general
and etymological significance, is a good one.
The English language has no better. In its primitive
Anglo-Saxon origin, it means the condition or
state of *worthiness*, or that quality in any object or
being which gives value, desirableness, excellence,
and attracts admiration and homage; and hence,
secondarily, it came to be applied to the acts by
which such admiration and homage were expressed
by other beings, and then technically and specially
to acts expressive of homage to Deity. Now, human
conceptions of Deity have been attended, of course,
with abundance of errors. Primitively, the *power* of
the mighty forces that seemed to control the universe
was more felt than their wisdom or order or
goodness, and man's ideas of that which constituted
the highest excellence or worth were necessarily
crude and low. Hence, the acts of homage toward
Deity or Deities, or the rites of worship which were
instituted, were often expressive of abject fear, and
were accompanied by many childish and even degrading
and cruel practices. With the progress of en-

lightenment, these crude ideas have been corrected, and man's conception of what constitutes the highest worthiness has been elevated and purified; and acts of worship have taken a correspondingly more rational and spiritual form. Something, indeed, of the old barbarian grossness often appears to survive in the religious ideas and ceremonies even of some sections of civilized society. Still, it must be said that enlightened mankind in general have a much nobler conception of Divine Being, and worship a much higher order of excellence than did their ancestors of the primeval ages. And, even though it may be claimed that, through the progress of modern science, the idea of individual personality and of personal providence will be eliminated from man's conception of Deity and he may come to identify infinite Being with the supreme inner energy, law, and life of the universe itself, still that does not kill the spirit and mood of worship, and need not kill the instituted practice of it.

As this last is a point on which there is a good deal of questioning thought, let us look at it a moment. My response to the question that might here arise would be that Science itself is a worshipper. It is a worshipper of truth. Truth is the supreme object of its homage and devotion. It has no self to set up in opposition to or apart from the truth. And is not homage to truth homage to the living spirit, or essence, or energy of the universe which religion has named Deity? Look, too, at the dominant spirit and mode of life of the true scientific man. I say the *true* man of science; for there are charlatans on the field of science as everywhere else. There are partisans and dogmatists among the class of scientific men as among theologians,— men who are bent upon advocating some pet theory, in which self-interest or self-pride is involved, rather than upon eliciting and establishing the pure truth. But take the *true* men of science (and, in taking these, we take really the great leaders in science, of whom Darwin, in our own day, may be cited as the most conspicuous example),— take these men, who have no other interest than the discovery and promotion of truth, who spend their abilities, their fortunes, their lives, in this unselfish search, giving no heed to consequences, but concerned only to elicit from the dark realm of the unknown the pure and simple reality of things,— and I know not where we shall find another class of persons who manifest more habitually that disinterested homage and devotion to a supreme object, which is the very essence of worship. And many of this class of men exhibit in their work the genuine religious emotions. In the presence of their great discoveries, they are awed into speechless and sometimes spoken adoration before the mysterious Power, the wisdom and purpose of whose hitherto secret ways they have traced and revealed to the world. We cannot say, therefore, that science and scientific men are antagonistic to the spirit of worship. They may reform and purify worship, but they do not destroy it. They may not often be found in the public places of instituted worship, but this may be because the kind of worship in these places is not generally as yet of so high and enlightened an order as is their habitual mood of homage. They are seekers and discoverers of truth. Truth is the lode-star of their lives,— their supremest attraction, their all-satisfying reward. How, then, can they be other, though they do not name him, than seekers and revealers of the Power that religion calls God?

Science, moreover, discloses within the universe to all our eyes, in the infinitely great and the infinitely little, new elements for inciting our adoring wonder: a law, majesty, order, beauty, power, an omnipresent ceaseless activity and life, such as, in their inner purport and in their relation to the life and development of mankind, the ancients never dreamed of, when they bowed down in worship before the outward objects of nature. Science has, in fact, revealed so much in the material universe itself, unfolded its heights and its depths, and lifted the curtain from so many of its wonderful energies, that, so far from the true spirit of worship being deadened in earnest and observant minds, there is rather almost cause for wonder that we do not to-day bow in adoration before the mystic energies that burn in the sun and nourish the earth, people the heavens with stars, and every year reclothe before our eyes the fields and woods with fresh life.

Look, again, at the artist,— not at the charlatan in art more than at the charlatan in science; not at the mere artist adventurer, who deals in tinsel and clap-trap to catch the popular superficial sense, but at the genuine artist whose imagination penetrates behind color and form and sensational sound to the pure realities of things, and who would reproduce nature's highest ideal. What is he but a worshipper of beauty? As the scientist gives his homage to truth, so the artist gives his homage to beauty. This is the aspect of nature that is his lode-star. It is his special gift and province to see the excellences, the wonders, that may be embodied in form, symmetry, harmonious sound, proportion, grace, color, light and shade; and these attract and hold him. These excite his reverence, elicit his grateful joy and adoration, impel his devotion, and determine his career and service. He is a worshipper at the shrine of beauty. There is the *worthiness* which wins his special fealty.

Again, there are those who render their chief homage to a moral idea,— to some external object of social reform or philanthropy. They may have nothing of the artist's capacity. They may know comparatively little of science, and have neither taste nor ability for its pursuit. Yet, no less than the artist and the man of science, they have their supreme object of devotion. They would live for the welfare of others,— for the righting of the wrongs of humanity, for the relief of the burdened, for the lifting up of the weak, for the opening of opportunities to the neglected and ignorant. Very likely this class of persons, too, may have little to do with the ordinary instituted forms of so-called worship. Many of this class of men and women in our time, seeing how little the churches in their organized capacity are doing for social reform and for causes of public philanthropy, are disposed to stand aloof from them altogether. They think that they can spend the hours of Sunday to better benefit for the world than joining in the customary church services. Perhaps they are inclined to say that humanity, at least in its most enlightened portions, has outgrown the need of such services. Nevertheless, these persons, though eschewing what is ecclesiastically called worship, have in their special aim and work the essential spirit and mood of worship in its general significance. That which draws and holds their highest homage, and commands the self-sacrificing devotion of their lives, is the idea of benevolence to mankind. This idea is to them the essence of the highest conceivable excellence, or *worthiness*. This, if they were to put their conception of infinite Being into words at all,— this idea, raised to the infinite degree, would be their highest definition of God. As he is the active power of supreme benevolence working for the welfare of finite creatures, so, they say, can they render the best and most acceptable service to him by the same kind of work for the well-being of humanity. For this class of persons especially, the old Latin proverb seems to embody the idea of worship: "Laborare est orare,"— "To work is to worship."

I have given these different illustrations for the sake of showing that, though we may discard what is technically called worship in the history of religion, we do not thereby free ourselves from the essential thing which the word *worship* in its general significance covers. Every true and earnest soul gives its homage somewhere; has some supreme and overmastering attraction that makes a worthy aim in life ; has some conception of worthiness above all others that moulds and determines life. It may be an idea, it may be some aspect of nature or the universe, it may be the inspiring example and character of some great person, it may be some grand aim of philanthropy, or it may be some grander, all-comprehending conception of universal excellence. Whatever it be, this is practically for such soul its object of worship. This creates the shrines at which it bows in its sincerest and most effective devotions, sets for it the goal of life, shapes character and career, and determines destiny.

It must be further said, too, that not only do the great, sincere, and earnest souls have such objects of worship, but little souls, and selfish souls, and souls that are full of vicious impulses and travel evil and pernicious courses, have also their worships. That idea or attraction or wish, whatever it be, which gives the dominant impulse in their lives, is the object of their homage. It may be a very sordid and degrading idea of life. It may be some vicious and criminal affection. It may be some poor, little, selfish aim that drags the soul down instead of lifting it up,—as the mere accumulation of money, luxurious self-indulgence, satisfactions of carnal appetite, ambition for personal power and distinction for their own sake. But, whatever it be, there is the god they actually worship. There is the shrine at which their hearts bow and their real vows are performed. Even if custom or policy take them to church on Sunday, and with decorous attitude and pious mien they go through with all the outward worshipful forms of the place, it does not follow that their hearts will be in the words of praise that may be sung, or of prayer that may be spoken : their actual worship may not be there. Wherever their strongest desires and affections may be, there will be their hearts, and there their real homage; perchance in some place the very farthest in its atmosphere and habits from a church, and amid scenes with which reverence, holiness, and purity could scarcely find a home. Their controlling aim in life, though itself unworthy, has become for them their idea of *worthiness*, and hence defines their worship. Such souls, indeed, are in the moral attitude of saying to evil, " Be thou my good."

The question, then, recurs, Will an organized public expression of religion, such as the ordinary Sunday service provides, be of any use in helping people to get away from this low plane of homage up to a higher,— away from sordid and harmful services to low aims and desires up to something more worthy and ennobling? Will, in other words, the technical institution of worship be an aid in purifying and elevating the actual worships of men and women in their daily living?

In order to answer this question aright, we must ask whether there is not some still nobler, at least some more comprehensive and universal aim in life, some grander and more commanding object of human homage, than any we have thus far noted. The scientific man, we said, is a worshipper of truth. The artist is a worshipper of beauty. The philanthropist gives his highest homage to the idea of active benevolence. And, on the other side of the moral line, the miser worships money. The ambitious demagogue worships power and popular applause. The voluptuary worships carnal pleasure. That is, each soul makes a specialty of any impulse or aim that is all-dominant with it. But is there not some one aim or impulse which is, or may be, the possession of all souls, which is never quite lost out of human nature under any conditions, which at least always appears in human nature under good conditions, and which will unite all souls in a common homage? Most certainly there is. And that common impulse or aim is *the moral ideal embodied in the highest conceivable excellence of personal character.* Here is one object which should have the homage of all hearts; one goal of attainment toward which all human beings need to set their faces, and strive toward, in order to complete their natures as human beings. Here is the central essence of all worthiness, and therefore of all genuine worship. However worthy and ennobling any special object of homage and devotion may be in itself, it may leave human character in some of its features quite undeveloped and incomplete. The man who is devoted to the truth of science may lead a most useful life and render vast benefit to his fellow-men; and yet he may be morose, ungracious, and even criminally neglectful of social responsibilities and obligations which he has assumed, — a one-sided, imperfect character. The artist may be enraptured with beauty, and bring forth productions which shall win the admiration and awaken the most reverent and noble feelings of all who behold or listen. Yet, from the very delicacy of his organization, he is peculiarly susceptible to those temptations which come through temperament; is open especially to personal suspicions and jealousies; and from his mood of exaltation, when his spirit mingles in the closest worship with his supreme ideal, so that whether in the body or out of the body he hardly knows, he is apt to be cast down into the depths of mental depression and despair. He needs, therefore, the balance of some larger and more universal principle to give him self-poise and serenity. And even in the philanthropist, noble as his work may be, we sometimes miss sadly some of those finer qualities of spirit that carry the charm of affection, courtesy, and good will into the personal relations of life. Thus, in general, the special aim and homage need to be included in some larger homage which shall balance, control, and complete the character on all sides; and only the moral ideal of the highest conceivable excellence, well-rounded and perfect at every point, can furnish the object of such homage.

Now, human nature at its highest has an entrancing vision of such an ideal; and human nature at its lowest has now and then a glimpse of such an ideal, — some little ray of light striking down from the shining glory even into its darkness. But we need all the helps possible to enable us to keep the vision full and bright; or to increase the ray of light, if we only have a little glimpse of it, and to hold our steps firm and steady toward it. There is so much in the ordinary course of human life that is disheartening and depressing, the demands and necessities of the body are so importunate, we are all so liable to be absorbed in the petty and selfish interests of daily care, there are so many temptations dragging at our feet and luring us to this or that fancied satisfaction, that it is with the utmost difficulty that we keep our gaze steadily fixed and our feet moving steadily forward to the goal of our highest moral ideal. We need all the helps possible in this contest.

And the Sunday service is one of these helps. For the world at large, it is a very important help. This organized public expression of religion ordinarily called worship is designed to represent and enforce the moral ideal of life. It upholds the standard of our highest faculties and aspirations against the rule of our passions and the sway of all lower tendencies. It upholds the standard of the spirit against the sovereignty of the flesh, of mental and moral satisfactions as more noble and enduring than material. It presents self-sacrificing devotion to a grand aim in life as nobler and more enriching than any possible form of self-indulgence. And it strives to keep before our eyes, amid the dissipating and illusive enticements of our every-day living, the attainment of a well-rounded, all-sided, perfect character,— perfect in its moral integrity, in its affectional sympathy and helpfulness, and in its equipoise of aspiration and trust,— as the one absolutely worthy goal of human destiny for all classes and conditions of mankind.

I know, indeed, how far the ecclesiastical usages of worship have fallen from a perfect accomplishment of this, their true aim. But they have not failed so far as to be consigned to instant disuse and destruction. I think we should all agree that even those forms of worship, in which there still mingle many superstitions and errors, may be better for those who really believe in them than no forms of religious service at all. And have any of us outgrown the need of some form of public recognition of religion? If the popular forms of religious service seem to us to fail of their highest usefulness because of the erroneous dogmas, irrational ceremonies, and sectarian exclusiveness that accompany them, all the more is it incumbent upon us to do our part to sustain some kind of public institution of religion, where reason shall be left untrammelled and thought be encouraged in its loftiest ambitions; where sectarian walls are thrown down, and no ceremony nor doctrine nor letter of Scripture is allowed to stand in the way of the free spirit of human fellowship on the basis of the moral ideal; where, in fine, the main question to be asked is not, With what sect or under what name or by what creed or ritual do you worship? but *What* do you worship? What is the controlling aim, the supreme homage, of your life? And we, friends, do profess to have some such idea as this in our Sunday assemblings here. Shall we not, then, as we come together again for another year of associated effort, come with renewed consecration of purpose, each to be faithful at his post, and, whatever his part may be, to perform it well, at whatever cost to personal and self-indulgent desire? With such consecration carried into deeds, we may make this house a rich sanctuary of benefit to ourselves and our neighbors,— a veritable gateway to heavenly integrity, strength, and peace for this community.

September 14, 1879.

XXI.
GOD IN HUMANITY.

"One God and Father of all, who is above all, and through all, and in you all." — NEW TESTAMENT.

"He who inwardly rules the sun is the same immortal Spirit who inwardly rules thee." — HINDU VEDA.

"Man is a mortal god. He leaveth not the earth, and yet dwelleth above, so great is the greatness of his nature." — ANCIENT EGYPTIAN.

THERE are doctrines in modern science which point to an identity between the power that exhibits itself as force and law in the material universe and the power that is manifest in human personality. Man seems to sum up in his own nature, under different and higher modes of activity, the various forms of energy and life that were anterior to him in the development of the world-forces. In him, the laws of material nature become perceptions and sensibilities. Instinct rises into intuition. Sensation opens into reflection. The blind physical attractions ascend to the height of conscious affections and moral choice. And thus the organizing energy of nature, as moral and intelligent being, is crowned with conscious power over matter. Now, if we follow out this thought,— the thought that the organizing energy, power, force, or formative and animating principle in nature, reappears, in a new and higher form of activity, in the consciousness of man, — we have a richly suggestive theme, which might be named "Man as the Highest Manifestation of the Power in Nature," or "Man as the Highest Worker in Nature," or, in more theological phrase, "God in Humanity." Perhaps, indeed, we shall have at some time a scientific doctrine of Incarnation.

And it is interesting to note how this thought, which science is now beginning to unfold and elucidate, has found expression in various religions through the lips of ancient seers, as, for instance, in the passages placed at the head of this discourse. These and kindred passages which might be selected show that, while religion has generally inculcated, especially in the teaching accepted by the masses, that man is under the rule of a Providence wholly external and supernatural to himself, there have yet not been wanting those who have had the insight to perceive the truth of the natural immanence of Deity in man, and to proclaim the corresponding truth,— that man, under the guidance of this immanent power in his own nature, was meant to be chiefly his own providence. The great mass of the people, under every form of religious faith, have been wont to look for some miraculous aid in the solution of life's perplexing problems. They have expected the heavens to open at their entreaties, and help to be despatched from a divine being believed to be enthroned in the upper world,— some Jehovah, or Jove, or Vishnu, or Krishna, or Christ,— to whose direct supernatural agency they have been accustomed to refer every good thing that has happened to them and all right knowledge of religious things that they have possessed. But the great religious teachers, though sometimes yielding to these beliefs of the people, have tried to hint of another kind of providential guidance, exclaiming with Jesus, "Who made me a judge or divider among you? Why judge ye not of yourselves what is right?" or with Buddha, "Self is the lord of self: . . . with self well subdued, a man finds a lord such as few can find"; or with the Greek philosopher, "The gods have not given everything to man: it is man who has ameliorated his own destiny"; or with the mystic Hindu, "By his own doings, one rises or falls. . . . Thine own self is the holy stream, whose shrine is virtue, whose water is truth, whose bank is character, whose waves are sympathy. There bathe, O son of Pandu! Thy inward life is not by water made pure." "How can teaching help him who is without understanding? Can a mirror help the blind to see?" "Fortune comes of herself to the lion-like man who acts. A work prospers through endeavors, not through vows."

If such shining truths as these could become general, how they would revolutionize prevailing religious beliefs and practices, not only among the people called heathen, but even in Christendom! For it has been and is to-day the dominant philosophy of the Christian Church that the divine Providence which cares for man acts through some channel of supernal influence exterior to him, and not through his own natural faculties; that Deity is a being of wholly separate and distinct individuality from man, necessarily communicating with him through some outward means of revelation ; that religion, to be genuine and trustworthy, must be something imparted at the outset by such external revelation, and that its efficacy in any individual case must depend on the continued act of supernatural impartation from this foreign source to each individual soul ; that religion, therefore, with all the graces and virtues it includes, is a form of life to be grafted upon man's nature from without rather than a natural growth, blossoming, and fruiting of his own native perceptions and energies.

I wish in this discourse to set forth the counter doctrine: that religion, with all its beliefs, institutions, history, is the natural product of the human mind; that the Deity that guides and saves the human soul is in the soul and works through the soul ; that the Providence that cares for humanity and acts specially for the good of humanity is in humanity, and acts chiefly through the human faculties. Yet let me remark at once, to prevent misunderstanding, that this is by no means to say that there is no Deity outside of man and no power or providence above or beyond man. Deity is immanent in nature no less than in man,— immanent in the whole universe of being, not only in that which comes under our cognizance, but in the whole possible universe. Wherever there is any kind of existence, wherever there is natural law, wherever there is any manifestation of power, there is the presence of Deity and of providential purpose indicated. Within and behind all phenomena there

is an organific energy and aim. A power that is
organific does not proceed by blind chance or caprice.
There is a divinity and providence in the affairs of
the universe, in the affairs of men. I do not dispute that proposition. But the proposition I would
maintain is this: that, whereas it is commonly
affirmed that man is connected with Divine Power
in some external and supernatural way, man's relation to this Power is really internal, and the Power
becomes a providence to him by operating in a natural way through his natural faculties. Man draws
upon the resources of Eternal Being for his own
life, but he does this through the normal action of
his own normal energies.

The first proof I would adduce in support of this
proposition is the history of religion itself. All the
more recent researches into the history of man's
religious development go to show that religion has
not come to man by supernal revelation, but that he
has slowly grown into it, and that it has gradually
developed its character and power precisely according to his growing knowledge and intelligence in
other matters. Defining religion as the expression
of man's sense of his relation to a mysterious power
or powers in the universe conceived as affecting in
some way the destiny of human beings, we find that,
historically, this expression has everywhere had its
source in the smallest beginnings, first appearing
in acts and beliefs that seem to the cultivated religious thought of a later time very crude and absurd.
These beginnings of religion with primitive mankind
are indeed almost lost in their obscurity, so slight

are they, so little illuminated by rational intelligence, and so mixed with matters that seem entirely foreign to the devout moods of the modern mind. That is, religion in its origin corresponds with the mental condition of mankind in that primitive era. And, in the historical development of religion, this same correspondence has been preserved, disclosing everywhere natural continuity and not supernatural intervention. When man was in a condition of mental childhood, or wherever he is in that condition to-day, his religion was and is that of a child. When the human race was a child *mentally*, it "spoke as a child, it understood as a child, it thought as a child," in religious things. Whenever and wherever man has been barbarian, his religion has partaken of barbarous practices. Whenever and wherever man has been intellectually narrow, his religion has been narrow, bigoted, severe, apt to fall into bitter propagandism and persecution. Whenever and wherever man has been intellectually imaginative, his religion has shown the characteristics of his imagination. With breadth of culture, wiser thought, increase of intercourse, and widening of acquaintance with the human family, and a deeper knowledge of human nature, has come a broader, profounder, and more charitable religion. Looking, therefore, at the historical development of humanity, it does not appear as if religion had ever been a gift to man direct and outright from the heavens, ready-made with its beliefs and institutions for human use, but that it has come slowly and gradually as the natural product of the human intellect itself, under the natural conditions of mundane experience. Man has grown into his religion as he has grown into everything else of value that really belongs to him. Religion has been evolved from the inborn capacities and functions of his mind, growing with his growth, under the various disciplines of experience, and strengthening with his strength. From its small beginnings in certain natural sentiments and perceptions of the primitive human mind, enlarging and deepening with the mind's growing thought under the manifold tuition of outward circumstance, of rough or agreeable contact with nature, of spur of inner and outer forces, it has thus gradually unfolded its great beliefs and institutions, its mighty power, its errors and wrongs, but also its immortal hopes and its sublime moral consecrations and sanctities. The creative power has been content here, as everywhere else in the universe, to work its way up and outward to self-manifestation by a process of slow gradation and growth. The human mind even, which was to become to so large an extent the instrument of the divine energy on this planet, had itself to be created by this slow process, and to be gradually adapted to its service by the training and strengthening of its faculties under the push and stress of the manifold forces of which the earth has been the scene.

And, if religion itself has come into human history through the natural action of man's natural faculties, then much more may we argue that the special aims of religion on which theology has laid stress, such as the providential guidance, education, and destiny

of the human soul, will be accomplished in the same
way; namely, not by a supernatural, mysterious
Power working outside and above the human faculties, but by a providence which works in and
through the human faculties themselves, and which
is none the less creative and divine because it is
natural and human. Let us turn, then, to this more
practical side of our theme,— to the question of
Divine Providence in respect to the actual condition
of humanity, individually and collectively, to-day.

The way in which the popular theology has met
this question — throwing, as it does, so much responsibility upon Almighty Power for man's condition,
so little upon man himself — has been, I do not hesitate to say, very demoralizing; though this demoralization has not shown itself practically to the extent
that it would have done, for the reason that, when
it comes to the practical matters of every-day life,
people are quite apt to leave their creeds and betake
themselves to the teachings of experience and common sense. Their own observation and experience
have, in fact, taught them a truer theology than that
which they have learned in the churches in Sunday
sermons or gathered from so-called religious books
and newspapers. The Church has told them of an
interposing Deity, working when and where he will,
by an instantaneous personal volition not to be accounted for, not to be naturally anticipated nor its
ways calculated, yet coming in response to zealous
human prayer; but, in their daily life, they have
learned of a Deity that is as regular as the sunrise
and sunset, that comes like "the seasons in their

order," and works everywhere through the method of natural law,— of a Deity, therefore, whose acts can be foreseen, whose ways can be depended upon. Theology has pictured to them a Deity whose " angels would bear them up in their hands " and save them from destruction, though they should violate nature's laws; but life's experience has shown them that the angels that come to the rescue of man from the dire result of broken laws which are never annulled, are either in the guise of human beings or of natural forces, or else they come not at all. The panic-stricken factory girls who threw themselves from an upper window of their burning mill found no angels to prevent their being dashed to death upon the pavement. The effective intervention for their rescue — which man's afterthought is now providing for such emergencies — would have been a permanent fire-escape attached to the wall. Thus it is that the experiences of common life and common observation are conducing to teach a truer doctrine of divine help and guidance for man than has been commonly inculcated by the ecclesiastical theology of Christendom. People are gradually learning that the grand providential resources for insuring human progress and happiness are stored within the keeping of human beings themselves,— that sufficient of Deity is naturally incarnate in humanity to endow humanity with the power of being a providence and a savior to itself.

If it be necessary to support these propositions by arguments, we can hardly go amiss of the illustrations in proof of them, to whatever part of human history or society we turn. Look at the progress of human society itself,—its progress in knowledge, in intellectual grasp and power, in natural science, in the arts, in political and social morality, in everything that concerns the well-being of man. How has it all been effected? Not certainly for man by a power outside of him, pouring into his nature, as if it were simply a passive receptacle, all these possessions and achievements of knowledge, virtue, and civilization; but they have all come by the laborious exertion of man's own faculties, they are the grand result of his own putting forth of effort. They have not been given to him; but he has acquired them, earned them. The human race did not have them at the start; but they are the wages of its toil, the achievements of its thought and enterprise through all the generations of its existence on the earth. And they are related to the great Power that is the ultimate cause of all things only by the fact that it was in the powers that produced them. The Deity that has made man what he is in civilized society to-day has not been shaping and moulding him so much from the outside as from the inside. The Divine Power has been manifest in the human thirst for knowledge, in the mental effort to resist or control natural forces, in the long struggle of humanity, and in the impulse at the bottom of the struggle, out and up from material and barbarous conditions of existence into a life of mental enjoyment and of social justice and love. We may say that Deity has done it. Yes; but it is Deity that had incarnated itself in the human race, that wrought in and through the very substance of the human faculties, that assumed flesh and became man himself.

Or look for illustration at some special points in the history of human society. The time was when bodily ailments and diseases were regarded as a direct visitation upon man from Heaven, either as a penalty for some sin or as a discipline for his faith. No one thought of tracing any connection between them and broken natural law. The remedy for them was to be found in prayer, in faith, in the impartation of some mystical spiritual virtue through the touch of a holy person or holy object. This doctrine of disease is taught in the New Testament. Now, a wiser knowledge is able to track physical diseases to human and finite sources, and only the most superstitious connect them with supernatural agencies, either as to cause or cure. The belief lingers, indeed, even in minds tolerably enlightened, that diseases are specially sent upon mankind for spiritual discipline; yet I have noticed that even such devotees of the old belief do not shrink from resorting to the common human and finite remedies, instead of the old prescriptions of prayer and religious penance, for ridding themselves of the disorders and the discipline together,— a symptom that the old idea is fast vanishing. The modern mind finds the seeds of bodily disease and suffering in some violated law of nature,— violated either wilfully or ignorantly or unavoidably,— though not always violated personally by the sufferer: he may suffer for another's transgression. It finds the cause in bad ventilation, defective drainage, unwholesome food, in false fashions of dress, in intemperance, licentiousness, and other abuses of physical appetite,— in short, in the thousand ways of physical neglect and abuse by which human beings, consciously or unconsciously, violate sanitary laws. And as the human mind has found the cause of physical disease within the finite conditions of existence, so it has found the remedy there. Since the cause is the violation of natural sanitary laws, the remedy, a preventive as well as cure, must be the knowledge and observance of those laws, with such temporary alleviation as medical science may be able to render by counteracting an evil already done. Here, then, is a plain case—and it is no small or trivial case, this whole vast region of human physical disease and woe—where it is now pretty generally admitted that man is his own providence, his own savior. To call upon an Almighty Power in the heavens to avert sickness or to change its results, to stay the ravages of a pestilence, to keep the cholera from a city, is beginning to be regarded by sensible and thinking people everywhere as the relic of a superstition which must soon take its place with many other beliefs which the world has outgrown and left behind. It is beginning to be seen that the Power has not to be summoned from afar, but is already here; that it has first made its presence known by the disorder and pain that have ensued on the infringement of some law of nature; that its presence is in that law, bruised and broken and indeed sinned against; that it is also in the human knowledge that has detected the fracture and raises the wholesome

warning of obedience; in the science that sends out
missionaries into regions of contagion in the shape
of disinfectants, and that has unfolded the momentous law of heredity and discovered antidotes for ex-
orcising the demon of poison from diseased blood;
in the public sentiment that establishes Sanitary
Commissions and Boards of Health, and demands
that streets shall be sewered and swept, domestic
premises be kept pure and sweet, and people be
taught to obey the laws of cleanliness. But not
only in these channels flows the Power that is a
providence for man in his struggle with physical disease. We may find it also in more tender guise:
in the faithful nursing and watchful care of human
sympathy; in woman's gentle fidelity in the sick-
room; in her instinctive tact and the magnetic virtue
of her presence and touch; in the unwearied, patient
devotion of a wife's, sister's, or mother's love, which
often, by its very unweariedness and patience, saves
the sick from the grasp of death. So that this is
a view of Providence of which it cannot be said that
it is all the cold operation of law: the great element
of love comes into it, and is at the very bottom of
it,— all the warmth and tenderness of the purest,
richest, human love,— of that love which is "the
fulfilling of the law."

And what has here been said of the way of Providence in dealing with man's physical diseases and
infirmities might, with a slight change of words,
be applied with equal truth to man's moral condition and progress. The great law holds good
here: that every violation of the principle of right,

every departure from virtue, brings, in some shape, the retribution of pain,— brings moral disease and disorder. The disease and pain do not come by any arbitrary fiat of a distant Deity seated on a throne in the upper heavens, but they come as the natural consequence of the moral transgression: they are the direct effect of an evident cause; and the Deity, the divine principle and providence, is there on the spot in that pressure of natural energy which inherently impels a cause to its effect. The Providence is in the warning given by the moral pain,— in the remorse, the stricken conscience, the loss of self-respect and of others' approbation,— to indicate that there has been moral disobedience; a warning given, therefore, in mercy to turn the transgressor back to virtue and to moral safety. The husks, the hunger, the swine for company, the disappointment and disgust of the prodigal son in Jesus' immortal parable, were the natural result of the vicious prodigalism to which he had yielded; yet there was a providence in them,— a providence inherent in the very severity of their discipline,— since they drove him back "to himself" and to the ways of righteousness. The Providence is in the law by which "whatsoever a man sows that shall he reap," and whereby "the way of the transgressor is hard"; and in the further law that, when man is warned by the hardness of his evil way, warned by penitence and remorse, of his transgressions, every effort which he then makes in virtue, every struggle against temptation, every step he takes in the returning way, will help

to bring him back to moral health and peace. The
power of help, like the power of retribution, is no
mysterious Being far away, acting through the
proxy of some transaction of atonement, but there
right at the spot of need,— in the penitence that
first turns his heart homeward to virtue, in the
aspiration and hope that light the way for him,
in the very strength of the moral exertion by which
he takes the steps that one after another are surely
bringing him back.

But does all this, though it may be efficacious,
seem cold? Law again, but no love? See, then,
how this same Providence, this Divinity in humanity,
becomes love! See it in the yearning tenderness
of a mother's love, who, if she be the true human
mother, never forsakes her prodigal son, but follows
him into whatsoever wearisome deserts of vice he
may wander. Or see it in the more general philanthropy that is seeking in all the dark and squalid
corners of society the welfare of human beings. It
is Divine Love that thus works in the love of man
for his fellow-man,— that goes down into the places
of poverty, vice, bondage, and crime, to carry, if possible, some comfort, to lift up, if possible, the most
degraded human beings into a capacity for a pure
enjoyment and into a place of moral health. It is
Divine Love that is working through the efforts of
benevolent men and women to put down intemperance, and to check the "social evil," and to emancipate human beings from every form of slavery, and
to bring into human society the elements of justice
and brotherhood. It is through this love of man for

humanity that Universal Love manifests its providential care, and gets its purposes for human welfare accomplished.

Behold the same providential aim, again, in different phase,— in the love that founds the home and provides for the family and permeates the household with all pure affections; in the love that shines out of the face of human friendship; and in that, too, which draws neighbors together in intelligent, helpful sympathy. What shall we say, also, of that passion for the truth which often comes into the human heart, that devotion to the right, that fidelity to conviction and conscience, whereby a man will endure peril and torture, and go down to death before he will swerve one jot from that which he believes to be the line of rectitude? What shall we say of the martyr souls of humanity,— those who face the dungeon, the gallows, the cross, or all the promises and frowns of the world, and still stand with manly uprightness to say or do the thing that seems to them right and true? Or of that later type of martyr spirits, blossoming right out of the materialistic enterprises of this business-devoted age,— the railroad engineers, brakemen, sea-captains, who, with their train or ship rushing into the very jaws of destruction, have stood unflinchingly at their posts of duty, and gone down to death with their hands still clinched to their tasks and their nerves serene with heroic self-command,— saving others by their calm courage and lofty presence of mind, while themselves they could not save? What can we say of any such deeds but that they are an exhibition in humanity of the

Eternal Power that makes for righteousness? A miscreant places a rail across the track in front of an approaching express train. The engineer, as he rounds a curve, sees it and the awful peril, throws his whole strength into one Titanic effort, reverses his engine, and brings the train to a stop just as the obstruction is grazed. The newspapers report it as a miraculous escape. But the miracle was all in the virtue of the Westinghaus brake and in the alertness of the engineer's brain and the skilled strength of his arm. The passengers go on, rejoicing, in their safety, while the hero who has saved them is taken from the train scal led nigh to death by the escape of steam caused by the very success of his exertion.

Illustrations like these, which might be indefinitely multiplied, make clear how it is that Deity manifests his power for human benefit and what is the main method of Divine Providence for man's guidance and protection. The great sanitary and redemptive resources, whether for physical or moral good, are stored within the human faculties, and are made effective through human activity. The divine energies are wielded through the human. They are involved in the very substance of human thought and forethought, sagacity and skill; in human courage, bravery, virtue, and love; in man's power to learn nature's laws and to put himself, through science and art, into harmony with them. Divine Providence is human providence. The Eternal Power cares for man, protects him, insures his progress, holds him, we may even say in the old Hebrew phrase, "in the hollow of his hand," but does it through that portion of the Universal Energy and Love which is made active in the mind, heart, and hand of the human race.

Does some one ask, then, Why say "Deity" at all? Why not say at once, with the Positivists, that Humanity is our God? Because, let me say in conclusion, when man finds a firm basis for his knowledge; when he adheres by an inward necessity to a conviction of truth; when he stands up courageously to defend the right and to keep his virtue; when, resisting temptations of selfish ease or pleasure, he shapes his actions by a pure impulse of love and charity; when he plants his feet so solidly at the post of duty that no threats of peril nor bribes to ambition can move him from his rock of conscience, — then he feels that he is acting with the strength of a power which, though it may manifest itself through his perception of truth and his individual adherence to right and goodness, is yet not of himself nor limited by himself, but is at the very basis of the universe and coterminous with the realm of all existence; because he is conscious that he is the instrument of a purposive process, reaching out, in respect to its root and its goal, as far beyond any purpose that centres in himself as the vast universe of matter extends beyond his little body of flesh; because he is conscious that his life, material, mental, moral, is but a part of the larger life of humanity, to which he is harmoniously or inharmoniously related in proportion as he follows or does not follow this inward monitor of truth and duty; because he is conscious that humanity itself, with all its achievements, with all its capacities and possibilities, is but a little larger part of the vast grandeur of the stupendous system of the universe, which in all its parts is animated with one life, by one power; and because he must needs believe that beyond and above humanity there may be other races of finite beings, as above our earth there are other and innumerable worlds, and that through all these infinite ranges of worlds and races there runs the unity of one vital energy. For these reasons, he says not Humanity, but Deity, when he would express the greatness, the everlastingness, the incomprehensibleness of this Power which comes to manifestation in his being, and works in and through his faculties, and is the source of the wisdom and love that are the guiding providence and felicity of his individual and social existence. Though standing in the strength of his own natural resources and faculties, and relying for present and future welfare upon his perfected manhood, he yet perceives that this strength and this manhood are but the partial revelation of a Power older and mightier than himself, older and mightier than the human race. And hence, before the unifying Energy that is working through the inconceivable vastness of things, he lifts his eyes in adoring wonder, and exclaims, " O God, I too, a speck of conscious dust, am thrilled with life from Thee!"

October 10, 1880.

XXII.

THE PERMANENCE OF MORALITY.

> " Possessions vanish and opinions change,
> And passions hold a fluctuating seat;
> But, by the storms of circumstance unshaken
> And subject neither to eclipse nor wane,
> Duty exists."
> W. Wordsworth.

"What Morality have we left?" is the title of a bright article in the *North American Review* for the current month,[*] satirizing those modern ethical theories (and particularly the system of Herbert Spencer) which many persons think are destined to supplant the old theological theory of morality as the revealed law of God. My answer to the question would be : I admit to some extent the force of this satirical criticism, though wholly ready to maintain that morality must find some other than a theological basis, and yet we have all the morality left in the world that there ever was, and a still growing quantity of it.

But morality and its foundations have been so implicated with certain theological creeds, the teaching has been so prevalent and dominant that the moral law is the directly revealed will of God, and is enforced by a supernaturally decreed system of re-

[*] May, 1881.

wards and punishments extending through all eternity, that it is not strange, when modern philosophy ventures to pronounce these positions untenable and it is plain, on all sides, that the old theological creeds are nearing their downfall, if there should be anxiety and alarm lest the very bulwarks of morality are to be undermined, and public and private virtue are to collapse. Nor should it surprise us if there should ensue some actual evil on this account, some temporary confusion of moral ideas, some lapses from moral conduct on the part of people for whom the old moral standard has been loosened by the loss of their old religious faith and who have not yet found any new standard either of religious or moral faith. It should not surprise us if some people should say — some are already saying it — that the moral law is just like religious belief: it is only this or that man's opinion ; it has no authority over others ; it is only individual and relative ; there is nothing absolute and unchangeable in it; at best, it is only the aggregate voice of the strongest number of opinions ; as a late writer expresses it, it is only what "society" at this moment may happen to demand of me. And, when morality is believed to be nothing more than this,— required conformity to the voice of public opinion,— there arises, naturally, in the human breast a feeling of rebellion to it. Public opinion may be a tyranny. What right except that of might have the majority of opinions to rule the minority ? Why is not my opinion of what I may do as good as my neighbor's ? Why should I act to please him, and not myself ?

Why not make my own interests and happiness the law of my action? Of what concern is it to others what I may do, so long as my action does them no harm? Why may not a man do what he pleases morally as well as mentally,— make a fool of himself, if he chooses,— if his conduct brings no injury to others? This is reducing the law of morality to the doctrine of extreme individualism of liberty, and making liberty synonymous with individual license. Yet such questions and reasoning may be heard; they even appear in print. And there is not a little of this confused, clouded, and practically pernicious view of the moral law among people for whom the old theological basis of morals is gone.

Nor should it much surprise us to find the Nihilists in Russia, or a portion of them, crying out in the same breath against God and against the claim that there is any such thing as moral right. The one type of theological teaching which they have heard is that God has revealed his will as the law of right through the Church, and that the head of the Church — God's vicegerent on the earth, sometimes even called God himself — is the emperor of all the Russias, the head of a government which they have never known otherwise than as a personal despotism, whose will was the law for them to obey. What kind of a God and what kind of a law of right has Russian absolute monarchy been teaching? What wonder if, under such theological indoctrination, the Russian people, in large numbers, have come to confound the very law of moral right with the will of the despotic government

which has crushed them, and even the being of God
with the tyranny they are struggling against! Thus
incensed, they cry out: "Away with them all,—
Government, Church, God, the Moral Law! To us,
they mean but one thing,— *Despotism.* And despotism is mental and moral despair!" Nor need it
surprise us that something similar has occurred in
France, where, among large sections of the working
people, the revolt against religion has also been, to
a large extent, a revolt against the moral order of
society. For here, too, the morality that has been
taught has been so implicated with a false theology,
and has often, too, found such poor exemplification
in the daily lives of the priesthood, and the Church
as a whole has really done or aimed to do so little
for the enlightenment and temporal improvement of
the people, that it is difficult for the people to draw
any clear line of distinction between what the
Church has taught as theology and what it has
taught as morality. They have a strong feeling that
the Church, with its orders of priesthood, with its
rich benefices, with its lavishly endowed monastic
societies, has somehow flourished at their expense ;
that it has neglected them, kept them poor and
ignorant and miserable,— has, in short, been their
oppressor and plunderer. And hence they have
declared war against the Church and all that the
Church stands for, without stopping to cull the evil
from the good. They would sweep it all away,—
theology, religion, Deity, the moral law,— level all
to the ground, that they may begin anew with absolutely fresh materials on unencumbered premises.

And yet, in spite of these evidences of a moral collapse of society in consequence of a growing disbelief in the old creeds of religion,— in spite, too, of dangers nearer home that I am ready to admit and would not wink out of sight,— to the question, "What morality have we left?" I repeat my answer, "All that there ever was, and a still growing quantity of it." By this, I do not mean that there may not be a temporary relaxation of the moral energies of society and a temporary depression of moral standards, especially in certain classes of people and in certain countries that have been most dominated by the old theologies. There have been such depressions, such temporary deflections and retrograde periods, in regard to morality in the past history of mankind. But the course of human history as a whole has been one of moral progress. The moral power at the heart of the race has always been equal to the emergency of overcoming and annulling any temporary aberrations from the line of healthy moral perception and conduct. And so I argue that this will be the case now: that there will be in human nature ample elasticity of the moral sentiment to insure recovery from any moral paralysis that may be caused by the decay and fall of the old theological basis of morality; that morality will still survive all disasters, as it has hitherto, and still grow and progress.

But I reach this conclusion not solely or chiefly by the argument of comparison with similar periods in the past. When I say that there is all the morality in the world that there ever was, and that it is likely to advance and increase instead of being overthrown, I mean that the source and vital elements of morality remain: I mean that the roots of it are not destroyed, are not touched, by any wind, however fierce, of theological scepticism which may for an interval be shaking down violently some of its foliage and fruit: I mean that the foundations of morality continue the same and undisturbed, whatever theological foundations may be undermined and whatever disturbances may ensue to those superficial ethical structures which have been confusedly built partly on theological and partly on moral bases. Genuine morality has always rested on a foundation of its own. Implicated with certain theological beliefs by the popular religious teaching, it is yet in reality independent of all theological beliefs, appears in connection with them or apart from them, and runs down to a root vitally its own,— and that root an ineradicable part of human nature itself. Morality is the best part of religion, but it has not necessarily part or parcel in any theology. And when the confusing teaching which has so long sought to make people believe that the moral law is an essential adjunct of certain theological creeds and not safely to be separated from them shall have passed away, and people shall be trained to trace clearly in their thought the moral law to its own simple and ineradicable root, and to trace with the same clearness, in respect to actual conduct, the practical moral law as it lies plain to sight in that *nexus* of natural vital energy which binds unerringly moral cause to moral consequence, then shall we

have a revival of morality. That sovereignty which
theological faith will have at last let go from its
loosening grasp will be seized by moral faith. The
standard of moral action will be lifted higher and
held with firmer nerve for the guidance of the
bewildered flocks that have lost their ecclesiastical
shepherds. There will be fresh-voiced, clear-toned
rallying-cries, summoning defenders for the right
and the true; an awakening resolution and energy
in all the moral factors of society; a movement
forward of the now theologically divided armies in
one morally united host against the forces of error
and wrong. Then may we expect new triumphs of
justice against long-entrenched usurpations and
iniquities, and the acquisition for man òf new individual rights and of more equal opportunity in the
name of human brotherhood.

But I may be justly reminded that this is a prophecy of rhetoric, and that what is wanted on this
question is thought and logic. Let me try, then, to
show what appears to me to be that abiding and
indestructible root of morality and source of all
moral power which will remain after theological
systems may have vanished, and which may be all
the more clear and the more powerful when they
shall have ceased to obscure the knowledge of it
and interfere with the right culture of it. First, I
cannot accept as satisfactory substitutes for the
theological theories of ethics those revivals of old
philosophies which are now urgently advocated and
with considerable apparent support from the scientific doctrine of evolution, whereby the moral law is

resolved into an inward impulsion to secure one's own greatest happiness or is explained on the altruistic utilitarian ground of an obligation to secure the greatest good of the greatest number. I do not doubt that, when a person has reached a very high and refined condition of moral culture,— what we might call the celestial heights of morals,— his own greatest happiness would only be possible when he was making the utmost efforts for the true happiness of others. But there are multitudes of people who have not reached that height; multitudes of people whose present and controlling idea of happiness is the satisfaction of self-interests, the gratification of certain personal desires and aims, the successful pursuit of pleasures of a merely material nature. With this large class of people, their ideas of happiness are so closely identified with the selfish enjoyments belonging to their low grade of life that they are incapable of even appreciating the motive, much less of acting upon it, of sacrificing their own present happiness for the sake of the higher happiness of making others happy. How are these people, who are living on the plane of this low idea of what happiness is, to be reached by an ethical theory which gauges moral obligation by an effort for personal happiness? So, too, I do not doubt that the ultimate result of the highest moral conduct is the greatest good of the greatest number. But, as a practical test for ascertaining what course of conduct is morally required at any present moment, this utilitarian standard of morality is worthless. At the best, it can be only an approximate test, never complete and absolute. For who would ever be able to trace all the results of his proposed action so as to be competent to say what kind of act would effect the greatest good for the greatest number of people who might in some way, at some time near or remote, be affected by it? If we had to go through with such a calculation before moral action, our moral action would often cease altogether, and could never come with that promptness of decision on which often its whole efficiency depends. And, even though the experiences of utility for successive generations may have come to be organized in mental action as intuitions, as is claimed, I yet fail to see how an analysis of the ideas of either utility or of happiness will yield the constituent elements of the moral sense as it has developed in the history of mankind. The essential elements of the idea of moral law and the essential elements of the ideas of happiness and of utility are, in my judgment, totally distinct, so that the latter cannot beget the former.

Where, then, shall we find the basis or root of the moral law? I find it in the native intuitive faculty of the human mind, though not in that developed form which the intuitional philosophy usually claims. The root, the ever vital germ of morality, is intuitive: it belongs to the human mind as such, to intelligence *per se;* but its development has been under the tuition of experience. Let us see how these statements may be substantiated.

According to the now commonly accepted view of the condition of primitive man, there was a time when man could hardly be called a moral being. The moral germ or capacity must have been within him, but it was unmanifested. There was only a fierce struggle for existence amid savage conditions of life. The deepest instinct was for life,—the instinct of self-preservation. Whatever threatened peril to life was shunned: it was an evil. Whatever promised help to life was sought: it was a good. The primitive man, thus seeking instinctively to preserve his life, would begin to classify things as good or evil according as they aided or hindered this instinct for life. And, anon, he would classify persons in the same way. If another man attempted to interfere with his existence, to deprive him of it, or to take away the things he had gathered for sustaining it, the intruder was an evil man, to be resisted. By the very necessity of such a condition of existence, the first reflective act of consciousness on the part of the primitive man must have been the instinctive feeling of a *right* to his existence, and the consequent right to defend that existence against any external assaults. But all this might have gone on without any active moral sense. It merely classified things (and persons) as good and not good. But as soon as the mental perception came to any individual of this primitive race that, if another individual had no right to attack his life or deprive him of anything he had gathered necessary to life, or harm his life in any way, so *he* had no right to attack that other's life or take away his sustenance or bring any harm upon him, then dawned the moral sense, then began the sovereignty of the moral law. It began in the mental transference to another of the same kind of rights as were claimed for one's self; it began in primitive man coming one day to think, and say to himself, "If I have a right to existence, then my neighbor-man there has a right to existence; and, if he has no right to harm my existence, then I have no right to harm his existence." And this is a perception that must just as certainly have come, as soon as there was intelligence enough to understand the relation, as came the perception that two and two make four; and in it is the germ of all morality. Generalized, *it is the intuitive perception of the necessary equation of rights between man and man in their relations to each other.* And this is my definition of the moral law. Its popular expression is the Golden Rule, which has appeared in substantially the same form in all the leading religions and nations of the globe; and its most central ethical word is justice. This definition puts morality on a basis as absolute and unchangeable as that on which the science of mathematics rests; a basis independent of the variable phases of theological belief, and that will remain after all the systems of theology that have ever been devised may have passed away. The idea of justice depends on no ecclesiastical creed, nor is it imperilled by any assaults upon religious faith; and the intuitive idea of justice is the corner-stone of ethics.

And, as we thus find the basis of the moral law in the eternal principle of equity, inevitably made manifest in the human consciousness when the mental perception came of the mutuality of social relations among men, so the enforcement of the moral law is guaranteed, perpetually and eternally, in the logical sequence of cause and effect. Reward for moral obedience, punishment for moral disobedience, are no arbitrary fiat of a distant Deity, reserved for some spectacular judgment-day at the opening of the future world, but they are principles or laws of physical, mental, and social life that are working right here in this world, and in all worlds where intelligent beings are living and acting together. These laws are a part of the very machinery of human action. Right action produces some kind of good fruit as its natural consequence; and wrong action produces some kind of evil fruit as its natural consequence. The good fruit is order, peace, happiness, physical health and power, mental and moral productiveness,— in fine, all the natural results of obeying natural laws of life, growth, and progress. The evil fruit is disorder, pain, misery, physical derangement, mental and moral incapacity and disaster,— or, in fine, all the natural disturbances, failures, and wrecks caused by a violation of the well-known laws of life, growth, and progress, in the largest sense of these words. Good action produces ever better and larger life; evil action is ever undermining the very forces of life, and tends toward its destruction.

In the complicated relations and mixed activities of human beings under the conditions of modern society, of course we do not always *see* either moral obedience or moral transgression working simply by direct line to its appropriate natural result. In the confusion and contradiction of manifold actions there may be mutually neutralizing tendencies; and yet the net product is the exact result of the really operative moral forces. And sometimes, too, there may be a superficial exterior action that may appear moral and may attain, yet also superficially, its moral rewards; and this for a time may veil our eyes against discerning the real moral transgression of the actor, and also against detecting the moral degeneration which is surely going on in his character and is the natural and unescapable result of his harbored vices. But such successful concealment of the process does not prevent the operation of the law of cause and consequence. It is just as impossible for a man to continue to do evil, however secretly, and still keep his nature good, and so go on perpetually to receive the rewards of goodness, as it is for a thorn-bush to bring forth grapes or a bitter fountain to give sweet water. At some time,— though possibly not in this world, and yet most likely even here,— all these disguises must drop away, and the character stand alone in its nakedness for just what it is, with no capacity for any companionships or enjoyments that are not in accordance with its own nature. But even if the disguises remain, though they conceal, they do not heal the moral disease nor stay the constant decrease of moral power within. No disguise is thick enough to evade the piercing sharpness of that punishment. Equally impossible is it for the character of genuine virtue to miss its highest rewards, however outward appearances may seem to belie the rule. It may be easy to take away from the deserving some outward crown of happiness and to press a wreath of thorns in its place. But it is the lot of the most virtuous that they care the least for the outward crowns,— that they are simply content with virtue itself; and there is no force in the universe that can rob them of that highest possible reward which can be accorded to any finite soul,— the growing power for virtue and diminishing susceptibility to any kind of evil influence.

Here, in this natural system of moral reward and retribution as the necessarily distinct and legitimate consequences of certain contrary courses of action, shall we find all needed sanctions for the practical enforcement of the moral law. And, when the theological theories of ethics, with their reliances upon methods of outward atonement for removal of moral guilt, with their decrial of personal righteousness as of less importance to salvation than mental faith, with their appeals to escape some indefinite curse and wretchedness in the world to come rather than a very palpable curse and wretchedness here and now as the result of violating laws of right,— when these theories shall have ceased to obscure and obstruct the natural moral vision of mankind, it will become, not as is sometimes said, more difficult, but really more easy, to appeal to moral motives in the conduct of life and to do it genuinely and effectively. Then will it be seen, as never before, that mankind is responsible for its own condition; that into the hands of human beings themselves, through their rational intuition of right in their relations with each other, through their capacity for intelligent understanding of nature's laws and their obligations of reason and conscience to co-operate with them, have been committed the progress, the happiness, the destiny of the human race.

More than ever, perhaps it will be charged, does this philosophy reduce human sentiment and conduct to "mere morality." It is a view of the moral law that does, indeed, detach morals from theology, but not necessarily from religion. Rather does morality, thus considered, blossom into religion. The moral law is detached from the outward authority of Mount Sinai revelations, from the dogmas of miraculous births and Mount Calvary atonements; but it is not detached from, but rather more fully identified with, the supreme aim and movement of the universe. Here, therefore, the central thought of our theme opens toward a higher sweep and wider horizons. What is religion in its strictest yet most generic sense but this: inwardly, in each individual mind, the feeling of relation toward a Universal Power and Law; outwardly, individual conduct in the service of that higher Law rather than of selfish aims? The moral law, in the dim primeval ages, had its prophetic germ in the instinctive feeling of the individual man that he had a right to life and whatever was necessary to life's preservation. When the mental sense perceived that others had equally the same right, then individual men found themselves inwardly constrained to respect this right in one another. Thus, the germinal instinct of self-preservation opened into *conscience*,— a common knowledge and confession that preservation was the equal right of all. But all this was on the lowest plane of life,— the plane of mere material life. That was what life first meant,— the perpetuation of physical existence and physical gratifications. But, as humanity progressed in development, higher and higher grades of life were discerned,— the life of the affections, sympathies, and charities, the life of thought, the life of inquiry and search after truth, the life of equity, justice, and rectitude; in short, the affectional, mental, moral life. And then, too, it became evident that man attained his richest and most satisfying manhood when he lived not in and for the body merely, but for the preservation of this higher life of mind and heart and soul; and that the lower forms of life must always be subordinated, often sacrificed, to the higher; that sometimes even the existence of the body, or the individual physical life, must be yielded up, in order to save the higher life of the mind's integrity or the heart's purity. And, when this point is reached, it is but a step to the central seat of the most genuine religion,— to the conviction that it is not the individual interest, the individual life, that the great world-process is bent toward sustaining and preserving, but some universal interest and life which the individual was meant to share and stand for and promote; but a step to the spirit that cries to the Law of Truth and Righteousness, "Though thou slay me, yet will I trust thee"; but a step to the practical devotion which, in utter self-forgetfulness, loses life to find it again in the finer, larger truth and in the bettered condition of humanity. And this is religion.

May 22, 1881.

XXIII.

THE PRACTICALITY OF THOUGHT.

"A thinking man is the worst enemy the Prince of Darkness can have."— T. CARLYLE.

LAST Sunday, I gave you what all, I suppose, would acknowledge to be a "practical sermon." It was concerned directly and solely with conduct and those springs of conduct that exist in the impulses and affections of the heart. It had nothing to do with theories or speculations or intellectual beliefs, except by implication to condemn them as tests of conduct and character. To-day, I am to give a sermon which may seem to some persons, at first glance, to be inconsistent with the tenor of my teaching a week ago,— a sermon on the Practicality of Thought. I propose to defend thought as an element of religion, even when it is largely concerned with considering theories and determining intellectual beliefs.

Yet there is no real inconsistency between the two positions. However strongly we may urge the conduct-side of religion,— so strongly that, when we hear a discourse with specially apt emphasis presenting that side, we are moved to exclaim: "*That* is all there is that is vitally practical about religion, all that is of any account; let us have that, and we may let all the beliefs and creeds and speculations concerning religion go,"— I say, however strongly we may urge this view, and maintain (and maintain truly) that preaching should be directed to this end, yet it may also be maintained, and with equal truth, that behind this *conduct*-side of religion there must be a solid, substantial *thought*-side, to give the conduct-side legitimacy. Conduct must have beneath it a logical basis of rationality, or else it lacks validity. It may not be always necessary, and often it detracts from direct practical effectiveness, to point out in detail the separate layers of this groundwork of sound reasoning; and yet it is there, if the conduct be true. It may have become so inwrought into the mental temperament as intuition and instinct that it may be appealed to more effectually in many cases without the construction of a logical syllogism; and that kind of direct moral presentation of the conduct-side of life is apt to be regarded as more practical, simply because it is more direct. But the thought-side is also practical. As an element in the progress of religion, even of what is called practical religion, thought is eminently the active power that effects the progress. Mankind would now be bowing down before idols of wood and stone as an act of religion, instead of doing righteousness, had not rational thought come in to clear away the superstitions on which idol-worship rested. And even at this day there are many superstitious beliefs which, with vast multitudes of people, are standing in the way of their seeing that the purest practical religion *is* the doing of righteousness.

Only the dispelling of ignorance, only the enlightenment of thought, can do away with the worship of beads and Bibles, and bring in the higher worship that is in spirit and truth.

The *Practicality of Thought*,— that, then, is our theme to-day. Religion in its completed wholeness is threefold. It is thought, it is sentiment, it is action. There may be a question whether it begins with thought or with sentiment, but there can be no question that its proper end is action. My own idea is that the elements of thought and sentiment appear together; that, if what may be called sentiment, or feeling, be excited in the beginning of religious development, whether in the race or in the individual, there must immediately arise some thought, some conception, of the object of the feeling, though it may be a very rude and very inadequate conception. Or, if anything gives rise to some conception or thought of a mysterious power external to man, such as has usually been the object of religious contemplation, then of necessity some feeling immediately arises toward this power,— a feeling corresponding with the thought. If the thought be chiefly of a being of terrible majesty and might, then the feeling will be chiefly one of fear and awe; but, if the thought be of a being of loving kindness and tender mercy as well as of power, then the feeling will partake largely of gratitude and love. So these two, sentiment and thought, go together. In the development of religion, they are simultaneous and reciprocal in their operation; and action, which comes after, is their legitimate product. Unless they result in action, they are sterile, and their existence is in vain. In the perfection of religious development, the three elements are combined in harmonious proportions. In this harmonious combination, sentiment is the impulse, thought the guide, and action the goal.

In this arrangement, it will be seen that thought is the specially important element. It is that which connects impulse, which in itself is blind, to its proper consequence in deed. Without this, impulse might rush unguided to some goal; but it might be a goal having no validity in the truth of things or in human benefit. If sentiment prevail with excessive preponderance in religious experience, we have that superlative emotional demonstration which may be called the hysteria of religion,— the ecstasy, trance, "slaying power," of the revivalistic meeting, where, for the time, thought and reason and even physical self-control are dethroned, and the resulting action resembles more the incoherent ravings of an inebriated man or the convulsions of an epileptic than the conduct of a rational being. Or, if sentiment does not preponderate to this excess, but still too largely dominates, there results a type of religion which spends itself chiefly in emotional religious ceremonies, and is afraid of thought as irreligious, and does not connect religion very distinctly with acts of daily life. But, again, it is possible that thought may preponderate too much over sentiment; and then there results a type of religion that may be morally correct and philosophically true, and yet *coldly* moral and true,— a religion wanting warmth, enthusiasm, and aspiration, and hence apt to be connected with a bloodless and nerveless kind of morality. And, still again, thought and sentiment may both be intensely active; but it is narrow thought and uncultivated sentiment,— the most mischievous and practically pernicious of all the possible combinations of the constituent elements of religion. Hence come the bitter spirit and deeds of sectarianism, bigotry, persecution, wars for enthroning beliefs, imprisonment and slaughter of bodies for the sake of saving souls. And the remedy is always a truer sentiment, that shall embrace humanity as well as imagined divinity, and a broader thought, that shall give a truer conception of divine being and divine law. And, yet again, what will seem, perhaps, most strange of all, and yet is a very common thing to happen, there may be religious action without thought or sentiment,— the result without the causes! This is where religious activity has become merely traditional, formal, and ecclesiastical. The causes have existed in the past: the sentiment and the thought were vital in the minds of people generations ago; and they produced certain institutions and habits of action which may go on acting of themselves and be participated in by men and women who no longer believe the thought nor feel the sentiment. And there is a good deal of this kind of religious action in the world: it is the formalism and hypocrisy, the crying evil, of instituted religion.

Such, then, is the general relation of these three elements of religion to each other and to the completed fulness of religion, whether historically in a whole people or in individual character. And now, on this general basis, I wish to show how practically necessary is thought in this combination; how that element which seems in itself to be the most speculative is in fact the most practically beneficial in the result.

And first, to this end, let us look at the province of thought in the general activity of human life and work. This age in which we are living is generally styled a practical, utilitarian age. It is an age of vast material enterprises and of intense devotion to the physical interests of the human race; an age of commerce, trade, mining, farming, manufacturing; an age of scientific discovery and invention, of marvellous progress in the useful arts, and of such successful appliances of inventive skill to supply the needs of mankind as even a hundred· years ago would have been declared simply miraculous. It is pre-eminently an age of activity, and of activity on what would have been called, in the religious phraseology of a half-century ago, the practical "worldly" side of human life. Of course, the age has other activities. But it is, by distinction, an age of *practical* affairs more than it is religious, more than it is literary, more than it is philosophical, more than it is poetic or musical or æsthetic in any form; more than it is military, frequent and bloody as its wars are; more, even, than it is moral or philanthropic. It is a commercial, utilitarian, business-devoted, science-learning, and art-inventing age,— an age of action and practicality *per se*. But where is the root of this action? *It is in thought.* It is in the human mind. The activity is not blind, unguided movement. If it were, it would not hit the mark of accomplishment so generally and precisely as it does. The things achieved are thoughts in somebody's brains before they are even begun. The practicality in all its phases, from the sailing of a ship to the discovery of a planet, is originated and directed by thought. Thought is applying itself to different problems than used to absorb the greatest thinkers, but it is thought none the less. Instead of bringing out a system of theology like Calvin's Institutes, it now brings out a steam engine. Instead of inventing a dogma for reconciling heaven and earth that were never estranged, it now invents a locomotive to go around the earth and bring into amity estranged nations. Thought is more dispersed than it used to be in earlier ages. It is not limited so much to the philosopher's brain or to the scholar's study. It stands with the mechanic at his bench. It is active in the manufacturer's brain. It throbs in the energy of the great magnates of the world's trade. It appears in miners and engineers, in the discoverers and inventors, and in a host of practical workers all through this busy world. If the great leaders of thought are fewer than once, it is because the number of thinkers is greater. The thought-army is made up of brigadiers. It was thought that tunnelled the Alps, and brought the lines of excavation from the opposite sides within an inch of each other, under the mighty mass of the mountain above. It was thought that scaled the Rocky Mountains with a railroad; thought that put a whispering wire under the Atlantic, and girdled the globe with an electric language; thought that is making night like unto day by the electric light; thought that has charted the ocean, and sails and steams across it; thought that organized commerce, banking, and government; in fine, it is thought that is the mainspring of all this bustling activity of the human world. It is thought that guides, controls, foresees, marks out the pathway, invents the machine, manages it when made, devises the instrumentality, and holds it to the purpose for which it was devised. It is thought applied to practical problems, but it is none the less thought. Indeed, it is one of the standing complaints of the churches that the thought of men is so much absorbed in these utilitarian and materialistic interests of life that little of it is left for the service of religion, so that church pews are empty and the old creeds go begging for believers.

Now, if thought be so important and fundamental an element in the very domain of these practical affairs of life, much more must it hold this master position in those departments of life which may be called mental, moral, and religious. The great thought-producers of the world have been the inspirers of human history and the sustainers of human action. Socrates, Plato, Kant, were mainly thinkers. They spent their lives in philosophy. Yet their thoughts have been, and still are, the sustenance of millions of minds. People who have never read a word that they said or wrote are yet mentally richer, and have had their own thoughts shaped and colored by the thoughts which such master thinkers as these left behind them. It is worth while even for a master mind, that is sure of its gravitating hold on a basis of fact, to soar into the empyrean of theory and speculation; for thus the lines of great truths are often discerned before scientific observation can climb so far, and imagination at least is fed, and poetry comes, if science does not. The heavens of science and the ideal heavens of the imagination have alike inspired poetic thoughts that are immortal. The poetry that is vital and creative is not the poetry in which sentiment dominates, but that in which the thought is as strong as the sentiment.

And, again, when we consider morality, thought is a most necessary, practical part of it. Even of the moral law, thought is as much the foundation as sentiment is. There is a sentiment of obligation, a feeling of *oughtness*, so to speak. Before, however, this feeling can arise, there is a mental perception of some truth that kindles it. Behind the Golden Rule, " Do unto others as ye would that they should do unto you," lies the perception of reciprocity of action,— the perception that the conduct which I demand from another as my right I owe to him as his right. This perception is the very root of the idea of justice; and upon it has been built, layer by layer, story by story, the whole practical system of law and jurisprudence. It is but a thought; but it is a thought that sustains the moral government of the universe, and all human governments, so far as they are stable and durable. And, in the moral problems that confront humanity to-day, nothing is more necessary than clear and wise thought as a practical element in settling them. Humane sentiment is good, and is needed; but humane sentiment alone cannot effect a solution. Excessive amiability may be, indeed, a hindrance to moral reform, granting indulgence where nature demands a retribution. Before such social problems as poverty, intemperance, licentiousness, criminality, while love and compassion may furnish the motive power, the utmost wisdom of thought is required to supply the remedial instrumentality.

When we come to religion, the practical power of thought is still more strongly illustrated. Behind all great religious movements there have been great thoughts. We greatly mistake, if we think that Christianity began mainly in a fresh development of religious sentiment, or that its dominant feature was a new kind of external religious action without any basis in thought. Jesus was not pre-eminently a thinker. He produced no philosophical system of thought. Yet he was one in whom thought, sentiment, and action were combined in an exceptional degree of harmony. And as, with reference to the existing religion of Judaism, his action was revolutionary, so was his thought. He continually violated its traditions and commandments, and taught men so. He distinctly proclaimed the abrogation of the Jewish law; and, in place of its ceremonial acts, as means of securing peace and blessedness, he inculcated the idea of the doing of righteousness. The Jewish Messianic conception he adopted, but transformed it, so that it became almost unrecognizable, with thoughts of his own. In fine, it was from such ideas as these which Jesus preached, and which Paul and the other apostles worked over, with large additions, that there came that great dramatic system of thought which was the strong motive power in the organization of primitive Christianity,—the scheme of a second coming of Christ in the clouds of heaven, and of a new-made earth and a Messianic kingdom, in which Jesus was to reign personally over the living and risen saints. Here was a system of belief, a creed, which, though it proved to be false in form, held thoughts which had a mighty sway over the unlettered people of that time.

Look at more recent history. The Protestant Reformation had its origin in the awakening of the human mind to a consciousness of its very right to think as against the authority of the Roman priesthood. And, when Luther came, he rallied the reformers around the idea of the Bible as the word of God, and each man to read and interpret it for himself, as against the idea that the priest or even the pope voiced the word of God. Behind the Reformation was this great central thought,— the Bible, and the Bible only, the rule of faith and practice, the individual reader of it being his own interpreter. It is a thought which later thought has had to correct; yet, for the time, it was a great step forward in intellectual development, and held the seed-grain from which the great Protestant movement has grown and spread until it has passed beyond the limits of a religion to become a civilization. Calvinism, again, derived its power to shape intellectually and morally the Protestant world, for two and a half centuries, from its thought,— not from the absolute truth of its thought, but because it had a definite, clean-cut, logically welded system of thought, put into words that the common mind could understand. Accept its premises, and you went on irresistibly to its conclusions; and it was not until within the present century that its premises were to any great extent denied within the limits of the Protestant Church. This system of thought, which became the staple doctrine of the pulpits and the mental and spiritual food of the pews, and which was meant to be accepted on its logical merits by the individual men and women who heard and read it, trained people to intellectual and moral robustness. Whatever may be said of its effect on the heart, it was a vigorous discipline of the mind and the conscience. By close alliance with the doctrine of civil liberty and political independence, it shaped the polity of States, settled New England, and became one of the strongest elements in practically moulding the political and social life of this North American continent.

The practical power of thought has been shown again in the progress of Protestantism and in the overthrow of Calvinism. As Protestantism had its origin in the awakening consciousness within the human mind of its right to think, so nearly every new denomination or sect or religious movement that has come in the course of Protestant history has sprung out of and been rallied around some new thought. The thought sometimes has been poor and narrow; yet it has at least shown the independence of the thinker, and has sought to win its followers by appealing to their thinking faculty. The advance of Protestantism is marked by these successive stages in the progress of thought,— when some new statement of truth, some new aspect of an old truth, some modification of an old doctrine, has challenged the judgment of the old church, and, if not accepted there, has gone out to form a new church.

The Universalist and Unitarian movements challenged Calvinism on some of its most vital doctrinal points. The challenge brought fierce conflict, and ended with two new sects, to denote the new watermark to which theological thought had risen. No: the conflict did not then end. The light of the new ideas has been reflected back upon the old denominations that rejected them until the very doctrines they once excommunicated are now shaping their own creeds. Unitarianism, in turn, after its separation from Orthodoxy, became too exclusively ethical and formal. It seemed to have spent its spiritual energy in a protest, and had no systematic religious philosophy of its own. Complaint was made that its sermons were good homilies enough on the plain, every-day duties of life, but arid and cold, without spiritual enthusiasm or sustenance. The Transcendental movement came with its spiritual philosophy and fresh enthusiasm for humanity; and Unitarianism at first fought it, persecuted its leaders, not by the fagot and thumbscrew, but by ways that were effectual to remove some of them from their pulpits. Yet, in moving them from Unitarian pulpits, it lifted them — like Emerson and Parker — to become teachers of the world; and Unitarianism, to a large extent, though not as yet very graciously, has finally accepted, to save itself from inanition and death, the very philosophy of religion which it had tried to cast out with these heretics.

And, to-day, it is *thought* again that is newly moving the religious world,— thought that has sprung from modern science and follows its method. The new religious philosophy, that is certainly coming in place of the old philosophy of supernaturalism in all its forms, is not yet definitely systematized. But it is in the air. Its power is felt, more or less, in all the churches. It is newly writing the creeds. It moulds the Biblical criticism of the Scotch Presbyterian, Robertson Smith; it revises the Bible in the Church of England and in the very heart of American Orthodoxy; it rewrites the Bible from the stand-point of rational historical criticism in the Dutch school of theologians; it is remoulding the time-honored institutions of France; it is even felt by the pope in the Vatican, and keeps him on the eve of flight from a rebellious populace. It appears in the secular journals and magazines as well as in the religious; in literature and in poetry quite as much as in the new treatises of theology. It especially is evident in science and in a broader social philosophy. It is in far-off India and Japan, and even in stable and stagnant China and in fatalistic Mohammedanism. Thus, everywhere the new religious thought is in the mental atmosphere of the age, dispelling the darkness of superstitions, scattering old errors, bringing in the light of larger truths. And everywhere it is shaping the faith of the future, — a faith which, when it comes, will be the most practical of all faiths, lifting the human mind into a grander and surer trust, laying upon the human heart and conscience a deeper sense of responsibility for the world's welfare, summoning States to a finer justice, trade to a stricter honesty, and welding society into a nobler bond of human brotherhood, in which, at last, *human* shall mean *humane*.

January 22, 1882.

XXIV.

THE GLORIOUS GOD.

> "God's glory is a wondrous thing,
> Most strange in all its ways,
> And, of all things on earth, least like
> What men agree to praise."

This little verse was the seed-text from which this discourse grew; and I cannot, perhaps, better introduce my subject than by telling you just how the growth started. The verse is one of five which stand together in our Hymn Book; but those five are selected from a much larger number, and the hymn to which they belong was written by the devout Roman Catholic, Faber. Though the general sentiment of the hymn is one to which our hearts might respond, there are in it certain ways of explaining religious truths (I refer more especially to the whole hymn as Faber wrote it) which would hardly accord with the thought of those of us who are accustomed to join in these Sunday services here. And, in looking over the pages of our book to select hymns for our weekly services, I have sometimes passed by this fine hymn, which for its general sentiment I wanted to take, because this verse in particular seemed to be contrary to my customary teachings. We believe, do we not, in a rational,

natural religion, immediately connected with the
practical, intelligible, every-day duties and dispositions of mankind,— a religion chiefly synonymous
with plain, simple goodness; with good aspirations,
good efforts, and good conduct; with knowledge
of and obedience to the natural laws that are
stamped upon, and the uplifting forces that are at
work within, the world of matter and the world of
man; and such obedience, such good dispositions
and good deeds, which, in our way of thinking, are
the best manifestation of divine power in humanity, it appears to us, men in general do "agree to
praise," when they clearly see and understand them.
This verse, on the contrary, seems to inculcate the
idea of religion as something strange and foreign to
man's natural experience; as something to come by
mysterious and special grace, which the natural
reason cannot be expected to comprehend nor even
to praise. Its key-thought, apparently, is that old
conception of Orthodoxy, that God's revelation of
himself, not only in history, but to the individual
soul, is miraculous,— an interposed visitation by the
Holy Spirit for purposes of conversion, and in
specially providential ways not to be understood nor
judged by human reason. And, very likely, some
such thought as this was in Faber's mind when he
wrote the verse. But Faber was a true poet. And
in every true poet, religious or other, there is a profounder meaning than can be translated by any
prose rendering. It is for this reason that many of
the old hymns and anthems, which conform verbally
to a theology which we discard, may yet do service

in the expression of a feeling that goes deeper than theology. And last Sunday, as I read this hymn to you to be sung, choosing it then as I had once or twice before with a silent protest against a portion of it, another possible meaning of this special verse came to me, and therewith the thought-kernel of this discourse,— which I bring you to-day,— over which I have ventured to write the words, "The Glorious God."

And yet, after writing the words there, I shrink from the theme. Shall any one venture to sound the depths of that mystery of infinite being in which we, and this universe and all things in it, live and move and have our being? Shall any finite mind have the audacity to attempt to portray the ways, the attributes, the aims of Infinite Mind? attempt to talk of an existence which, by the very fact that we call it *infinite*, we admit to be boundless, incapable of being described, incapable of being comprehended? Does not the old text meet us, to forbid the essay at the outset,— "Touching the Almighty, we cannot find him out"? We can understand how the believer in a miraculous revelation of Deity, the believer in a scheme of theology which is alleged to contain a celestially illuminated chart of God's entire nature and dealings with mankind, should venture to speak of his power and glory as something which man can define and describe. But how can one to whose thought Deity is and must be, by the very necessity of the case, largely hidden, one to whom infinite Being means literally and actually unbounded and illimitable being,— and the unfathom-

able unknown must ever be more than the known,—
how can such a one dare to attempt any expression
of such a thought as the glory of God?

But, on the other hand, if we can retain, with the
natural exercise of our faculty of reason, anything
of the religious sentiment; if we are to define religion as anything more than or different from morality,
then it is necessary that there should remain some
such thought as this; and, if the thought, then also
some possible way of giving it utterance. Words
may not utter it fully,— this thought of the possible
divine glory: music may often sound its depths
deeper than words. Yet words may suggest the
interpretation, even though not able to make it
complete. And at this day, when positive knowledge is our boast and the tendency is so strong to
confine thought to the limits of the world of phenomena; at this day, when we go to the scientists
and the cyclopædias to explain all the mysteries of
the world-forces, and the theologies in which we
were bred are vanishing like the fairy stories of our
childhood, and what we once read as history is
turning into uncertain tradition and legend and
myth; at this day, when the archæologists and
biologists are following back the trail of unbroken
evolution in the history of man and the history of
the planet he occupies, for vast ages back of the time
where we used to put creation, and the words "heredity" and "law" and "force" are applied as labels
to whole regions of life formerly thought to be under
the direct control of a personal deity; at this day,
too, when, on the other hand, what cannot be thus

studied and explained, mapped and labelled as positive knowledge, is apt to be put aside as unworthy of consideration among practical men and women,— as a country not only unexplored, but unexplorable, not only unknown, but unknowable,— amid such tendencies of thought, there is some danger that not only much of the mystery, but much of the beauty, poetry, and power of uplifting sentiment, which have been associated with religious ideas, will also vanish. I think it very necessary, therefore, that those of us who accept the results of the new science and of the new methods of studying man's history on the earth should be ready to set forth, if we can, any truer and grander thought of Deity which may have come to us in lieu of the old theological conceptions which science has displaced.

And we may say, in the first place, that our thought of the divine power and glory meets the test of the verse that is our text in this,— that it is, of all things, "least like" what men in general, thinking of that power and glory, "agree to praise." What is the idea of God held by the vast majority of the people of Christendom? It is the idea of an Almighty Being seated in majesty and magnificence on a throne above the skies, after the pattern of a human sovereign, touched with paternal benignity, but ruling the world from that distant heavenly throne by a double system of laws and special providences. It is of a being who made this universe in the first place either out of his own nature, calling the very atoms of matter into existence, or out of material atoms existing co-eternally with himself,—

building it thence as a master mechanic fashions a machine, — and who then impressed upon it the laws and forces necessary to keep it in operation and peopled it with living creatures, while he retired to his celestial abode to govern it henceforth by these general laws and by occasional startling interventions of supernatural power. It is of a being who, in primitive ages, visited the earth in the form of man, walked upon its surface, talked with its first inhabitants, commanded them what to do and from what to abstain. Ay, it is of a being who was once born on this earth of a human mother, and grew here from babyhood to manhood, and then lived for a brief time a devoted life of goodness, and was put to death on a cross, and ascended again to heaven, where he remains to judge the world of mankind as death shall summon them before him. This is the central conception of Deity believed in by the great majority of the Christian populations of the earth. And this, with its various accessories of creative and sovereign power, of monarchical magnificence, of arbitrary judgment mingled with paternal compassion, of almighty will and all-knowing wisdom, is what the mass of the people in Christian congregations "agree to praise" in their worship. Or go into other religions, the same anthropomorphic idea of God prevails. It is God a great and powerful ruler, a king, at best a sovereign father; God, too, who once lived on the earth in the form of man, or perhaps even lives there to-day (like the Grand Lama of Thibet), surrounded with power and arrayed in the habiliments of glory.

But the divine glory that we would seek is, of all things on earth, least like what these people have in mind as God. We do not look for it in the god Jupiter, nor the god Jehovah, nor the god Osiris, nor the god Thor, nor the god Brahma, nor the god Jesus. All these were honest and sincere but ineffectual attempts to express the inexpressible, to define the undefinable, to personify an existence and power which in its essence must forever remain above all human conceptions of personality. They served their historic time and purpose. They marked some aspect and direction of human thought in its effort to grapple with the problem of the ultimate cause of things. They were reaches after the Divine, approaches toward it, but none of them revealed the fulness of its glory. In all the religions, and in Christendom especially, people have been too much wont to glorify their own metaphysical speculations about Deity, their own mental conceptions of him; to take these as his revealings, and to pass by the actual revelations of divine power going on right around them. What a vast amount of religious energy and devotion, for instance, has been spent in setting forth the glory of the Divine nature and work according to the purely metaphysical conception of the triune personality of the Godhead! The assertion may be safely risked that no person ever succeeded in getting a logical, rational idea of this doctrine. Indeed, the last resort of all argument upon it has always been that it is a doctrine not to be understood by reason, but to be accepted by faith. But the time has passed when any considerable num-

ber of thoughtful minds, awake to the thought of
this new age in which we are living, can be content
to look for the divine glory in these metaphysical
creeds wherein men have put their own conceptions
of Deity; or in any names, however sacred and ancient, which have survived from man's earnest but
futile effort to define and personify the power in
which and by which and amid which he felt that his
own being was embosomed and kept in existence.

"The glorious God," — where, then, shall man
look for the living counterpart, if there be any, of
this thought? Where but in the universe — this
universe of nature and man — which is the only possible presentation of divine power that comes within
our knowledge? This universe is itself the shining
garment by which the divine power is made visible.
While people have been looking away into the past
and trying to keep hold of their belief in God by
holding to the creeds and conceptions of him that
were framed centuries ago, and saying to themselves
and repeating in their churches, "What a glory was
then revealed to the world!" lo, here is the same
God, existing apparently as he has always existed,
working as he has always worked, right in the familiar scenes of nature and human life, close around us
every day. It is not because the divine glory is so
far off that it is becoming dimmed, but we miss
seeing it because it is so near. Let us lift two or
three of the curtains from these hiding-places among
the every-day facts of our lives, — just lifting a little
the drapery of these very phenomena with which
science deals, and in the knowledge of which we

have such an advantage over the ancients; and *because* of our knowledge of which it is sometimes boasted that we have no occasion for any God at all this side of that curtain of the absolutely unknowable which can never be lifted at all. If I mistake not, we shall find the glory, "wondrous" and "strange in all its ways," shining all around us, just behind and through the most known and familiar things.

Every year, before the winter has loosed its icy grip upon the earth, you begin to see the animal wonder of a new spring-time. Under sheltering fences or the sunny side of your houses, and close up to the warm stones of your doorstep, which have been heated all day in the March sun, you may have seen the grass springing up and putting on its dress of living green. It was the first streaks of the dawn of that coming glory of life and color, of leaf and flower and fruit, which in a few months are spread over all this northern zone of earth. It comes so steadily and surely, and we have become so accustomed to its coming year after year, that we do not see the wondrousness of it as we should, were our eyes to behold it for the first time. Could we see it for the first time, indeed, we should stand amazed, if not worshipful, before the spectacle of the awakening life and beauty. And you say, too, that you know the cause of it,— that the earth in its annual circuit round the sun turns at this season its northern hemisphere, by reason of the angle between its equator and the ecliptic, more directly to the sun's rays, and hence receives more of the sun's heat.

But the process is none the less wonderful, though you may give its reason and even scientifically analyze all the details of it from beginning to end. It is, to begin with, a sufficiently stupendous fact that that luminary in the heavens, ninety-two millions of miles away, should be the yearly incubator of life on this planet. What is the secret power behind that glory? But the process of it, as science unfolds it, is a tale more wonderful than any legends of genii or deities which the old mythological religions taught or stories of fairy spirits that belong to nursery lore. How is that blade of grass at your doorstep linked with the sun? Mechanically, by a gossamer web, as it were, of ether, spread invisibly within our atmosphere and through all the interplanetary and interstellar spaces of the heavens, and acting as the conductor of both light and heat. Heat, you know, is a mode of motion. In the sun, it is the resultant of the constant motion of the sun's constituent matter. This motion is transmitted — transmitted as heat — to the contiguous atoms of the ether, which are set to vibrating, and these hand it to the atoms lying next, and these to the next, and so on, until, precisely as motion is communicated through a whole row of marbles which a boy strikes at one end, the heat of the sun is communicated through the ninety-two millions of miles of the vibratory waves of the gossamer web of ether, and strikes your doorstep, and touches the dead-looking grass-root in the crevice below it. And, when the sun's rays become sufficiently vertical to make this touch powerful enough, it starts that activity in the root which soon shows itself in the green blade above and harbingers the spring. It sets an energy to work in those rootlets by which they seize from the earth and air just the chemical particles needed to build that green leaf of grass ; and these particles then are sent upward in the sap by the principle of a suction pump, to be digested and separated by the leaf itself.

And this is an epitome of what the sun is doing by its magic art at every spring-time over all the expanse of the meadows and in every forest, every shrub and tree and bud, all round the globe. But more than this : the sun has been scientifically shown to be not only the annual renewer and preserver of the vegetable life of the earth, but the source of all life, animal as well as vegetable, and of all physical power and beauty, that are anywhere manifest on this earth. It is Tyndall, remembering the law of the correlation of forces as well as this immediate effect of the sun's heat, who says : " The sun rears the whole vegetable world, and through it the animal ; the lilies of the field are his workmanship, the verdure of the meadows, and the cattle upon a thousand hills. He forms the muscle, he urges the blood, he builds the brain. . . . He builds the forest and hews it down, the power which raised the tree and which wields the axe being one and the same. The clover sprouts and blossoms, and the scythe of the mower swings, by the operation of the same force. The sun digs the ore from our mines ; he rolls the iron ; he rivets the plates ; he boils the water ; he draws the train. . . . There is not a hammer raised, a wheel turned, or a shuttle thrown, that is not raised and turned and thrown by the sun." Well may this enthusiastic devotee of science add: "Presented rightly to the mind, the discoveries and generalizations of modern science constitute a poem more sublime than has ever yet been addressed to the intellect and imagination of man. The natural philosopher of to-day may dwell amid conceptions which *beggar* those of Milton." And to this I may add that, though Milton's conceptions were theological and these are scientific, these are none the less concerned with Divine things. What is behind this glory of multitudinous life that marches over the earth with every spring? Have we reached its primal source in the sun? Nay: the sun is but the shadow of some power older and mightier still. The sun is but one of many millions of suns, each with its family of planets, which it warms and lights and peoples with life, and arms with power. We should have to lift the whole curtain of the starry heavens to behold the revelation of the inconceivable glory of which the sun is but one ray.

Let us lift another of these curtains of phenomenal facts in the domain of positive knowledge. Many of you, I hope, have read, some perhaps have heard, that incomparable sermon by our friend, William C. Gannett, on "The Treasures of the Snow," — one of the four miracles of the year, he calls it. You who have heard it, or you who have read it, know with what exquisite poetic touch he unlocks the snow-flake, and tells what may there be see nunder the powerful microscope, or is scientifically inferred from what the microscope discloses.

Yet, exquisite in poetic feeling and expression as is his description, the poetry, beauty, and wonder are all in the simple facts themselves. The dryest chronicles of science tell them all,— how every tiniest snow-flake is made up of crystals which are put together in upwards of a thousand different varieties of form : in prisms, three-sided and six-sided ; in pyramids, and in prisms capped with pyramids ; in star-shapes, the lines radiating from a centre of glory, star sometimes within star, and these within a third and a fourth ; in prisms capped with stars at both ends ; in fern shapes, with all the varieties that are found among ferns in the forests. But through all this mingling of different forms there is no disorder, no misfit. The lines, the joints, the angles, are all drawn with mathematical precision. No deft fingers of the most skilled and patient workman in China can copy their exactness. And through all the variety there is identity, too. There is one mathematical law that pervades the whole structure. To quote now from my friend : " Snow-nature is bound by a law of sixes. The sides of every prism and pyramid meet at one angle,— that of sixty degrees or its multiples ; the rays of every star diverge at that one angle ; every vein upon those little fern leaves joins its stem at that one angle or its multiples. The snow-stars are all six-rayed or, rarely, twelve ; the centres all hexagonal. Watch the flakes of a whole winter's storms, climb Chimborazo, go to the pole, or make your mimic snow-storm for yourself inside a chemist's bottle,— never will you find a finished star with five rays or with seven, or with that law of the angles broken. The rays themselves are broken, but never that creative law. Bruised, shattered, huddled together, the snow-flakes reach us; but, through all bruise and shatter, that law of sixes lies plain upon them. By that they are born and live and die." Well may my friend add, "Is it not very impressive and full of awe even,— these mathematics carried down to the microscopic measurements,— the grand legislation of the universe laid thus upon its invisible atoms?" Surely, *some* power has its *shechinah*, not only in the majesty of the storm, but in this glory of every single snow-flake that falls at our feet or that melts away unseen in the air.

Shall we lift another curtain on a somewhat different scene? Look, then, at the cell from which comes all animal life. In its first original stage there is nothing to distinguish whether bird or beast or man is to come from it. What shall come depends on some hidden formative principle in itself, inherited from its ancestry, and upon the environment to which it is to be subjected in its development. Suppose it is to become human. It then draws to itself in time, by a mechanism which man's inventive genius may wonder at, but cannot imitate, the materials for building that most consummate of all nature's structures, the human body. The animal, vegetable, and mineral worlds are drawn upon for tribute to build it. But, beyond all animal structures before it, this human body becomes a *thinker*. Its brain is not simply used instinctively to push its own fortunes in the struggle for a merely

animal existence, but it becomes an instrument of
conscious reflection upon the very work and purpose
of nature itself in bringing it into being. It dares
even to assert — this human brain — that it sees
nature's aim, understands the intelligence that is
impressed on the snow-flake and planted in the seed
and that struggles through all the graceful or un-
couth forms of animal life; and it has the audacity
— this human brain — to say further, " I can help to
complete this plan : I see that mathematics in the
snow-flake means the law of justice in mankind ;
that order in the material universe means morality
in human society; that the relation of mutual dependence and helpfulness evident between the forces
of nature means brotherhood among men." And
thus this human brain, whose pedigree thirty years
before we could not distinguish in the cell nor whose
future prophesy, becomes, under the laws and forces
of its own existence, not only a thinker, but a doer
of righteousness. Here it becomes a Plato, there
a Washington, and there again a Jesus. And, in
hosts of humbler men and women, it manifests itself
in deeds of loving-kindness and tender mercies. It
is a builder of states, a ruler of nations, a creator of
the arts of civilization. It discovers the secrets of
nature, learns the management of her forces, edu-
cates and transmits its own power, organizes philanthropy for the improvement and preservation of the
race to which it belongs. The potent life-forces
hidden in that tiny cell have unfolded into a power
and glory that may well be called Godlike in their
character.

Let us draw aside yet another veil in the world of scientific fact, and one behind which is promised a near view — almost, indeed, a veritable revelation — of the central mystery of life itself in its most elemental forces. A few years ago, the scientific journals were thrilling with fresh interest over a new discovery. It seemed as if, at last, human research, through the agency of the microscope, were to be rewarded with a sight of the primordial substance in which all organic life had begun, and which is the necessary substratum of all continued vitality. *Protoplasm* was the word coined to name this wonderful and unique form of matter, which appeared to carry in itself the " promise and potency " of all modes of terrestrial life. Let us look for a moment at its nature and habits through the eyes of a man of science. Putting under the lenses of a powerful microscope a section of the leaf of an aquatic plant peculiarly adapted to disclose the protoplasmic life-current, and supposing his readers to be gazing at it with him, a scientific professor[*] says : " You behold a series of cells. But through the thin wall of any cell appears a flowing stream. . . . A very river it seems as it rushes on, wave after wave, up from the depths below, across the field of vision and down again, over and over or round and round, in ceaseless rotation. Now, the current catches in its course this little particle, now that, hurling each along, now up, now down, now over, now under, without weariness, without hindrance, hour after hour before us. And now, as the stream goes on so grandly, think, for a moment, what it is at which

[*] Prof. T. H. McBride, in *Popular Science Monthly*, July, 1882.

we gaze. We call it protoplasm; but it is the current of *life*, the 'physical basis of life,'— the common bond which binds in one the whole kingdom of organic things. Think, too, of the antiquity of that stream, of its lineage. The brook that 'goes on forever' is as nothing to it; for here the stream has come flowing down through ages, which are to us an eternity, ever since life began on earth. The mountains have been hoary with years, and have disappeared beneath the level of the all-producing sea; but this stream is older than they. Continents have grown old, worn out, and been renewed, rebuilt from the débris of this same stream, and life has again flooded those continents; but this stream is older than they. . . . [In the interminable past] the vast procession of life begins, rises before us, spreads away in variety, activity, in beauty, in wonderfulness, incomprehensible." Verily, this seems like lifting the veil in the Hebrew temple, behind which was conceived to be imaged the Eternal *I Am*,— the Being that was, and is, and is to be, from everlasting to everlasting.

And so we might go on, lifting the curtains from this familiar life all about us, and of which we are ourselves a part; and on every side, from every nearest or remotest or obscurest corner, there would be revealed to us the same ineffable wonder of activity, of order, of arrangement, of beauty, of power, in the great and in the little. We need not go outside of the sensible universe for the demonstration of a divine glory beyond anything and everything that the theological creeds have ever been able to give us in their conceptions of Almighty Being.

But, though we thus keep within the limits of
sensible demonstration, there is something within
the revelation at every lifting of the curtain of phenomena which the phenomena themselves do not
explain,— something which they suggest, manifest,
but do not account for. There is always one secret
unrevealed. We see into the glory, we are amazed
and awed before it, but we see not the source of it.
There is always one question unanswered. Touch
nature where we will, follow science up her road-
ways and byways in whatever direction we may, we
shall find everywhere the wonder, the power, the
glory ; but behind all curtains that are drawn aside
there remains one inner curtain that is never lifted.
Science shows us the wondrous material atom containing within itself the potency for all forms of
organization and life, but the secret of that *potency*
she does not disclose. She takes us to " vital force "
as the formative, guiding principle in every living
organism ; but whence and what the *vital force* she
has not yet explained. Even if she prove it to be
chemical force, that is but a step farther back. She
carries us back to Force itself as a primordial element in the origin of things, to Force as eternal and
imperishable, remaining one and the same amid all the
changes and correlations of it in the manifold forces
of the universe ; but she has not told us how we are
to conceive of this mighty primal energy, in and of
what it consists, or what the philosophy of its existence. She points us to the infinitesimal nerve-
cells of the human brain where this wondrous primal
energy, after the civilizing discipline of millions of

generations of organic existence, sets up housekeeping as a rational thinker and a doer of righteousness. But how the connection has been established between the nerve-cell and the thought, and whether, with the dissolution of the house, the *housekeeper* also ceases existence, are problems which science has not solved. She bids us look at the protoplasmic current in its ceaseless flux and reflux, and almost promises there to unlock for us the final mystery of the secret of life. But whence the beginning, what the cause of the protoplasmic current, she has made no revelation. We may look in and see, as behind a glass case, how the work of life goes on; but we see not the secret power that starts it and sustains it. If we touch with a needle the wall of the current at which we have been gazing, thinking to investigate closer, instantly "the charm is broken, the mystic river ceases to flow, the tiny particles settle into unbroken peace." That cell, in fact, on which we gaze is then dead, while all the others remain alive; and so the curtain falls upon the secret unexplained. So, turn whichever way we will, back of the boundless glory that we behold lies the mystery of a power unrevealed.

Shall we say, then, that God is only in the hidden mystery? That he is not revealed at all, because the very paths which are lighted for us by the glory lead us finally to barriers beyond which we cannot pass nor see? That, because we cannot know him wholly, he is, therefore, wholly "the Unknowable"? That he is in the infinity beyond that barrier, but not in the finite beauty, order, power, majesty, goodness, love, whose source we have traced up to that line? Nay: by the very discovery brought to us by science, that all force or energy is one and self-persistent, however manifold its forms, our logical intellect may leap that barrier to unite the phenomenal glories on the hither side and the sovereign substance of being unrevealed beyond in the inseparable links of one all-pervading power and life. Life infinite and life finite are but one life. As one force, one law, bind together and penetrate this common earth which we daily tread and the heavens into whose star-populated depths we gaze, but which we can never wholly fathom, so is this whole universe of our senses bound to and pervaded by the unfathomable sovereignty of being that escapes all tests which our senses can meet or our science devise.

And an added glory comes into the universe of phenomena, because of this very mystery of sovereign being in which it is embosomed. Our world — this little earth — takes on dignity and majesty from the infinity of things, unseen as well as seen, of which it is a part. Imagination, reason, conscience, are alike spurred to finer achievement by the problem of the world's relation to the unseen Infinite; while the heart may rest serenely upon the confidence, than which there can be none surer, that its destiny is linked with the forces which make the very integrity and stability of the universe itself. As to what is in the mystery behind him and in the mystery before him, man need have no fears. It is enough that this present circuit of life in which he shares, and which is flowing out of the mystery of the past toward the mystery of the future, is glorious with intelligence and measured by advances in moral benefit.

I have seen a child in its mother's lap gaze up with a sudden wonderment into the beaming benignity of the mother face and into the loving depths of the mother eyes, as if its infantile mind had just caught some new revelation there and was trying to comprehend the fulness of its meaning,— perhaps stopping in the midst of a frolic or of pain and crying, with this wondering, searching, upward look, and seeming to be impressed with a sense of a power manifest there that understood all and could do all and was full of good will; then nestling down closer and in quiet into the mother's lap. So we are children still in the lap of our mother Nature. And sometimes we are hushed into a tender awe, it may be in the midst of our pains, or it may be in the midst of our pleasures or our work, as if a mysterious, mightiful power were bending over and holding us. We lift our gaze upward to see not only that we are held in the embrace of Law, but that through Law shines the glory of Love; and, at that answer, our hearts are at rest.

April 22, 1883.

NOTE.— This discourse was given first in March, 1882, but not in the completed form as here printed. At the date stated above, it was delivered, in its present form, before the "Free Religious Society" in Providence, R.I.; and was thus redelivered in New Bedford in 1884.

XXV.

A TWENTY-FIVE YEARS' MINISTRY.

*"And, for success, I ask no more than this,—
To bear unflinching witness to the truth."*

ON Wednesday, the 28th of December, 1859, just twenty-five years ago this day, and at this hour, I stood here to be invested with the office of preacher and minister to this society. The ceremonies of induction — though considerably too long, I remember, for the frigid inclemency of the weather — were of the simple form common to the most liberal Congregational societies. The society had already completed the contract of settlement with the candidate, whom it had heard and called of its own free choice; and no questions were put to him concerning his creed or his ecclesiastical standing. Several ministers were present from this city and elsewhere, some of them having formerly been connected with the society, who conducted the services in a way that expressed both the natural solemn dignity of the occasion and the spirit of cordial good will and good fellowship that should exist between neighboring churches. Having thus been officially made your minister, I preached here my inaugural discourse on the following Sunday, New Year's day of 1860. To-day, then, we exactly complete a quarter of a century of life together as people and pastor.

A quarter of a century's ministry,—what memories press upon me as I write those words! Memories that almost overwhelm the purpose which I have in mind to-day in this anniversary discourse. In these years, one generation has nearly gone, and another has come. Mingled with your faces as you sit here this morning, I see another congregation, more numerous than that which usually occupies these seats,—the congregation of our risen dead. They take no room among us; but, through my memory's eye, I see the space between these walls alive with the faces of this benignant company of our departed membership. But into this field of reminiscence I can hardly trust myself to enter. Nor do I propose to-day to take up any time with the statistics of the parish and of parish work. The number of marriages and deaths in the society in these twenty-five years, the changes from year to year in its membership, the condition of its benevolent agencies, the state of its Sunday-school, the advances which may have been made in the external equipments of the society both with regard to its Sunday services and its benevolent and social objects,—all these are matters of a certain personal and parochial interest, and it is usually expected that they will be brought forward in anniversary sermons. On previous anniversary occasions, I have referred to these points, and at times somewhat in detail; and to-day, though we have no boasts to make, the external condition of our society might be presented in a way of which we should have no cause to be ashamed. But my thought presses in another direction at this time.

One remark only will I make on those matters which concern our external prosperity as a society, touching merely the one point where our affairs are the least promising,— the fact, namely, that the increase in the population of our city brings little or no increase to our numbers here, and that it is even doubtful whether the gradual passing away of the old families, from which the strength of this society has been largely drawn for the past sixty years, is made good by their descendants. Even with regard to this one point, it may be said that, counting our morning and evening services together, it is doubtless true that the services of this church during these twenty-five years have reached and are still reaching a larger number of persons in the community than has been the case in any previous twenty-five years of its history. And so long as the society has this opportunity and can wisely use it, there is no pressing cause for anxiety concerning the future.

Leaving, then, these externals, let me proceed to the purpose I have most at heart on this occasion, which is to trace, in a measure, the more interior development of my ministry among you, and to sum up, in pretty definite shape, the convictions — the articles of faith, I might say — which have been the substance of the teachings of this pulpit during this period. I say "the substance of its teachings"; for there has been a development — a growth, I trust — in my own thought within this time, so that truth comes to me in somewhat different form from what it did when my ministry began ; though this change, perhaps, is more marked in respect to the mode of statement than in respect to the substance of the matter stated. In some particulars, however, my beliefs have undergone a change,— so gradual that possibly it may not have been noticed by my hearers, yet a change nevertheless,— under the influence especially of the widening and deepening scientific thought of this modern era. But not to anticipate this point, to which I shall recur by and by, I now ask you to go back with me to the beginning of our work here together ; and if, talking on these matters that are so near our hearts, I make unusual use of the first personal pronoun, you will, I am sure, pardon the offence to-day.

My ministry began near the opening of a stirring period in our national history. In that last week of December, 1859, when we took here those mutual vows of trust and fidelity which bound us together as people and pastor, the country was flushed with the excitement caused by John Brown's memorable expedition into Virginia. That hero's life had just ended on a Virginia gallows by Virginia law. However the act for which he died may be judged in the cold court of the prudent understanding, it was one of those deeds of chivalrous heroism which always win human hearts and kindle human consciences as with coals of fire from heaven. Even Virginia's governor was compelled, as he has confessed, to admire the character of the man, while he signed the warrant to hang him. And John Brown, dying on that Virginia gallows for daring to confront human law and human constitutions for the sake of the slave, became the sign in the sky, by which the two hostile and warring ideas in the nation, liberty and slavery, began to gather and align their respective hosts for the coming conflict of arms. Before the first year of my ministry was finished, in the expiring months of Buchanan's administration, with the election of Abraham Lincoln as his successor to the Presidential chair, we heard the ominous rumblings of the earthquake which soon came in the terrific shock of civil war, with its vast armies of national brothers fighting against each other, and its four years of battles and carnage and sorrow. And then when peace came, with its triumphal decree of emancipation to the slave, there followed the still longer and more anxious period of reconstruction, culminating in the final triumph of the ballot and of equal rights of citizenship before the law to black and white alike.

During these two eventful periods, my ministry was turned largely to national questions by an inward force, a moral compulsion, which I could no more have resisted than I could have resisted the sun in his course. From the first day to the last in that dreadful contest, this pulpit pronounced, with no uncertain sound,— and oftener than was agreeable, perhaps, to all the membership of the society,— not only for the national cause, but for the national cause as it meant, or should be made to mean, liberty and justice to the negro,— equality of rights to all the inhabitants of the land. And there is no part of my ministry to which I look back to-day with more satisfaction than to this. It is a special cause of joy to me now to recall that I never from the first had the slightest question as to what were the principles which the pulpit should keep paramount in discussing the issues of the great conflict; that, in the very first discourse I gave upon the matter, several months before the war actually broke out, I struck the key-note, which I never afterwards lost, that, as slavery was the cause of the nation's troubles and perils, so emancipation must be their remedy; and that, again, when Fort Sumter was attacked, and President Lincoln called upon the loyal States for troops, and the northern section of the country was in that Pentecostal flood of enthusiasm for defending the dishonored flag, when many warmly patriotic souls thought it injudicious to risk disturbing the sentiment of loyalty to the Union by introducing the issue of slavery,— that even then I could not hesitate to declare that the one thing which imperilled the Union was slavery, and the one thing which could permanently save the Union, and the only thing which could give to our armies a cause worth dying for, was *liberty with justice.*

I do not recall these things in any spirit of boasting. Far from it. I was by no means alone in such pulpit work; nor did I have much to do, at the time, in determining my course by reasoning it out and nerving my will to it. All that had been previously done for me in my education and moral temperament. Rather do I recall this part of my ministry in devout gratitude that the mighty moral forces which were then surging through this nation to lift it to a higher plane of righteousness found and used me as their instrument. I recall it, too, that I may give due thanks to you of this society for the untrammelled freedom you gave me for such utterances. This work was not mine alone. We did it together. You gave me the freedom, and I used it. On no other terms than those of free expression, as my deepest convictions compelled, could I have remained your minister. But, though my discourses on these themes may not always have been in accord with the judgments of all who were in the pews, never did I receive from you a hint or sign that you wished this pulpit to be other than free. Whatever it may have been able to do for our country's cause during this eventful period, you shared the work.

I may here add that the freedom which I then used in speaking in this place on matters of vital political concern, I have continued to use whenever it seemed to me that, in pending political issues, questions of deep moral import were involved. The ordinary questions on which political parties are separated have their appropriate discussion elsewhere, and do not properly belong to the pulpit; though the minister as a citizen should have his views on such questions, and should be expected, like all good citizens, freely to act upon them in his personal capacity. But, whenever political issues or party action distinctly involve ethical questions and come into the domain of practical morals, then the pulpit has a legitimate right to express itself on such issues and action, and will be very derelict to its duty, if it fail to do this. It is a very delicate and difficult duty with which the preacher is thus charged, calling for the faculty of strict mental justice and for entire freedom from the spirit of partisanship. He should be able to speak in such a way that his hearers, if they can listen with the like candor, will feel that it is the moral, and not the political message that is dominant in his mind. It is in this way and spirit that I have always endeavored to approach and treat such questions here,— with what success it is not for me to say.

But, I think, I may safely say that the freedom of this pulpit for a wide range of topics has been established beyond recall. As wide as are the applications, to national, social, or individual conduct of the fundamental principles of justice, honesty, purity, humanity, brotherhood, so wide at least must be the freedom of any pulpit which has any good reason for existence in this last quarter of the nineteenth century. On this ground, I have been wont to consider that not only political questions which involve moral principle, but all questions of social and moral reform, are fitting themes to be treated in this place. Temperance, justice and equal opportunity to woman, the treatment of crime and criminals, the national duty to the Indians, social purity, marriage and divorce, the secularization of government and of the public schools in this country as a matter of equal rights for all classes of citizens, the better reconciliation of the interests of labor and capital,— these and any other themes pertaining to the social amelioration and elevation of mankind, I have been accustomed from time to time to bring to this pulpit, that we might view and weigh them here from the stand-point of religion. The religion, indeed, which I have tried through all these years to present to you in my preaching covers all these great themes and objects which are so vital to human happiness and progress.

Yet there is a popular distinction between religious themes and themes pertaining to social reform and philanthropy; and, at this point, I turn to survey those beliefs underlying my ministry, which by this popular usage would be called religious beliefs. And here it is that the gradual development of thought, involving some changes of opinion, of which I just now spoke, is to be noted. When I first came among you, I could have said that my views accorded more nearly, perhaps, with the system of belief which had been preached by Theodore Parker than with the views of any other representative man. That is, I discarded the supernatural, the prodigious, the miraculous, as evidence of religious truth or attestation of a special revelation from Deity, and accepted religion as only a natural revelation of moral and spiritual truths. Between the so-called revealed religions and natural religion there was, to my mind, no distinction. All religions were natural,— that is, were the natural unfoldment and ascension of the human mind in the discovery of ethical and spiritual truth; and yet all religions so far as they possessed any truth were revealed,— that is, truth, wherever found and in whatever religion, was from Deity, being a part of his very nature. Jesus was an exceptionally great religious teacher and prophet, but a natural, finite, and therefore fallible human being. It was only his clear and extraordinary insight into truth that gave him authority, and not any special credentials, attested by miracle-working, which were given him from heaven. Christianity, historically, was a development and accretion of many beliefs and forces, some true, some false ; and it could only be called the absolute religion when reduced to the simple principles taught by Jesus,— love to God and man. Christianity might, however, be properly thus defined, and thus be accepted still by the rational mind as synonymous with absolute religion. And the three primary ideas of absolute religion — God, Duty, Immortality — were to be regarded as given by direct natural revelation in the human consciousness, and hence needed, and could have, no stronger attestation of their truth through any kind of outward evidence addressed to the senses. This is a brief, imperfect schedule of the leading features of Theodore Parker's theological beliefs.

And this, in substance, would pretty well describe the chief points of my theological views when my ministry began, except that I questioned whether the doctrine of immortality could be philosophically said to rest immediately on the testimony of human consciousness ; whether it was not rather a logical inference from certain facts of consciousness ; and except also that I was not so pronouncedly theistic in my conception of Deity. The very first sermon I ever wrote, and one of the earliest I gave in this pulpit, was criticised by our professor in the Theological School as too strongly infused with Pantheism. I had then, as I have always had since, a logical difficulty in separating Deity from the living law and energies of the universe itself, as an individual, self-existing being, who might be conceived as existing alone, in his own solitude, though there were no universe at all; for, to my mind, the universe itself was infinite in its range and life and possibilities of power, and, hence, to conceive of God as a separate infinite entity apart from it required the logical impossibility of believing in two infinite beings. Therefore, my thought tended to identify Deity with the inmost powers, life, and development of the whole possible universe; as, in some sense, the soul, of which the universe was the body, though this comparison, drawn from our knowledge of finite organisms, could only very inadequately and imperfectly express the actual relation between Deity and the natural universe. In his essence, Deity must, indeed, remain uncomprehended by the finite mind, though his existence and power must be necessarily assumed. With these exceptions, my thought at that time followed pretty nearly in the line of Mr. Parker's religious views, as they may be read in his books to-day. In brief, my religious philosophy was that of the New England Transcendentalists. I believed that man had by nature an intuitive faculty by which the great religious and moral truths were self-evident to him. These truths were a transcript in the human mind of the attributes of the divine mind, or they were the divine nature as mirrored in the individual human soul. And to this philosophy I was predisposed by the Quaker doctrine of the

Inner Light, to which I had been bred from childhood, and which I may even say I possessed by heredity as well as by early training.

And, now, as to the source and nature of the change which has come in these beliefs. In the year 1859, Darwin's *Origin of Species* was published, — that epoch-making book, as the Germans say. This book I read in the first year of my ministry. With the evolution theory of creation I was already acquainted, and in a general way accepted it as much more rational and credible than the popular belief in special creative acts. Several years before, I had read that little book, *Vestiges of Creation*, whose authorship was not discovered until last year, when William Chambers, the veteran Edinburgh author and publisher, died. Then a friend, with whom the secret had been deposited, revealed to the world that William Chambers wrote *Vestiges of Creation*. That publication for its time, though now displaced by later works on the same theme written from the vantage-ground of wider scientific investigation, was also for many minds an epoch-making book. It was so to me. From that time, though I saw that there was not a little of hypothesis in the development theory, as it was styled in that work, I was an evolutionist, in the sense that this seemed to me much the more probable way in which the various organisms and species of life had come into existence; while my mind was by no means shut against further evidence, nor was then conscious of all the logical implications of the evolution doctrine. The book opened to me, however, a new earth and new heavens, and planted in my thought the seeds of a grander and more fruitful conception of Deity than any which I had found in the old theologies. Darwin's famous book brought the further evidence, gathered so carefully and from such wide fields of research and long-continued study. And it was all confirmatory of the development theory advanced in the older book. Other contributions, from various authors, rapidly followed on the same theme in its different branches.

Soon, it became evident that here were truths of science, which would profoundly affect the intuitional system of philosophy as it had been applied to religion. Here was science, not only going behind instinct in the animal to explain it, defining it as "inherited habit,"— the habit of doing certain things having been formed through a long series of experiments in natural selection to find the conditions most favorable to life,— but here was science also going behind the social affections, sympathies, charities, and even conscience in the human soul, and confidently offering similar explanation of them. And, if this explanation were true, what would become of that idea of the intuitive philosophy that these human benevolent affections and the moral sense, or conscience, are a direct impression made by the divine mind upon the individual human mind? or of the more mystical idea that, when these attributes exist in specially large measure in any human soul, it is because such soul is specially open and receptive to a direct incoming of divine power, as from a personal source of inspiration and enlightenment apart from its own organism? Through the pressure of questions like these, I was led to review the positions of the intuitional philosophy, especially in its application to religious truths, with the result of considerable modification in my views. I saw especially that the old idea, a favorite of the intuitional school of thought,— that the divine mind, as a present personal entity, impresses the individual human mind with certain qualities of affection, or inspires it with certain thoughts, or endows it outright at birth with certain mental gifts,— was no longer tenable. I saw that this idea of a commerce of finite minds with the infinite mind through the air, as it were, without the medium of any organism, was really a relic of superstitious faith; and that, under the figurative language of God's attributes being mirrored in the human soul, or being impressed upon it from some entirely external source, as if God and man stood over against each other as two distinct personalities, was concealed the delusion of a false philosophy.

But I was not long in reaching a new position, nor was there any serious conflict in my mind between the new and old. I said science must be the criterion for testing our beliefs, for science discovers the facts of the universe; but science, observe you, only in its actual discoveries,— not science, merely in the domain of the material world and its forces, but science as it embraces the whole realm of facts in the world of the human intellect and heart, and in all phases of human history. A belief or a sentiment is not necessarily to be discarded because science fails to explain it. It will be time enough to discard it when rational knowledge has positively shown that it rests on error. The circulation of the blood went on by natural law in the human frame before Harvey discovered the true theory of it. So there may be in man's mental and moral organism the natural exercise of certain functions called spiritual or religious, which have hitherto performed their service for human life in connection with theories of them wholly erroneous. But it does not follow that the functions themselves are an illegitimate and artificial excrescence upon human life. They may be as necessary to the higher moral life of man as is the circulation of the blood to his physical life. If distinctly proved to be founded in and maintained by error, then, of course, they are to be abandoned. But, until then, they have a right to stay, with the presumption that they have a legitimate cause; and the true explanation of them may yet be found.

With regard to the relation between man and Deity, these scientific truths which are involved in the doctrine of evolution only compelled me to recur more definitely to that pantheistic conception of Deity which the Cambridge professor had criticised, and to adjust all related beliefs and the language for expressing them to that central thought of the identity and oneness of Deity with the living law and energies of the universe itself. Instead of man being connected with Deity as one finite person with another, the two communicating in some mysterious way through the intervening spaces, man is connected with Deity through that natural organism of his own faculties, by which his life is woven in one piece with the life of the world-forces around him, and with the unfolding order of the forms of being and life anterior to him for countless ages. I have found no science which dispenses with the necessity of a causal and sustaining power whence all beings and things have come and continue; nor have I found any science which does not acknowledge that man is in necessary vital relation with this power, whatever it may be. And this is the power which, in accordance with a strictly scientific philosophy, wells up in the human consciousness as thought and moral perception, as personal will and humane sympathies. Here, therefore, I find ample ground, not only for a religious philosophy and for religious institutions, but also for all that was most valuable in the intuitional philosophy,— namely, its assertion of divine Power and Life as immanent in human life; of the moral sense as the perception of an absolute distinction between right and wrong; and of mind as the dominant element in the evolution of the world-forces,— or of mind, instead of matter, as riding in the saddle of the powers that have evolved this world of nature and man which comes under our knowledge. Why should we imagine the divine Power to be brought any nearer to us or to be any more real to our thought, if we conceive it as in some way external to us and inspiring and impressing us by an *afflatus* from the skies, than if we conceive it as welling up within us as the vitalizing force of our mental and moral perceptions and the very power that constrains us within to follow the true and to do the humane and the right? By this latter view, we are set, indeed, in the very current of the divine energy. It is that which has created our mental, moral, and affectional organism, and still supplies vitality to all their functions. The mighty Power sweeps in and through us, itself the light by which we see, itself the law of righteousness which commands our service, itself the force of the truth and beauty which impels the adoration of our intellects and lifts our lives to noble aspiration and purpose: only, in the exquisite structure of this organism by which we live, we are, in a measure, free to ignore and resist this vital influx and upsurging of the Eternal Energy in which our being consists; or, on the other hand, we may keep the natural channels of our faculties open to its ceaseless, benignant flow, and even increase their capacity, and thus work in and by its power to fulfil its purposive movement in the great world-process.

Further study, also, of Christianity in its origin and history, and by comparison with other religions, convinced me that it had no special claim to be considered as synonymous with absolute religion. I saw that just those things in it which are permanent and make it acceptable to the rational mind to-day are the mental and moral perceptions which it holds in common with all the great religions of the world; while those beliefs, and particularly that of the Messianic authority of Jesus, which especially mark it as a distinct religion, are the beliefs which the rational mind to-day questions and which are transient and perishable. The conclusion was forced upon me that it is presumption and arrogance to claim as "Christian" those ideas and those virtues and graces of character which may be equally found among enlightened believers in other religions than the Christian; and I came to the conviction that the progress of humanity would now be greatly aided, if the barriers between the religions, which are kept up by their special claims and names, could be removed, and people from various faiths should be drawn into one fellowship on the basis of absolute liberty of thought, of pure aspirations, and of earnest endeavor to know and to keep the law of righteousness, recognizing no other authority than that of truth itself. I believed that the time had come for distinctly inculcating these ideas; and I have, therefore, during the larger part of my ministry given myself to this work, here and elsewhere, in connection with what has become known as the Free Religious movement. I have hoped that these ideas would gradually permeate the minds of people, in the churches and outside of churches, and in time organize religion on natural and rational grounds and in new and more effective forms for the benefit of humanity.

And, now, let me briefly draw into serial form the leading articles into which these fundamental principles of my religious faith naturally branch, stating them succinctly without argument, the argument having been given from time to time for these many years. The statement may be called my creed: mine, though not necessarily yours.

1. I believe in God as the power eternal, immortal, invisible, omnipresent, within and behind all phenomena, unknown and yet known, working in and through nature, producer and sustainer of all forms of existence, vitalizer of all organisms and life, welling up as mental and moral energy in the consciousness of man, and striving in the development of human history to establish righteousness as the law of life for the individual and for the race, and as the surest, amplest providence for human guidance.

2. I believe in man as the highest consummation and expression of the eternal energy in that part of the universe which comes within our knowledge. Beginning on the level of animal existence, springing from the lower forms of life that were anterior to him, I believe that in him the eternal energy has fashioned such an organism that he has been able to rise from the plane of animal life, through the various grades of savagery and barbarism, until he has reached the heights of civilization, enlightenment, and power, which he holds to-day. I believe that he has made this progress, and has capacity for indefinite progress in the future, through his natural faculties of reason, conscience, and affection, which are a manifestation in him, under finite limitations, of the eternal energy itself, and which may be so vitalized as to make man a secondary creator in co-operating with and carrying forward the eternal world-purpose.

3. I believe that the moral law, or conscience, is man's intuitive perception of the equation of rights between human beings in their relations to each

other. I believe that a certain stage of intelligence through the disciplines of experience had to be reached by primitive man before this perception became possible, just as a certain degree of intelligence was necessary for perceiving the relation of numbers in the multiplication-table; but that, when this degree of intelligence was reached, the perception of the equation of rights between man and man would follow as necessarily as the perception of the relation of numbers. I believe, therefore, that morality rests on as permanent and irrefragable a basis as does the science of mathematics.

4. I believe that religion is the expression of man's relation to the universe and its vital powers, or to its living, sustaining energy. From connection with and dependence upon this energy, it is not possible for man to escape. The fact of this relation is established by science; and science, in its broad sense, must be depended upon to give the true theory of it. But, in all ages, man has been conscious of it; and his expression of the relation has threefold form,— through thought, through feeling, and through action. Through one or another or all of these forms of expression, he has sought to perfect his relation to the universal forces and laws. I believe that from this fundamental idea have grown all the special religions, while their distinguishing beliefs and ceremonies have been shaped by the intelligence of the people holding them. I believe, therefore, that all the religions have a natural origin and a natural development; that, by virtue of their common root, they are sects of one universal

religion ; and that, notwithstanding their differences and antagonisms, resulting from their special doctrines and claims, there are among them certain underlying unities of belief, aspiration, and moral sentiment, by which they are bound together in one fellowship.

5. I believe that the sacred books of the various religions have the same natural source,— the human mind, in its effort to express its relation to the infinite Power. They are the religious literature of the race or people producing them. Various in merit, they all contain important truths ; and the truths in all of them are mingled with errors. As a transcript of what humanity has thought and felt, as it has struggled with the great problems of life, they are invaluable. But they are to be read to-day, not as infallible authority for truth, but with that discrimination which can separate truth from error, and find refreshing for the heart and moral stimulus for conduct instead of a creed to bind upon the intellect.

6. I believe that the founders and prophets of the religions were human beings, of superior intellectual endowments or moral insight ; holy men and seers, who became the natural leaders of the people about them, and around whose lives, through the pious imagination of their followers, there afterwards gathered legends and myths, to express the people's wonder and admiration for their greatness and power. I believe that the lustre of the moral example of Jesus is not dimmed nor the power of his character for moral inspiration impaired by thus

placing him in the natural line of humanity, and in a group of kindred souls, who have lived, wrought, and died, and borne brave testimony to truth and right, for the guidance and healing of the nations.

7. I believe that reward and retribution for deeds done in the body are assured by the natural law that binds effect to cause; that moral error, or wickedness, produces as its inevitable consequence pain and wretchedness; that, if continued, it is suicidal in its agency, and tends to the ultimate destruction of its own power; that moral good, on the contrary, is self-perpetuating, and leads ever more and more to larger and higher life, to realms of purer happiness, and to ever greatening capacity for virtue and for virtue's service.

8. I believe that, on the ground of the strongest and most rational probability, though it be beyond the realm of knowledge, man may entertain a confident hope — nay, a faith — in his own personal immortality; that the eternal energy, having achieved self-consciousness in the wonderful personality of human character, with its power of progressing upon its own nature, will not lightly throw away such a being and such an advantage after a few years of earthly life. I believe, however, that, while man may entertain this hope and hold this faith, his first of duties is not to dream of the life hereafter, but to work zealously for the amelioration of human society on earth; to show himself less anxious about saving his own soul for eternal bliss than concerning the salvation of other souls around him from present ignorance, wrong, and wretchedness, so that they

may become capable of intellectual, moral, and spiritual life.

9. I believe that, as God, the eternal living energy, is ever seeking and striving to embody his power more and more in man, soliciting him, by inward constraining impulse, to truth, goodness, and moral beauty, so also may man correspondingly seek and find God; for

> "God is seen God
> In the star, in the stone, in the flesh, in the soul, and the clod.
> And, thus looking within and around me, I ever renew
> (With that stoop of the soul which, in bending, upraises it too)
> The submission of man's nothing-perfect to God's all-complete,
> As, by each new obeisance in spirit, I climb to his feet."

10. I believe, finally, that these lines of Browning aptly express religion's threefold form of manifestation, through thought, emotion, and conduct. They hint a philosophy of Deity and man, and of the relation between them, and they picture the emotional attitude of the human mind in all genuine worship and prayer; as also the brave endeavor and deed that are necessary to bring human life and divine law into practical harmony.

Thus, friends, have I given you my creed, not, of course, to impose it upon you, but as the substance of the religious philosophy which underlies my ministry. One doctrine implied in my creed is that every person is responsible for his own,—that freedom of thought is both a right and a duty which all human beings should hold sacred.

But higher than any creed is the deed. Better than any other kind of faith is the faith that takes shape in pure and upright character. This has been my constant theme through all the years of my ministry. It has sometimes seemed to me that, whatever the topic I treat, my sermons always come, in the practical application at the end, to this one goal,—*character, true and beneficent character*,—this above all things, this forever and evermore. But is not this the proper goal,—the end of all endeavor, of all aspiration, of all living? What but this makes life worth living? What is nobler, what fairer, what more beautiful and entrancing than the life of a noble soul? O friends, if my ministrations have led any of you in these years to see this truth more clearly, to feel it more deeply, and if my services have thus in any way inspired you to purer, truer living, I ask for no higher satisfaction. That, and that only, is the measure of my success. My first sermon to you as your minister, New Year's day, 1860, closed with these words: "If I can lift any souls among you to more ennobling truth, to purer love, to stronger virtue, if I can quicken your spiritual vision, and lead any of you to see more clearly the infinite beauty of a life proportioned to the laws of eternal rectitude, then will these New Year's vows of consecration be crowned indeed with blessing, being followed in due season by seed-time showers and hopes, maturing summer suns, and autumn harvests of ripened souls." Dear friends, if my ministry has been in any measure instrumental in doing for any of you such a service as I here pictured in my hope, or if I was permitted to do it for any of that congregation of our risen dead, our "cloud of witnesses," who have joined

> " the choir invisible,
> Whose music is the gladness of the world,"

then indeed will the young man's vow of consecration, twenty-five years ago, have been lifted, to become to-day my manhood's crown of rejoicing.

December 28, 1884.

APPENDIX.

LETTER TO MR. POTTER.

Dear Mr. Potter, — Many friends desire the publication of a selection of your sermons, and they ask that the volume may contain such as you may choose from those you have given from our pulpit during the quarter of a century you have been settled over the First Congregational Society of New Bedford.

They also ask that an engraved portrait of yourself with your autograph be bound in the volume, and that the account of the Reception on your twenty-fifth anniversary, including the addresses, as published in the papers of the day, be annexed. Your friends wish to make this volume a part of that celebration, and a permanent *memorial* of the value to them of your twenty-five years' service and of the gratitude they feel toward you as pastor and preacher.

Will you kindly attend to the compiling of this volume, in such form as you may deem best, and thus gratify this general desire?

In behalf of these many friends,

Cordially and faithfully yours,

S. GRIFFITTS MORGAN.

NEW BEDFORD, 1885.

In accordance with the suggestion in the foregoing letter (to which this book is the answer), the matter contained in this Appendix is added.

A PARISH RECEPTION was given to Mr. Potter on the evening of Dec. 29, 1884, in celebration of his having completed on the previous day twenty-five years of service as minister of the First Congregational Society.

At the opening of the Reception, the following hymn, written for the occasion by Mr. William G. Baker, of New York, a former member of the Society, was sung by the Sunday-school, accompanied by the presentation to the pastor of a basket of roses: —

>A sower went forth sowing
>In Eastern fields one day,
>And cast in lavish handfuls
>The seed along his way.
>But, ah! the sun was burning,
>The weeds and thorns grew fast:
>'Twas only in the "good ground"
>The seeds sprang up at last.
>
>Like seeds cast by the sower
>Through ev'ry passing year,
>Our teacher's words have fallen,
>That still we love to hear.
>Our hearts shall be the "good ground"
>Wherein the seeds shall spring,
>To blossom with the beauty
>Of these fresh flowers we bring.

After social greetings by the Society and guests, a collation, and singing by the choir of the Society, assisted by a chorus, the assembly was called to order by T. M. Stetson, Esq., who spoke as follows: —

ADDRESS OF THOMAS M. STETSON, ESQ.

Ladies and Gentlemen, and Children and Grandchildren,—

Do you know that in this Society there is a dread and awful power? It wears the garb and aspect of a gracious lady, but its decrees are more imperious and absolute than those of the council of Venice. It has decided that in this our festival — and nobody can organize a symposium better than Unitarian ladies — there shall be speeches instead of the walnuts and the wine. I told her it might have a disastrous and centrifugal effect upon the liables (for I cannot style them reliables) of the parish: that next time my Brother Crapo would have "Alabama claims" in Washington requiring immediate attention; that Judge Prescott would drop his cane and fly off to Westford; that Mr. Rotch, Mr. Clifford, the new mayor, and myself would vanish where no feminine committee could find us. But it was of no use; and I am ordered by our high priestess to bring Mr. Potter up here, because she says he needs to be spoken to,— that this is no ordinary occasion,— and she says it will be only seventy-five years more for the completion of his centennial service with us, and he wants to know what reply we have to make for his twenty-five years of preaching. This may be so. I once read a sermon of the greatest writer that ever lived. The clergy present will at once know that I mean the Rev. Mr. Tarbell, of Lincoln, who left six thousand sermons, each equal to fourteen printed pages of the *North American Review*. He said that, after writing some four or five thousand of these, the saddest doubts came to him whether he had not survived his usefulness, and whether the earnestness and bloom and fire of his youth had not departed and left no substitute. Perhaps our pastor has his periods of doubt and depression; and I presume he would like to know what record his ministry has made, not merely upon sermons docketed and filed in his desk, but in his parishioners' minds and hearts.

Let us tell him to-night.

How events have marched since you, sir, became our minister! How you have been interwoven with the dearest associations of this people! How many marriage ties you have consecrated! Over how many strong men — men of business, of affairs, men of the world, men of the State and of the public — have you spoken the last benediction of faith and hope! How many gentle women, too, have passed away, whose lives had filled their homes with joy; not of the world, knowing its ills and woes only through their sweet charities, living afar from its tides and tempests, and seeing in their stormy waves only the deep blue of heaven, and yet, oh, how useful in God's scheme for human welfare and felicity!

What tides of action and of thought, of peace and war,

have swept by since you, a youthful acolyte, stood at our temple's gate, with your priestly brethren, and the solemn invocation went up,—

> "Since thy servant now hath given
> Himself, his powers, his hopes, his youth
> To the great cause of truth and heaven,
> Be thou his guide, O God of truth!"

Our right hand of fellowship was given you then. It need not be given again, for it has never been withdrawn; but, to-night, we are celebrating your silver wedding to this church.

What a congregation it was when you undertook the cure of souls, and especially what predecessors you had to follow!—the sturdy old logicians and expounders, Samuel Hunt and Dr. West; the masculine orators of the liberal faith, Dewey, Peabody, and others; Weiss, a very Chrysostom of the modern pulpit. What a mantle fell upon you! Nor was it an ordinary society, nor of that weak mental pliancy which can be easily moulded by any able divine. It contained people of strong and diverse thoughts and methods and views. What a history it had, too! The *Mercury*, usually so accurate, erred this morning in attributing our birthday to the year 1795. Why, our first minister died over sixty years before that. Nor were we an offshoot of the meeting at Acushnet. We were the whole of it: we were the "Bedford precinct" for nearly a hundred years before that date, and for thirty years after, too, till our name was changed by law to "The First Congregational Society in New Bedford." Nothing happened in 1795 excepting the building of a new edifice. Ours is the oldest legal church organization in this part of the colony, and was established to be a bulwark of the Protestant faith here, and with legal powers and safeguards that would startle you to hear. It had legal control over all religious affairs here, and over all men, religious and irreligious ones, too. Its powers were enormous. Its taxes were laid on every man who lived in the precinct territory,— on his poll, his lands and estate,— and this was collected by force of law. Every stranger who came here was taxed in the same way, irrespective of his faith, unless he could get a certificate from the clerk that he belonged to some other church approved by the government. Just one hundred years ago this winter, a poor Baptist, who had but one cow, and that necessary for the support of his family, in an inclement winter, was jailed for nine solid months because he would not give up that cow to pay a ministerial tax to our society. Those were the days when parish funds collected easily. The sheriff and the law did it, and it did not need the zeal and assiduity of any John R. Thornton of that century to keep the parish treasury full.

And if the town or precinct, as the case might be, was negligent, and did not provide a minister, in such case of a "defective" town (mark that phrase: a town was "defective," if a minister was lacking), then the county court stepped in, selected a minister, and saw to his installation and settlement. Fancy such an ordination as that, Mr. Potter! Instead of an induction into our pulpit by the grave and reverend seniors who did it, fancy it done by the county sheriff and his mace!

And it was not safe in those elder days for any discontented subject to grumble and scold improperly about the quality of the preaching. For the first offence, he was "convented," — whatever that may be I don't know, but it sounds like something that might hurt. For the second offence, he had to stand on a block four feet high. Doubtless, our sweet ancestors of Plymouth colony deemed a block four feet high conducive to devotional thoughts.

No rival church was tolerated here in our early period. If any man set up such without the consent of the government, he lost his vote in town meeting and had to receive such other punishment as the court should inflict; and it was made the duty of the county court to purge out such as were " perniciously heterodox."

The future of the church was also provided for by law. It was the legal duty of the selectmen of the town to see that children and servants were made to understand the grounds of Christianity, so far as " necessary to salvation." This was a grave task for a selectman of old Dartmouth on his dollar a day.

The church was militant then. It had to be. The laws provided that every man should take his gun to meeting with him and at least three bullets. The same chapter also provided, however, that he should not shoot at any game except an Indian or a wolf.

These were halcyon days for the clergy. They had no rivals to fear and no grumblers, no loss of parishioners and no bother about salary. Before you came, Mr. Potter, these, our lofty prerogatives, had one after the other vanished, and the voluntary system prevailed. That had some advantages, though I remember the experience of Rev. Dr. Barnes when it began. He heard that his flock were assembled in parish meeting, and were talking of increasing his salary from $300 to $400. He seized his hat, hurried to the meeting and begged they wouldn't; for he said it was as much as he could do to collect $300 out of them.

You came to us when these tremendous safeguards of the law had ended. Your relation to us and ours to you had to stand upon its merit alone. You came to a congregation of various views, habits, and culture. The elder ones were strongly attracted to the ancient faith and the ancient ways; watchful and rather suspicious of all novelties, but not hostile to honest inquiry into the records of revelation, nor into the infinite and unrecorded revelations of the earth, the universe, and of man's own consciousness. There were others who had passed into more liberality of faith — possibly some might deem, had travelled too fast or too far. Observances differed too. Some, after a week of figures and finance on wharf or at counting-house, when the Sunday came hungered and thirsted after righteousness spoken; and yet others, raised on three services a day, a Sunday-school, mid-week meeting, the "great and Thursday lecture," the perfunctory morning and evening prayers at college, where prayers answer the purpose of the military reveille and tattoo, found when the Sunday came that physically and mentally they needed loneliness, and the silences of the forest and shore, and in the very stones found sermons.

Yet, whatever our differences of ways, of observances, of creed too, your ministration has united us in a deep satisfaction when Sunday comes that you are at the helm and that our beautiful church is always open for its appointed work.

All Unitarians have one thing in common. We do like and must have good preaching. We always have had it,— have it now and always will have it,— whether we hear it from you, or from Dr. Dexter, who has occupied our pulpit, or from Mr. Julien and other gentlemen who will have an attentive and appreciative audience when they do come.

Possibly some outsiders, knowing as little as outsiders ever do of an inside, have deemed you a crank, because, forsooth, you would not turn any accepted crank, and would not deem that all the truths of the infinite now and hereafter were known to the writers who have preceded us. You have promoted inquiry into all domains of religious thought. You have aided thoughtful people in their gropings, questionings, doubts, and darkness, with an inquiry free but always reverential toward the faiths of the past, always deeply reverential toward the hero of our faith, than whom even the most expanded culture and incisive thought of the present never has produced, depicted, or imagined a diviner man.

Yours has been a twenty-five years of progress; and we wish to say now — not in mere cordial phrase of personal regard, but weighing our words — that the zeal and earnestness of your early service could not equal in interest to us the zeal and earnestness and widening scope and more comprehensive insight of your present. Yours has been a life of industry, fidelity, and growth. A soldier of the Church, you have never slumbered on your arms, nor shrunk behind any red-cross shield, but have met the advance with unprotected breast. You have not taught us that religion is a mere means for personal advantage, however exalted, nor a private solace or balm of however lofty a nature. You have never based your instructions upon the selfishness of the entoderm, but have advocated reforms of every kind, and with all the care and prudence such preaching requires; and by that I do not mean with faint heart or half speech, — but the treatment of every reform of old abuses requires a care commensurate with the limitless importance of success. Reforms are not altogether lovely. The serpent sheds not his old skin without pain. Reformers, too, are not always and altogether lovely. They are spinous. They bristle and sting. We have never found the unloveliness of the typical reformer in you. Your many sermons, in all ways and means for human improvement, have pervaded, imbued, and permeated us like the gentle dew of heaven. Yes, — to use the phrase of your own journal, — you may be our ectoderm to your heart's content, but you will never be an echinoderm.

How well it attests the value of your ministry here — in spite of the fact that our Society is by no means homogeneous, and includes various beliefs, methods of thought and culture — that there is now a sterling unity among us and universal assent to and devotion to every serious and honest inquiry into the mysteries of life and of Deity, and that we are one shepherd and one fold! Our temple has been no place for discord. Too many prayers of tender hope have shed a perfume through the place.

And now, with a united society and united hearts and with all signs gracious as rainbows, we welcome you to the second quarter-century of your ministry.

On closing, Mr. Stetson called upon Mr. Crapo for remarks.

ADDRESS OF HON. WILLIAM W. CRAPO.

Ladies and Gentlemen: —

Twenty-five years is not a long period in the lifetime of our church parish. Its organization dates back to the early days of the settlement of the town. It was an influential factor in the religious and moral development of the community prior to the Revolution. It has a history, not remarkable simply for its longevity, but for the conspicuous and creditable service it has performed, and for the marked and distinguished men who have presided over it and who have ministered to the spiritual needs of its people.

We will not discuss the wisdom or necessity of church organization. For the development of truth, in the effective accomplishment of moral growth and spiritual culture, it is requisite that there be co-operation and cohesion, unity of purpose and unity of action. Some go farther, and say there should be discipline, even if forced by compulsory rules and arbitrary regulations. They say that, as the contentious and disagreeing partner in business affairs, that as the impracticable and mugwump in political action, are elements of weakness, so in like manner the dissenters and come-outers, who break the ranks of established church organization and are stragglers along the edges, impair the solidity and force of the assault when made against ignorance and error. I do not undertake to weigh in the balance the merits of adherence against the merits of independence. Our fathers, here in this locality, were never very submissive to church rule. They were free thinkers at the outset. They believed in regulating their religious exercises and in selecting their religious teachers according to their own notion, even if it defied an act of the General Court. I confess I have always had an admiration for the early settlers of this town when they defiantly declared, in the face of persecution, that they would have for themselves "perfect liberty in all matters of religious concernment." Our pastor was born in this town of Dartmouth,* where the principle was boldly asserted and successfully maintained. This principle of freest thought and the freest

---

* New Bedford was once a part of the original township of Dartmouth.

exercise of conscience was the inheritance confided to him, and with courage and fidelity he has endeavored to transmit it. Independence of thought and persistency in maintaining it were born with him. What more natural or logical? If you plant an acorn, you must not expect that there will grow from it a bending, shrinking, shivering weeping willow or an æsthetic sunflower.

But I am preaching a sermon, which is a very improper thing to do upon an occasion of festivity and congratulation. Let me, however, add one suggestion. When it is asserted that our church has swung away from the moorings of the true faith, when the indictment is presented against us by the religious community that we have committed or are committing heresy, and it is charged our pastor is not according to the orthodox pattern, we will answer back with the same identical words which our fathers sent from the Dartmouth town-meeting, in 1705, to the quarter sessions at Bristol: " We understand that our town is presented for want of a minister according to law. To which we answer that we have one qualified as the law directs,— an honest man, fearing God, conscientious, and a learned minister, able to dispense the word and gospel to us."

Such a man, Mr. President, we have had as our minister during the past twenty-five years.

The history of the First Congregational Society, which is our parish title, shows the remarkable concurrence and harmony which have existed between its pastors and congregation. In early times, Dr. Samuel West was its religious teacher, occupying its pulpit from 1761 to 1803, forty-two years. It is said of him that he was a man of great learning and equal piety, a lover of disputation, and vigorous in theological argument. I do not doubt that he preached political sermons; for he was an active partisan, and rendered zealous service in promoting the independence of his country.

Within the last sixty-one years, we have had four pastors.* There was Dr. Dewey, who instructed this people with great stores of knowledge, and with profound, vigorous, and original thought. He was a ripe scholar, a wise teacher, and sound religious guide.

Then came Ephraim Peabody, the warm-hearted, lovable, companionable man, who, with great good sense and a strong mind, made piety to grow in the household as well as in the church.

After him, John Weiss was for many years our minister, a man of marvellous brilliancy, with a genius and inspiration which seemed heaven-born. Bright, piercing, far-sighted, he fascinated and captivated us, and lifted us heavenward.

These are the men who, in the past, have strengthened the faith of this people, and have guided them to a higher, purer, and better life.

* Only the longest and leading pastorates were here named. But the society has had other faithful ministers in this period. The now venerable John H. Morison, D.D., was a colleague with Mr. Peabody for several years, the two having been settled together at the beginning of the latter's ministry. Dr. Morison is the only one of Mr. Potter's predecessors now living. Between Mr. Dewey and Mr. Peabody, Rev. Joseph Angier was settled as pastor for about two years; and Rev. Charles Lowe was settled as colleague with Mr. Weiss for one year.

We have met to-night to greet our friend, who is their successor. We can speak freely of those who have finished their record. But I find it difficult to express — or, rather, I find it difficult to refrain from expressing — the feelings and sentiments of this grateful, loving, and admiring audience, when speaking of our pastor in his presence. I know his hatred of adulation, his contempt for honeyed words, his scorn for fine-spoken, fulsome praises. He who so loves the truth will resent the truth, if spoken of himself. I will not affront him to-night by telling you in his hearing of his virtues, of the work he has done for us, and of the blessed services he has rendered, of the debt we owe him, and of the love we bear him.

Were he not here to-night, I could speak of his courage, — that intellectual and moral courage which dares to follow convictions wherever they may lead, that shrinks from no encounter with the truth, and that boldly accepts the result. I could speak of his integrity of thought, which permits no evasion nor sophistry nor subterfuge, but which, with inflexible honesty and with even justice, seeks to find the pathway to eternal right. For twenty-five years, with high character and upright life, he has labored with us and for us. He has pleaded for rectitude, for loftiness of purpose, for exalted purity, and for righteousness. We will not undertake to measure his usefulness.

Mr. Potter, we have asked you here to-night that we may thank you for your modest, patient, faithful work.

We greet you with warm hearts. With cordial good will and fellowship, we declare our gratitude, our esteem, our affection. We congratulate you, not simply because your pastoral charge of twenty-five years remains unbroken, but because of its duties well performed. This festival is the token of the tenderness of our sympathy and the loyalty of our friendship. We wish you much happiness and long-continued usefulness.

Mr. POTTER'S remarks in response were entirely extemporaneous, and only a meagre report of them was made. On being summoned to the platform, he said that he had some difficulty in keeping a consciousness of his own identity amid such novel circumstances and facing the addresses to which he had just listened. After seeing, indeed, the morning paper, with its purported biographical sketch, sounding so much like an obituary notice, he had had a feeling all day as if he ought not to be around hearing such things; and perhaps it was for this reason that the few thoughts which had previously come to his mind as proper for him to say on this occasion, should there be any call, had slipped irrecoverably away. He could, however, if he still knew his own heart, say that he felt, felt deeply — far more than he could express — a most grateful appreciation of all the kindness which had been shown in these utterances and in all the arrangements of the occasion, as in the many other more private ways by which his friends had been revealing their hearts to him during the last few days. But he wished, too, that this might not be wholly an occasion for mutual congratulations over the past, but that out of it might come new consecration and new strength for the duties of the future; and he concluded with an earnest appeal to the Society, which he meant also for himself, that all should stand ready to seize and use any new opportunities for labor in behalf of the good of the community which might come to them as a Society, so that the light of this church of their fathers should not only continue to shine, but should shine with increasing clearness and brightness, for the blessing of the living, the honor of the dead, and the good of generations yet to come.

www.ingramcontent.com/pod-product-compliance
Lightning Source LLC
Chambersburg PA
CBHW020739020526
44115CB00030B/633